Art by Tim

Sketches and Selected Work
by Tim Dowling

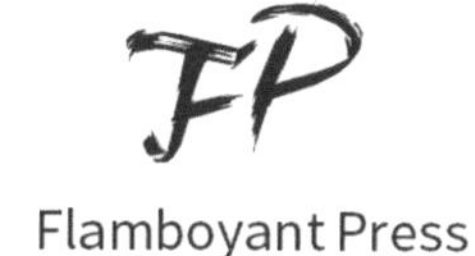

Flamboyant Press

Illustrations & Text - Tim Dowling

www.flamboyantpress.com
www.tim-dowling.com

ISBN- 9783946610076

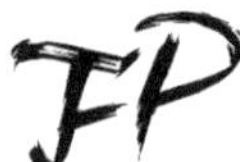

Published by Flamboyant Press
Dennis Timothy Dowling Verlag
Im Wengert 33, 71287 Weissach, Germany

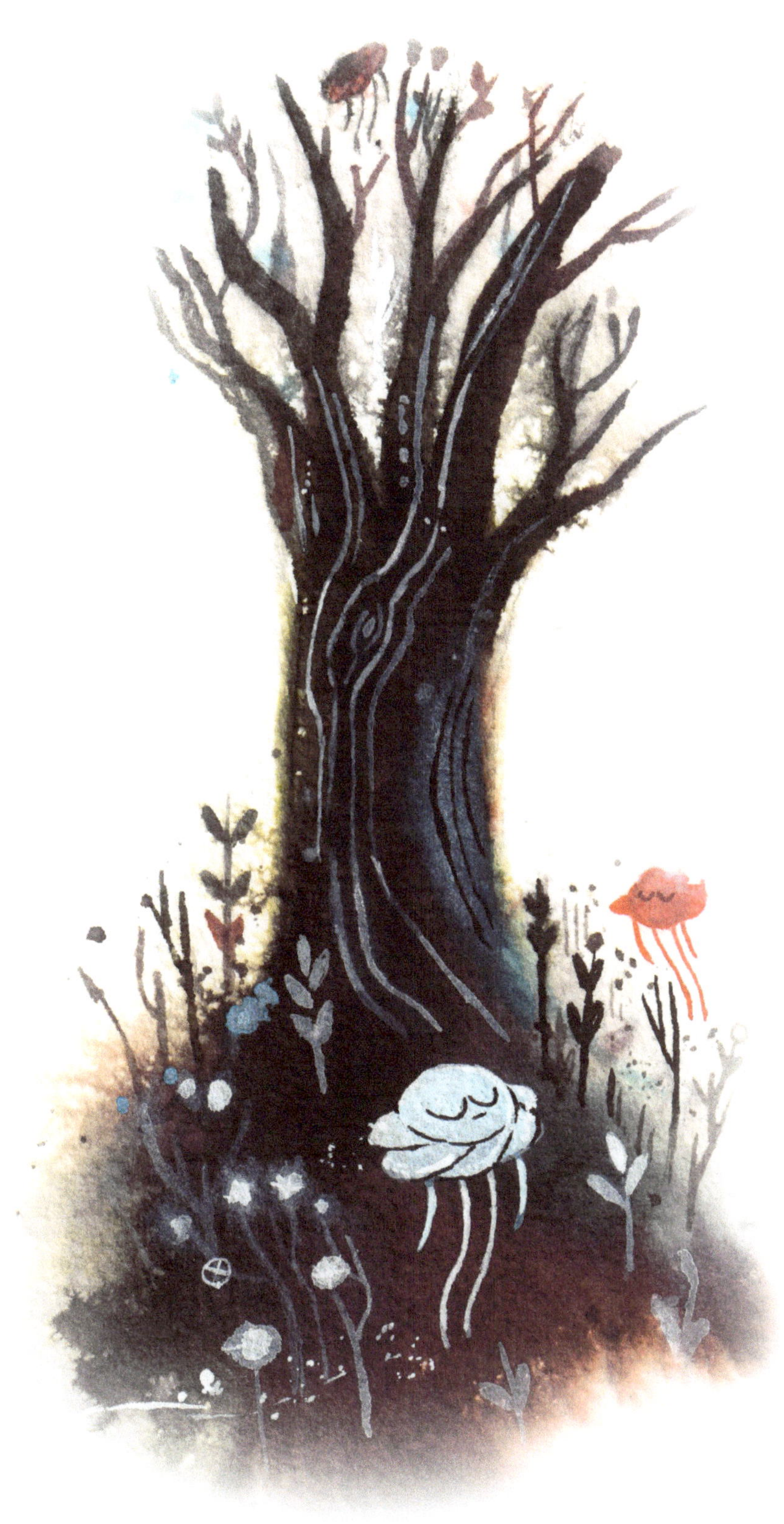

Art is the last
form of Magic
that Exists

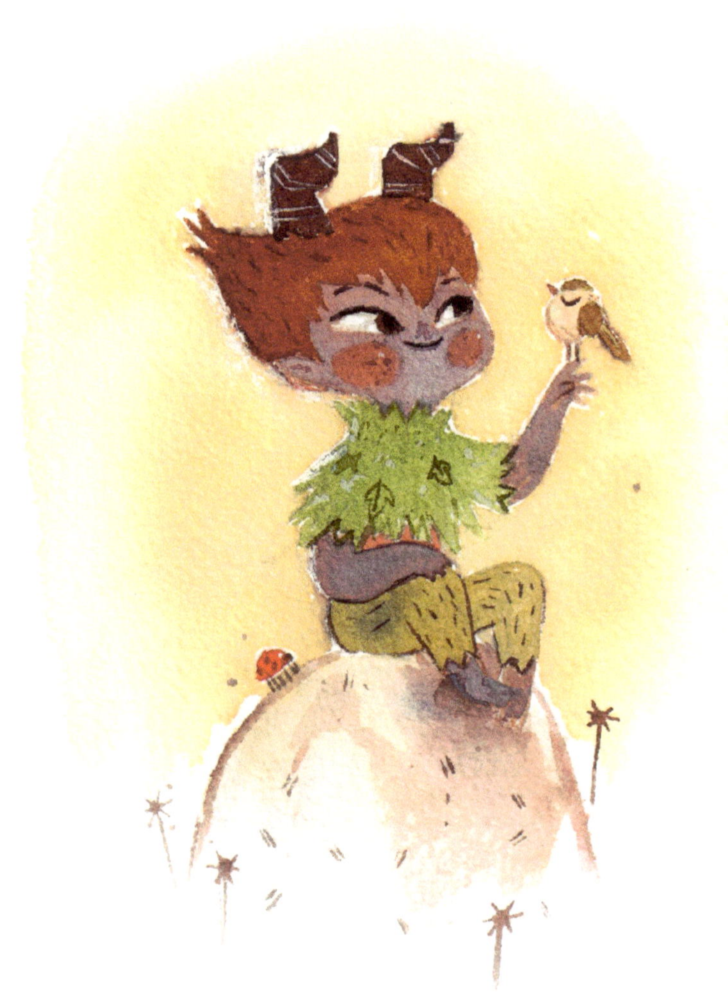

.Table of Contents.

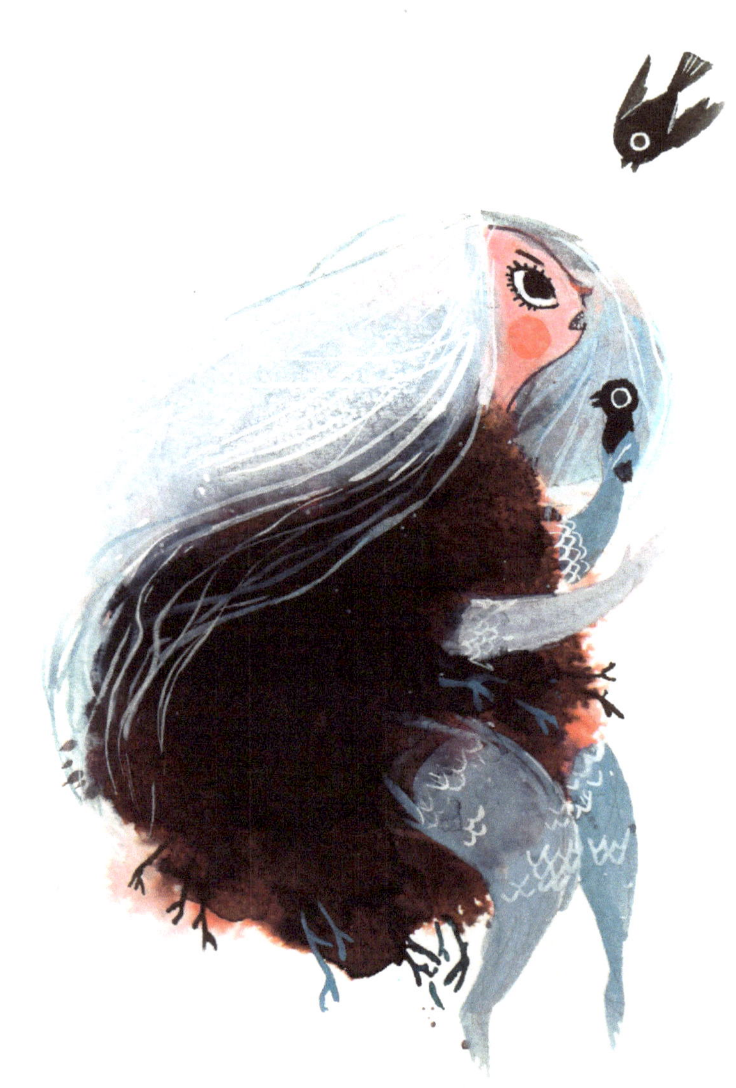

Introduction

My name is Tim Dowling and I am artist and writer; to give you brief history about
myself, I was born and bred in St. Maarten, Netherlands Antilles (a small island in the Caribbean)
As a child, I had a strong interest in drawing.

I discovered animation quite young at home when on a special occasions my father would set up
the Super 8 mm projector to watch family films. After the family films we would watch 2 or 3
Disney short-films, that lasted no more than 4 minutes. My mother would act out the voices
as there was no audio. The projector got jammed often enough and my father would cut
the area of film away that got damaged and splice it back together. He showed me the tiny
pictures on the film and explained how the projector made the pictures move; basically
he explained how animation worked. Ever since that moment I was hooked on animation!
Secretly I would take the old Disney reels and study them under the magnify glass.
Sometimes I would also draw onto the film so I could watch my own animations.

After secondary education I got into an animation program in Dublin, Ireland (BCFE) where
I learnt the basics of drawing and animation. The real work began when I started my professional
career in 2D animation. I learned a lot! My first animation job was working on Cartoon Network's
Foster's Home for Imaginary Friends with Bouldermedia, since then I have worked with the likes
of Disney, Nickelodeon, Cartoon Network, Brown Bag, Cartoon Saloon and Kavaleer.

Coming from an animation background though and diving into the world of illustration proved
to be particularly challenging. In animation one is required to adapt quickly to different styles,
in illustration one needs to have a singular style to be recognizable. My work is still in transition
and probably always will be as I approach projects conceptually.

In this book you will find selected sketches, illustrations, character designs and more
which I have done throughout my career as an animator and illustrator.
I have also included "the making of" my latest children's picture book;
"The Truth about Monsters"

I hope you enjoy this book as much as I had making it.

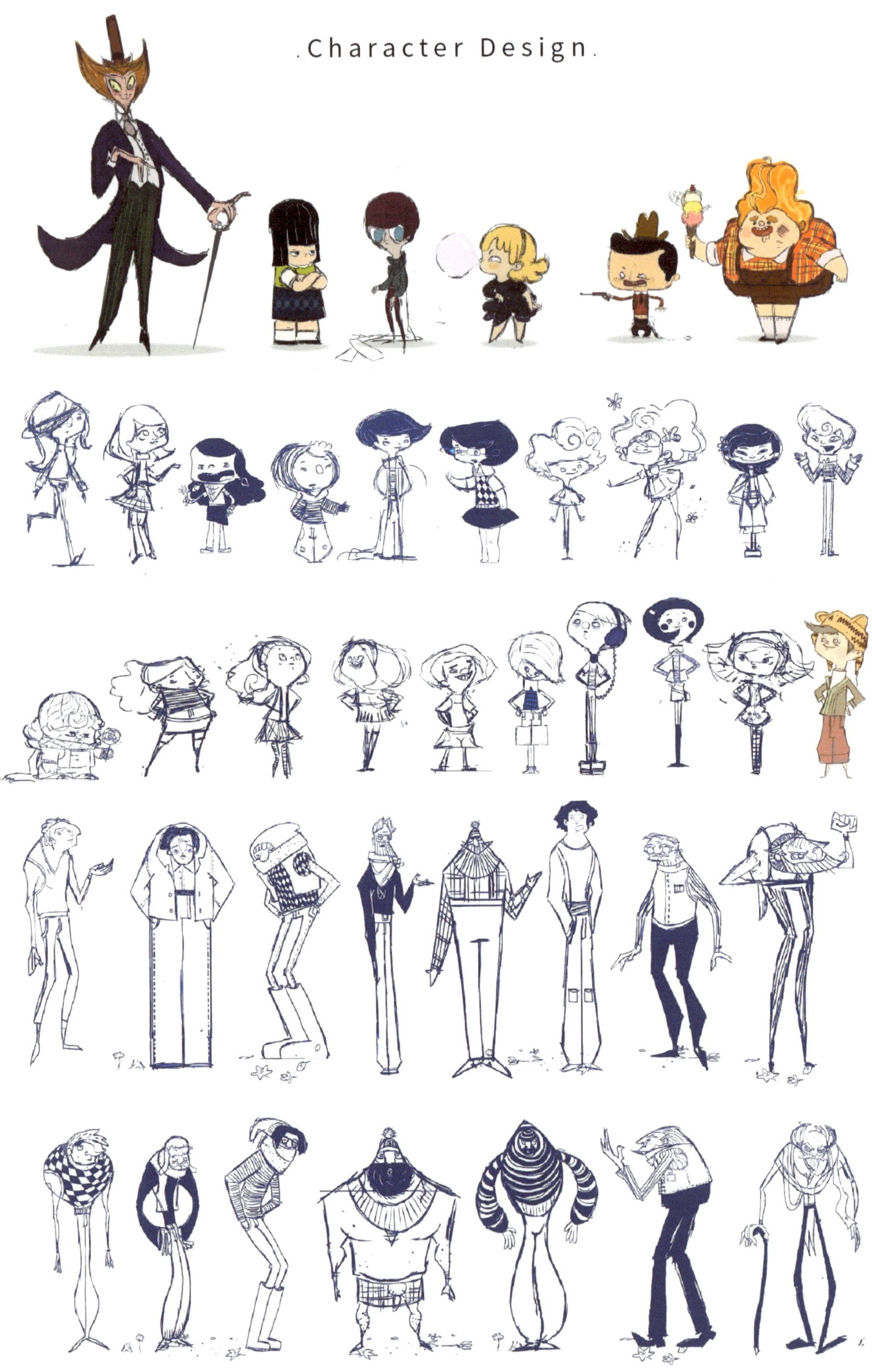

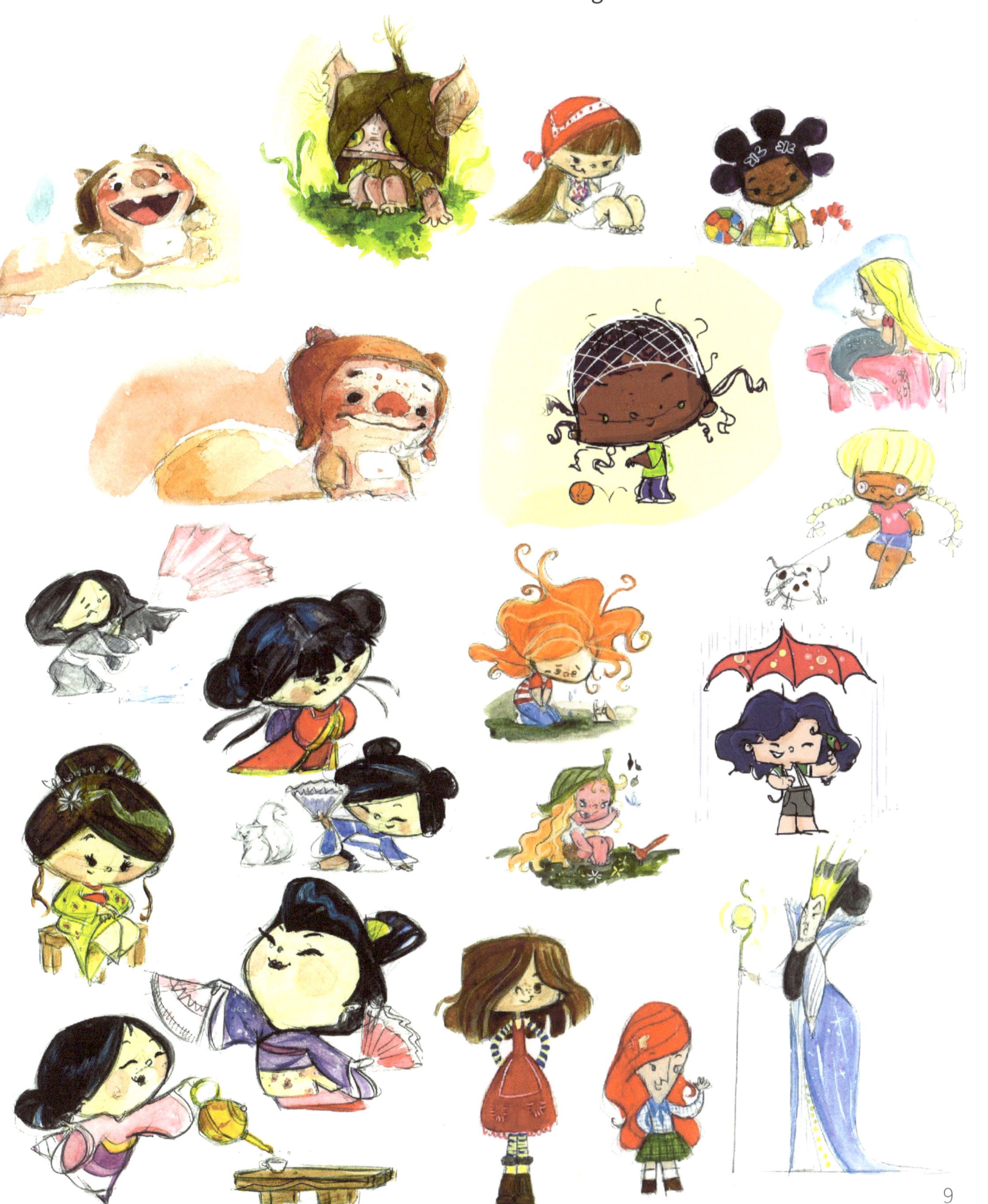

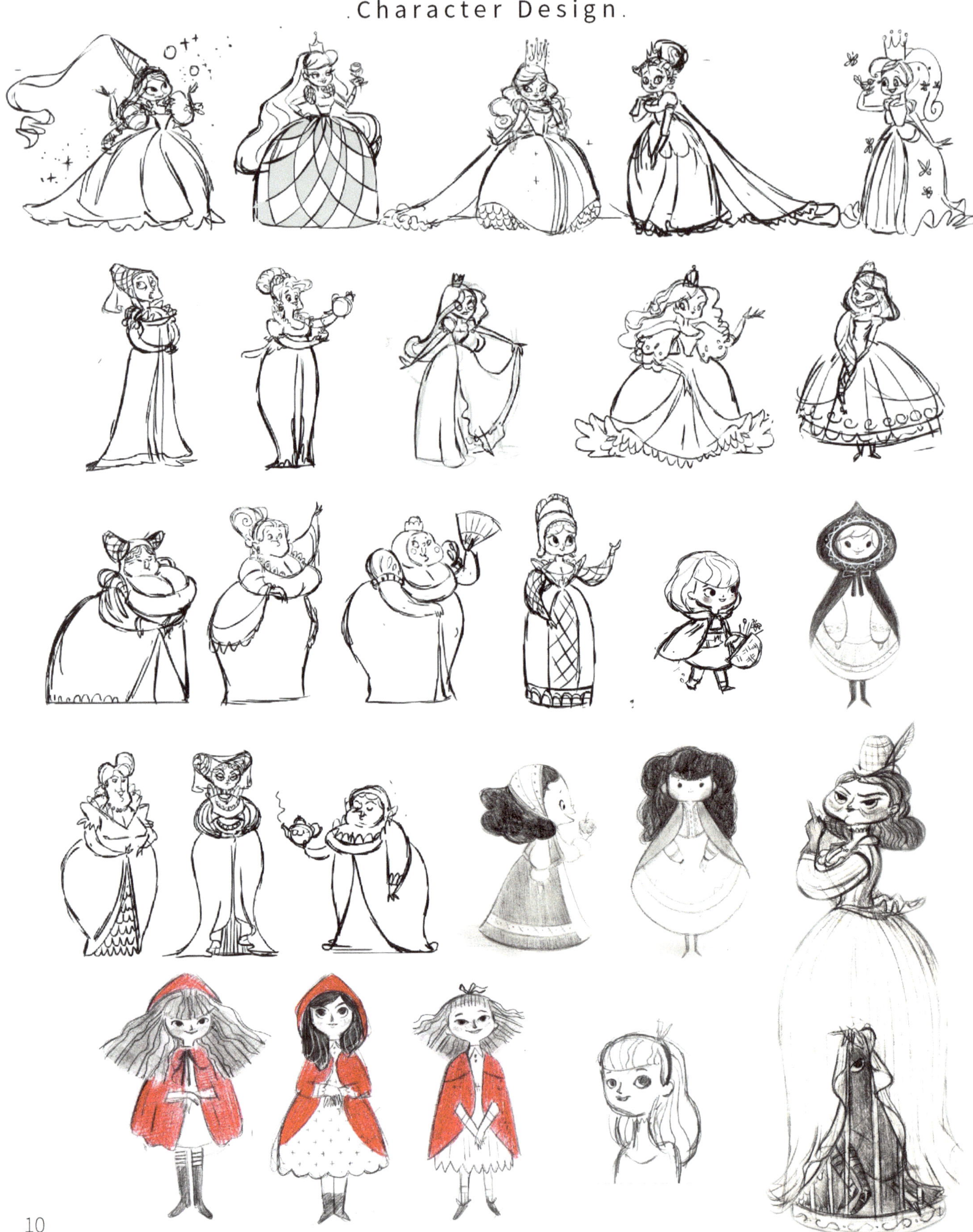

Character Design.

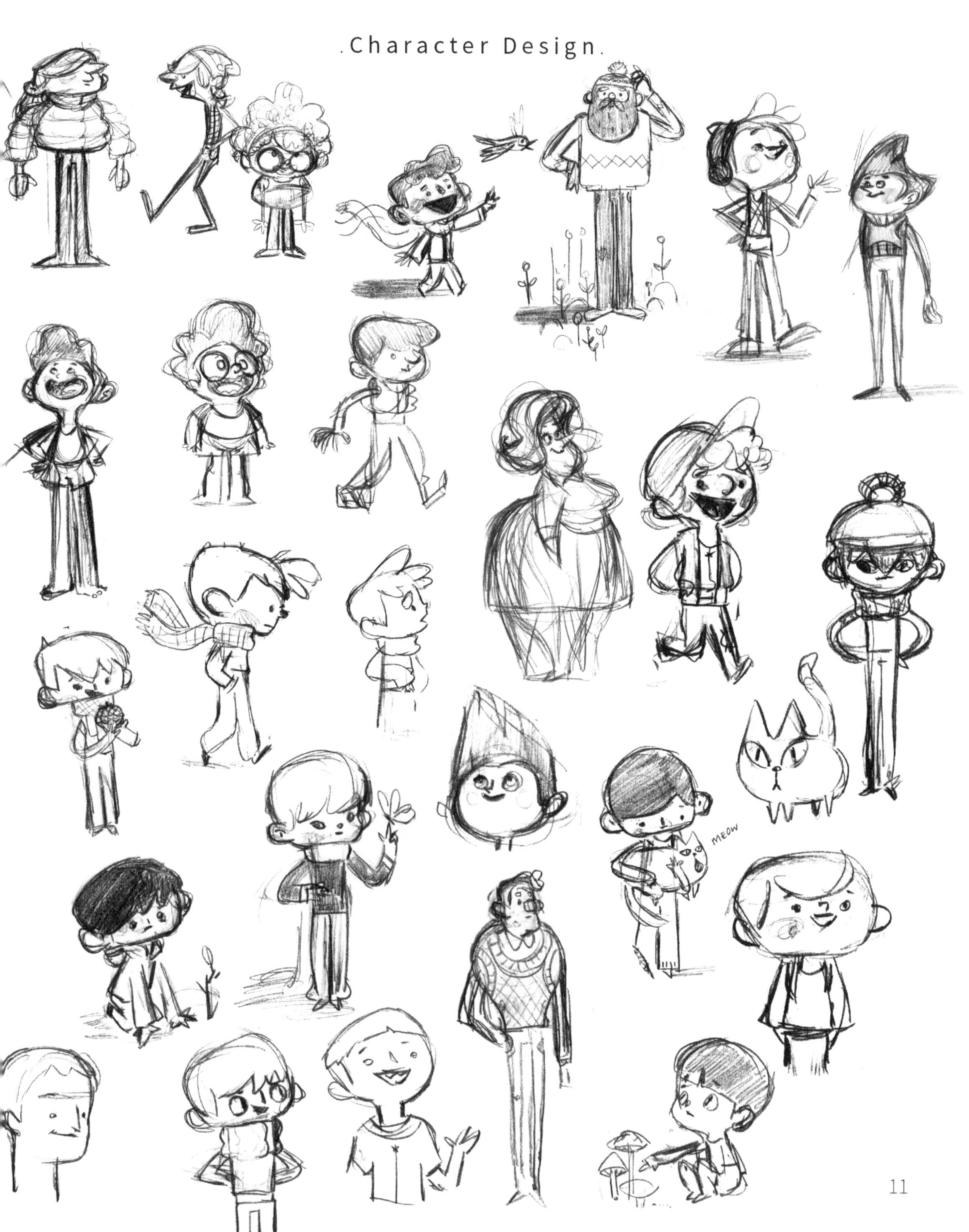

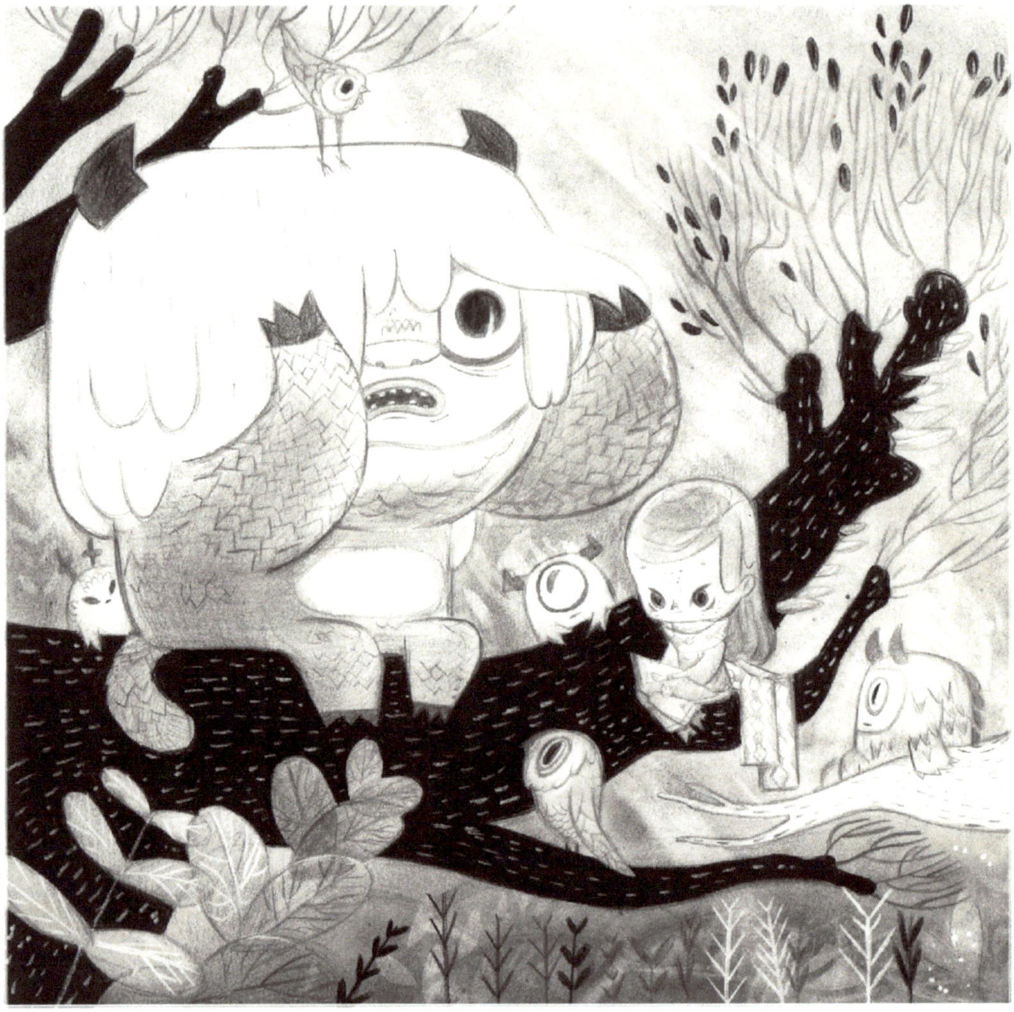

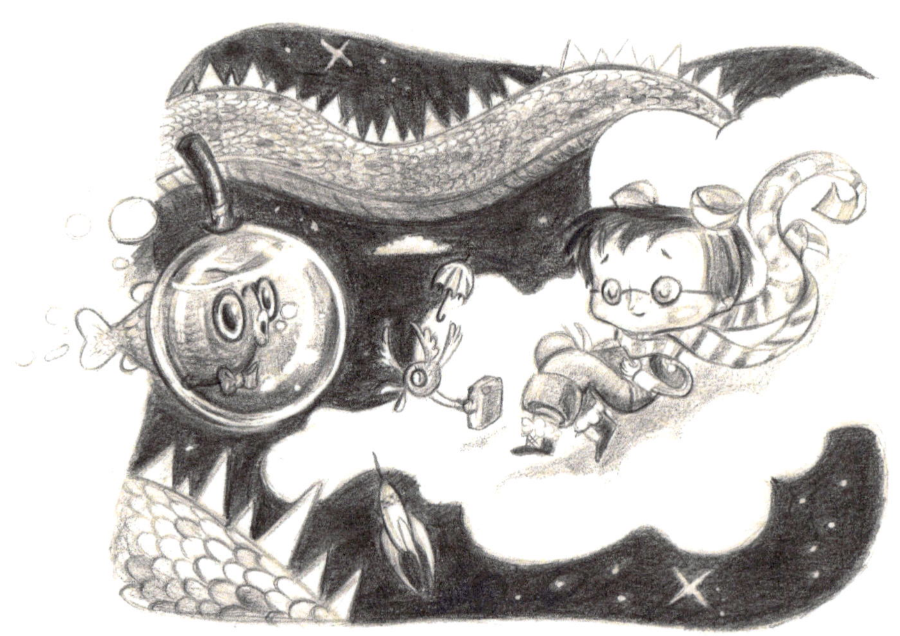

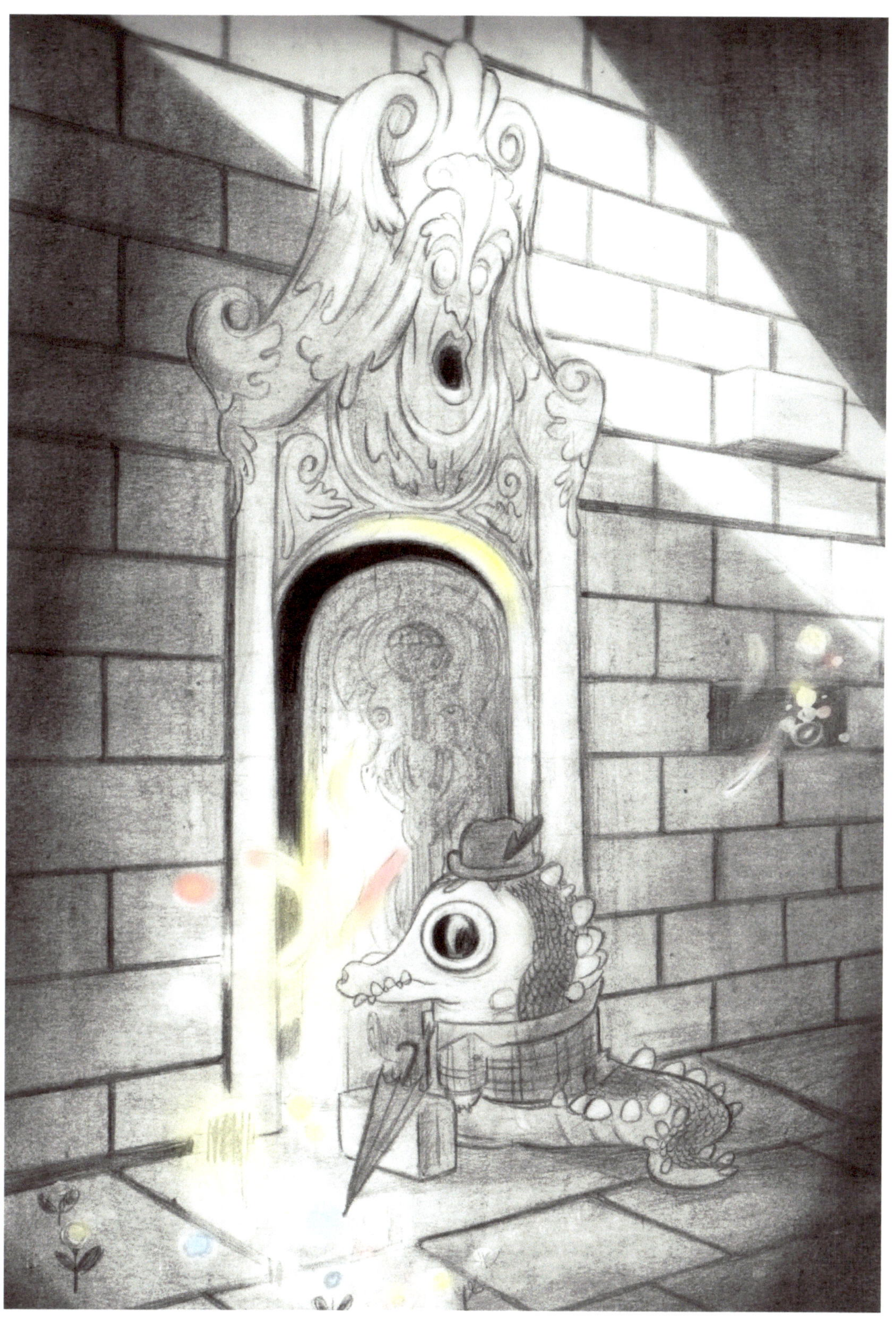

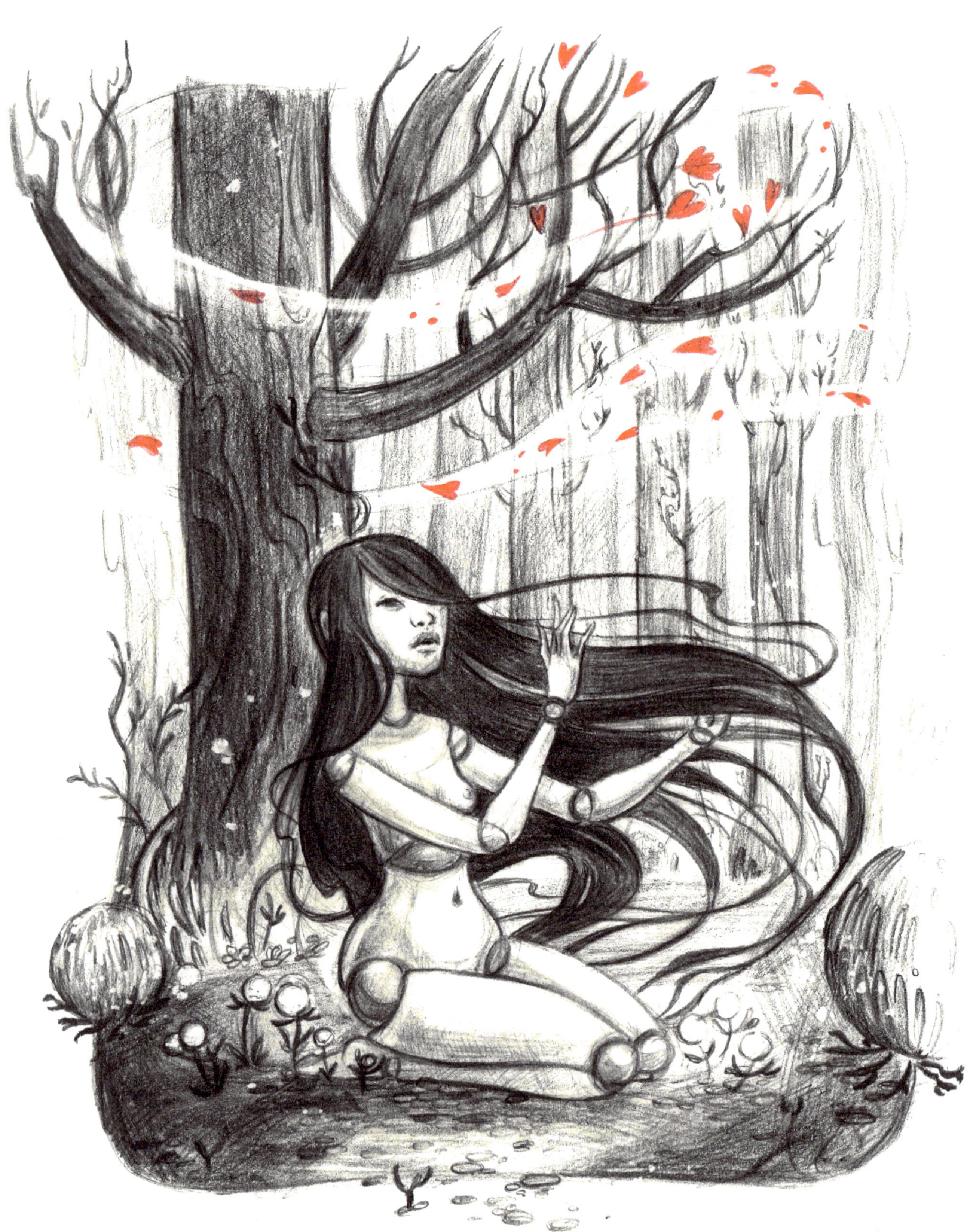

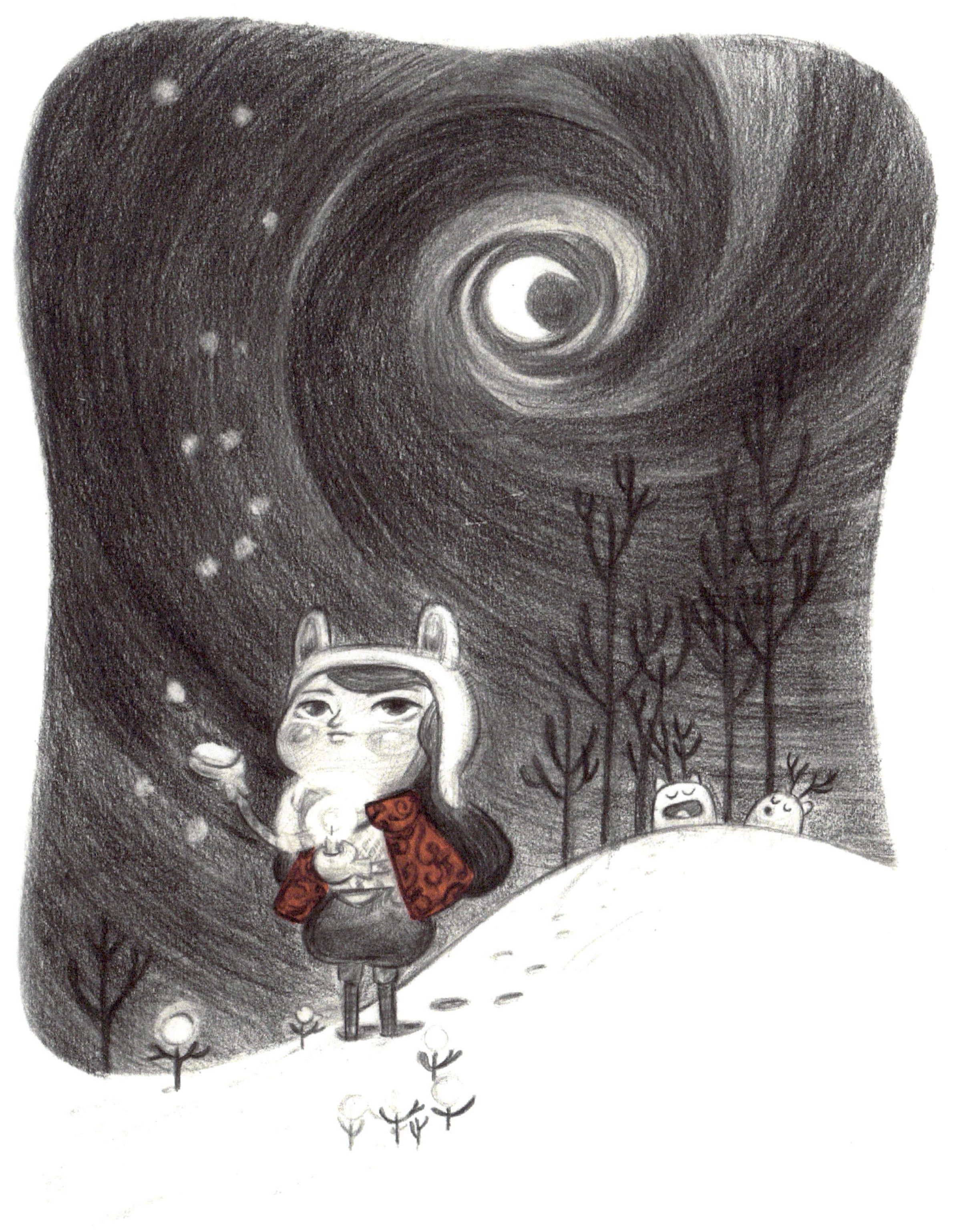

.Pencil Illustration.

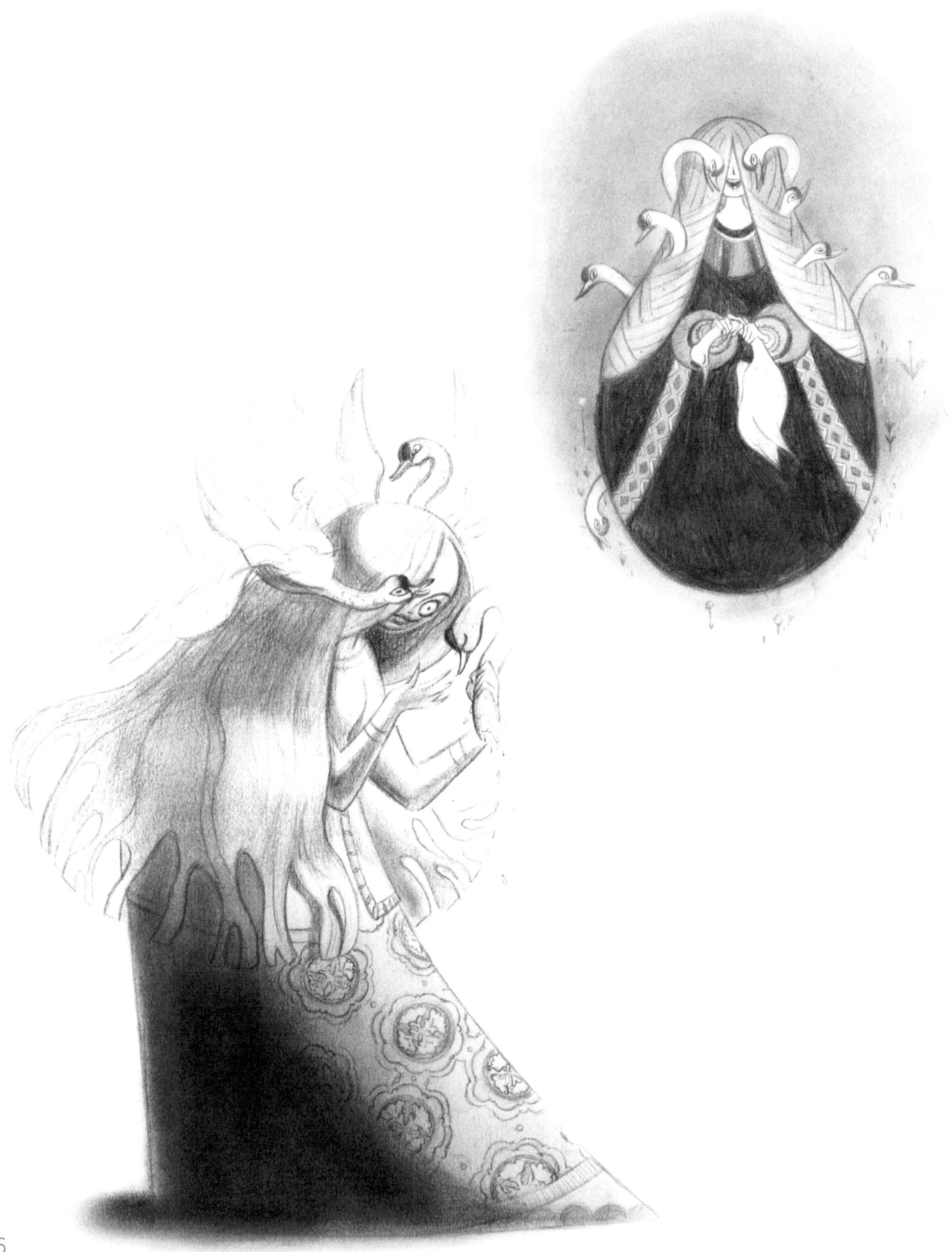

. Pencil Illustration .

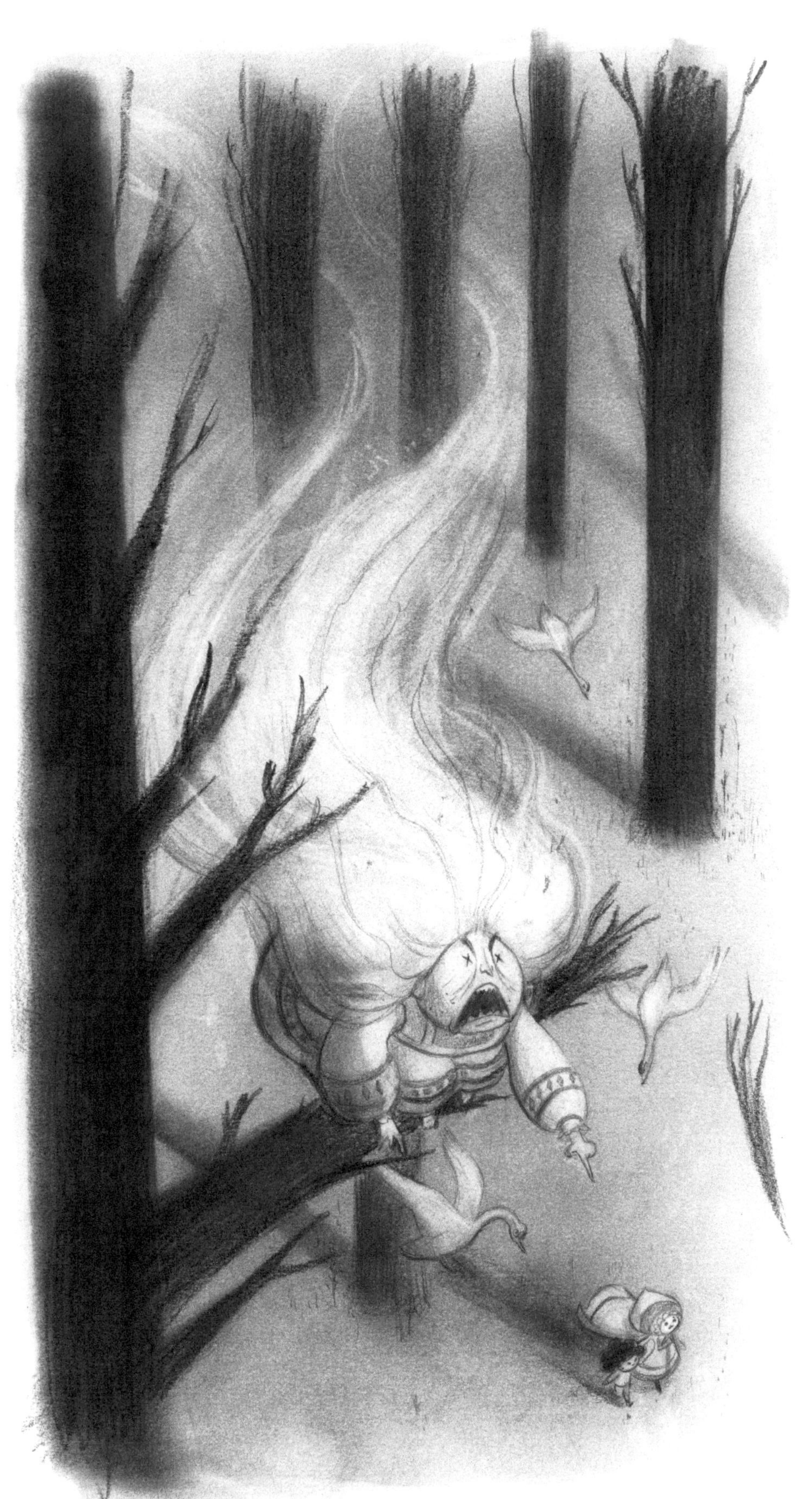

17

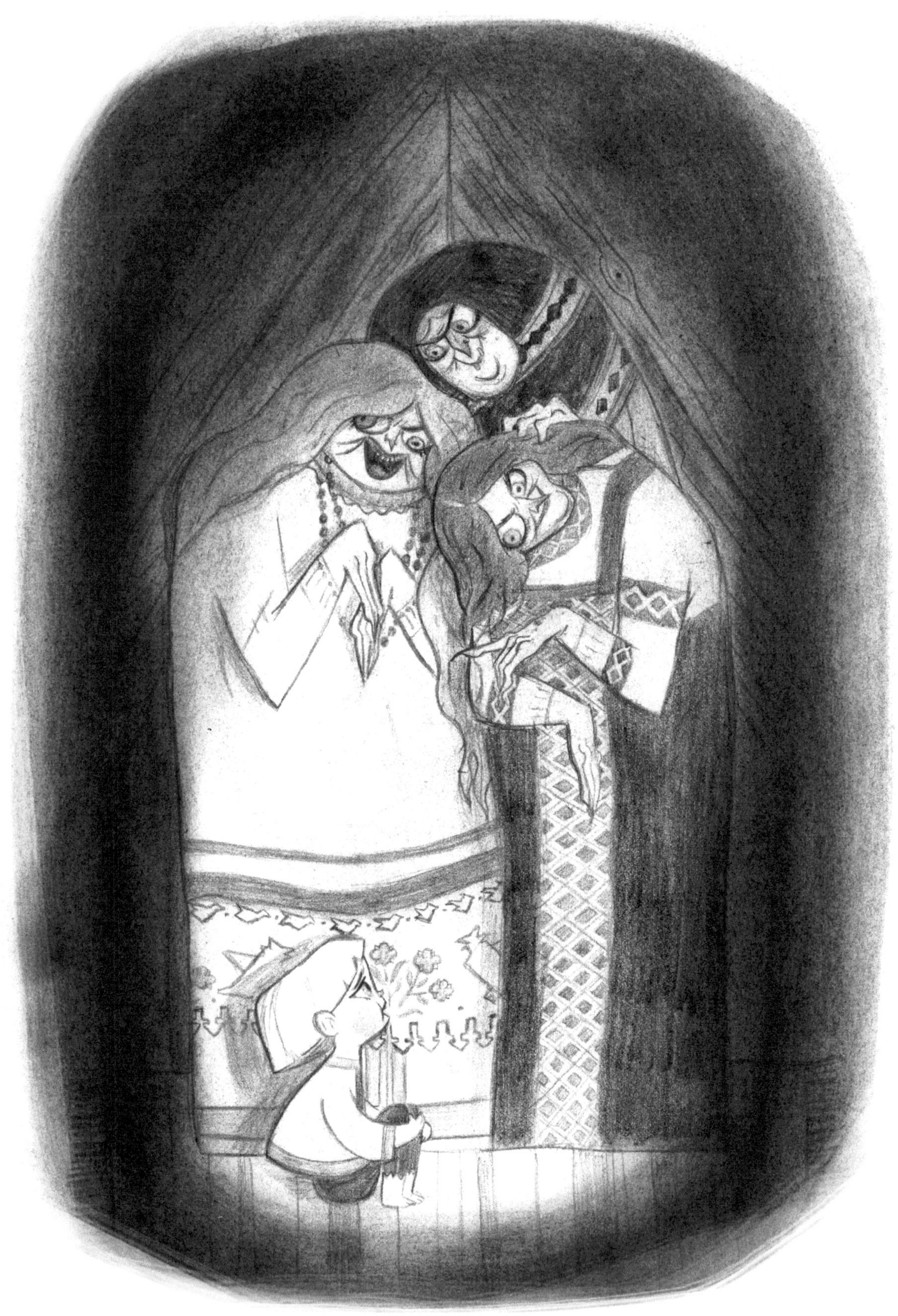

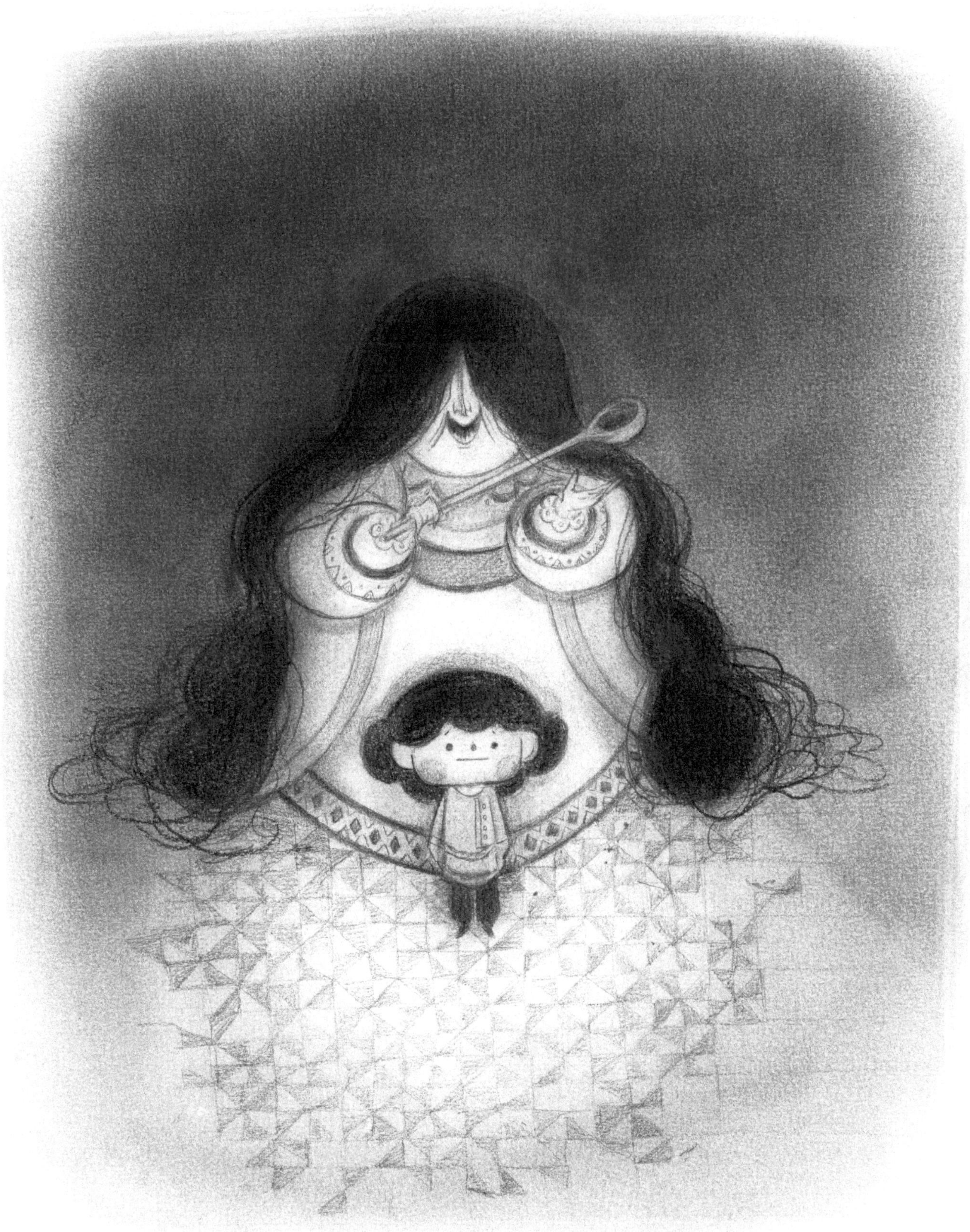

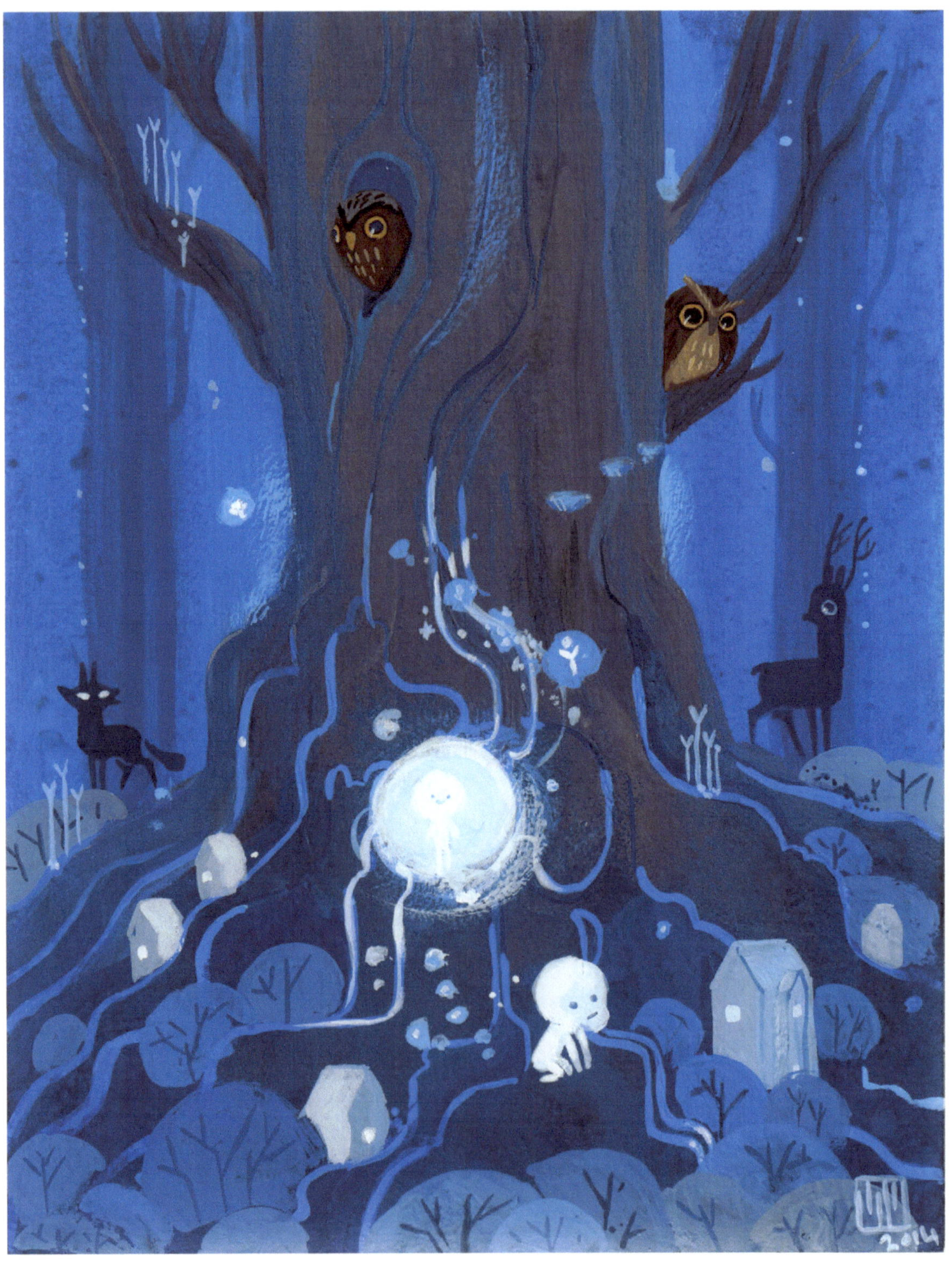

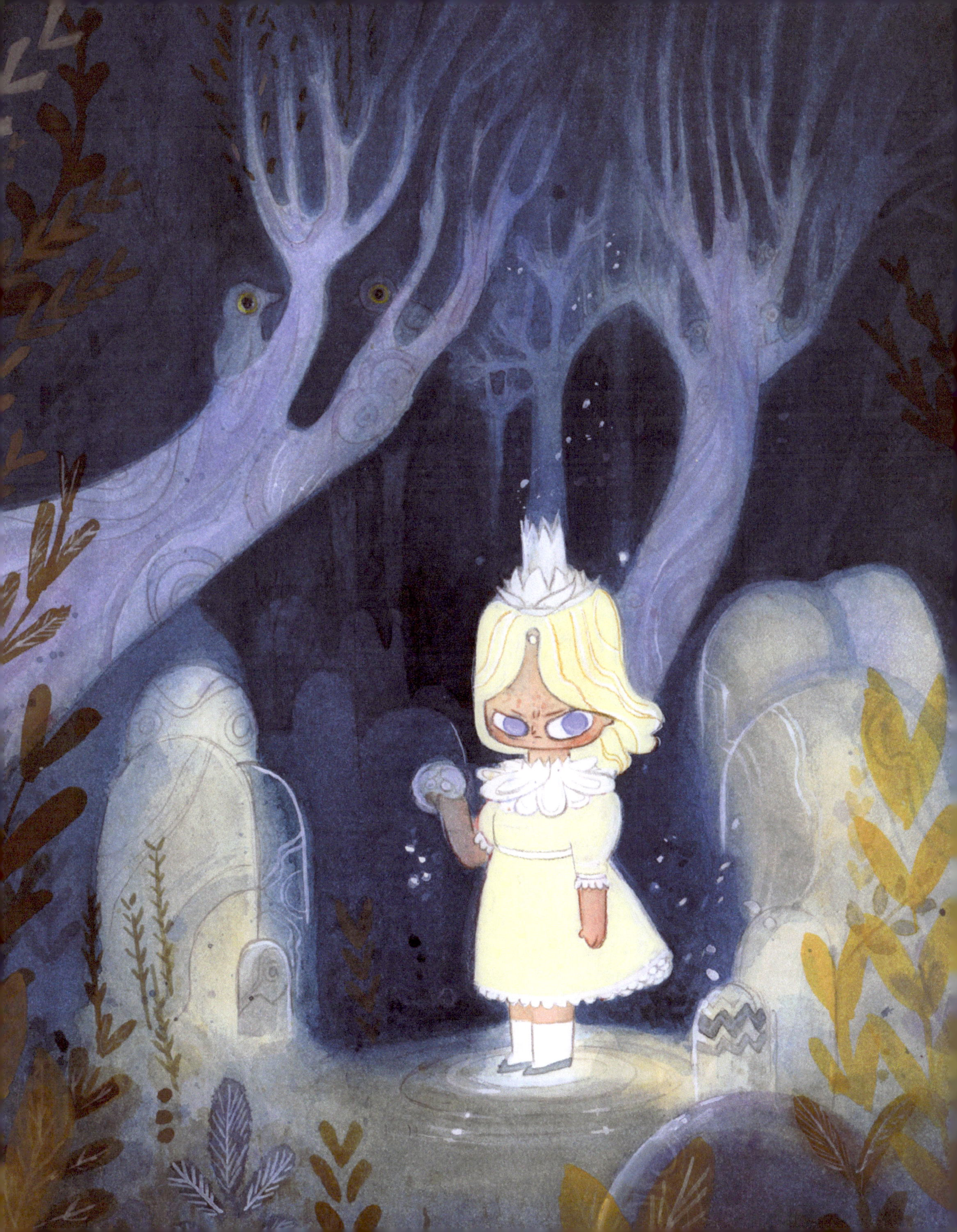

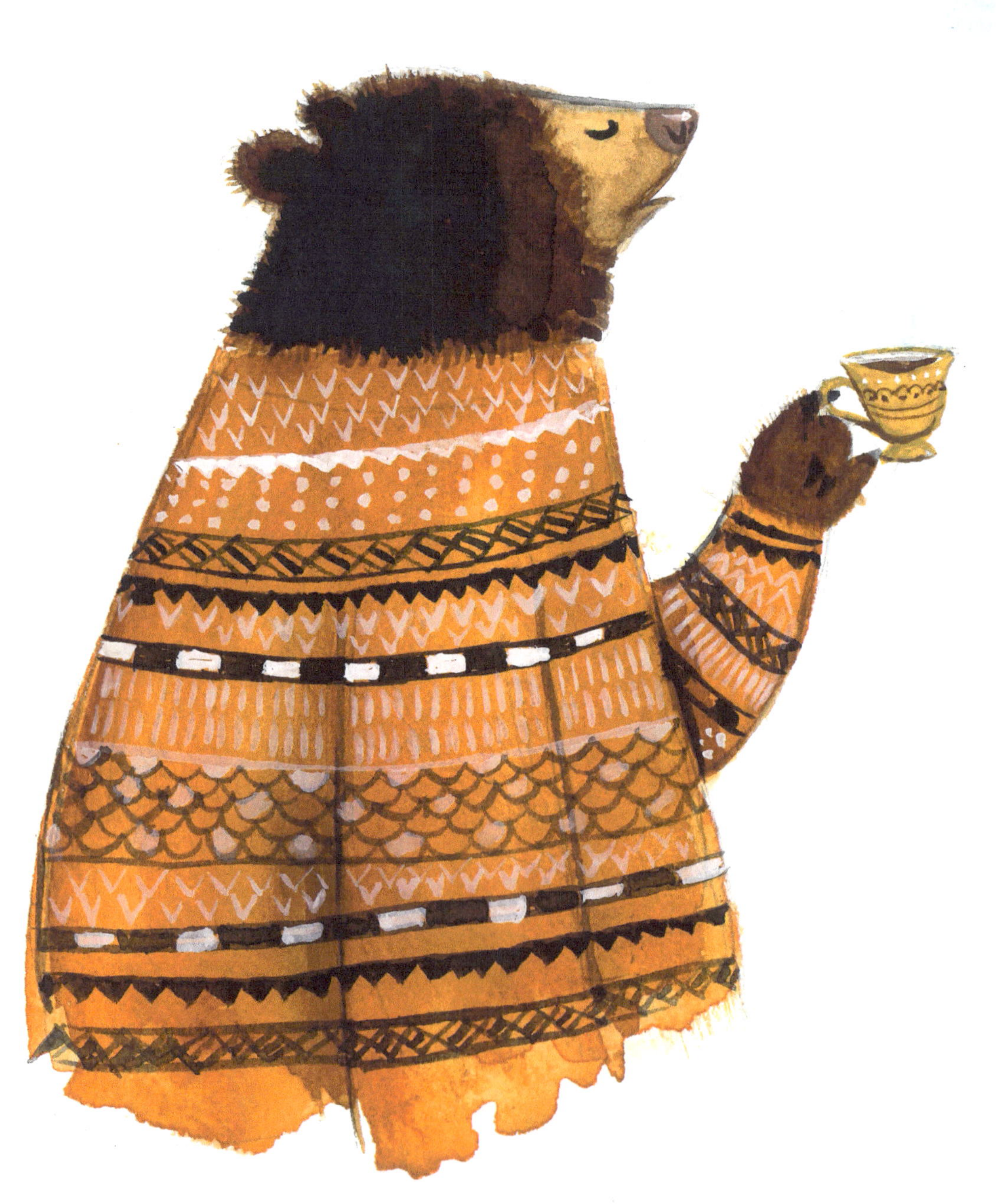

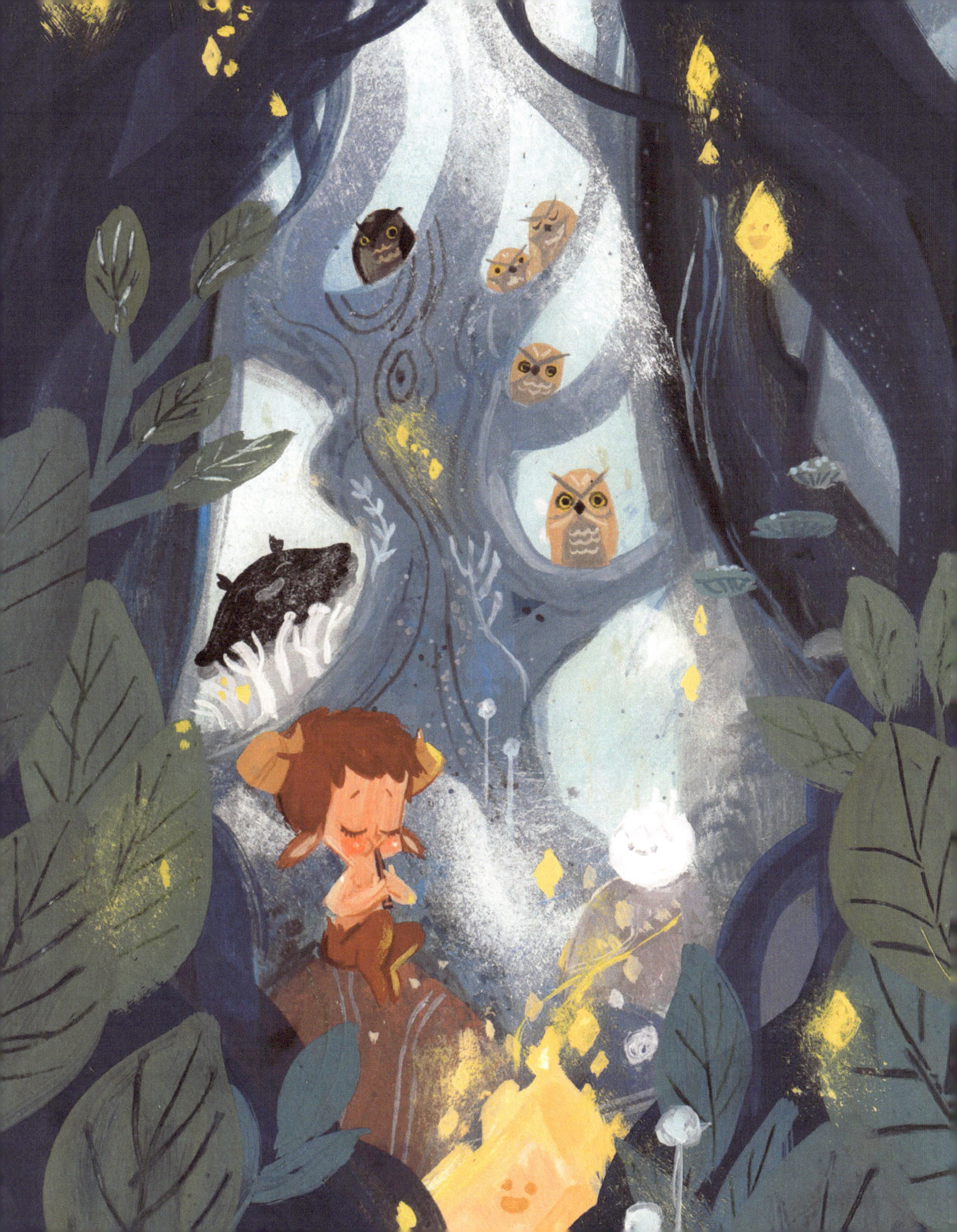

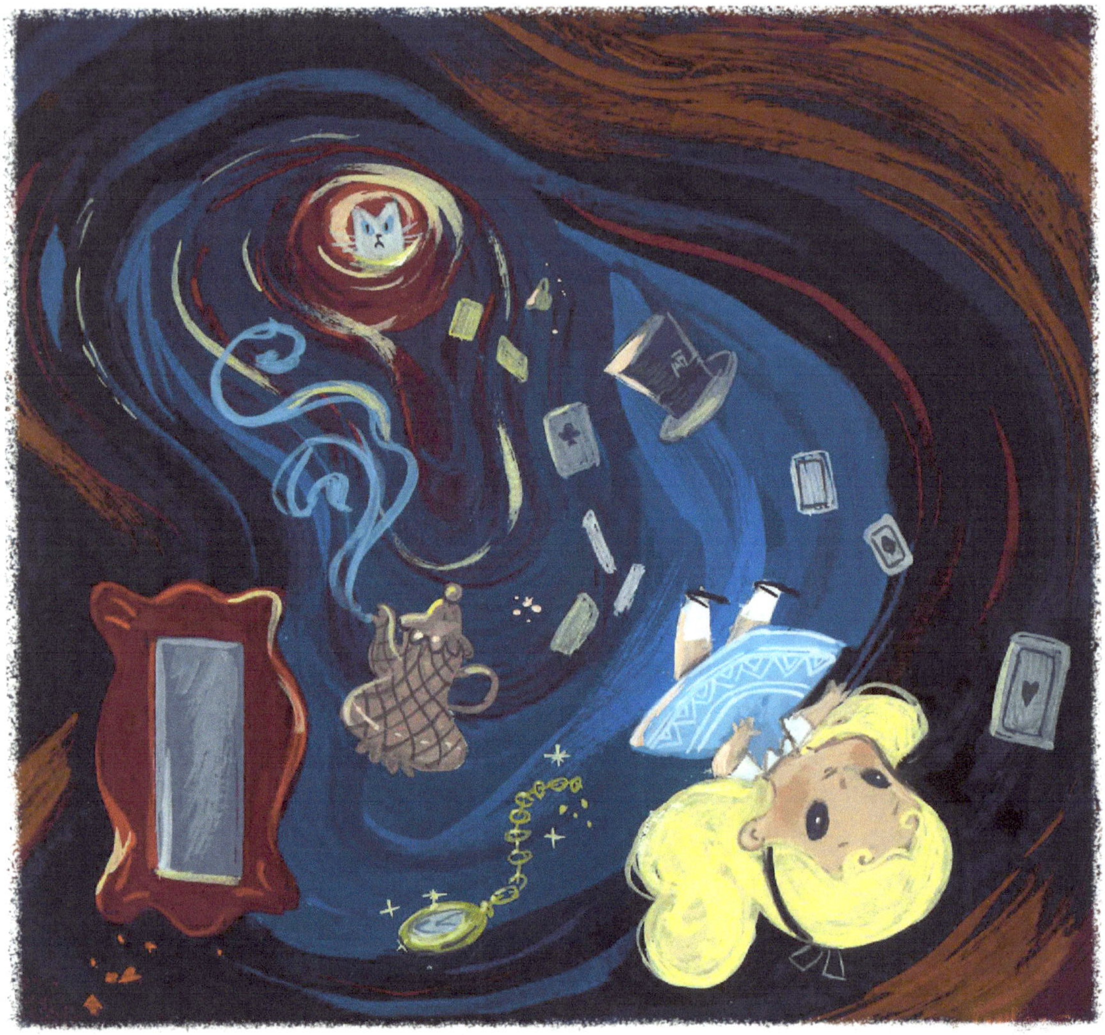

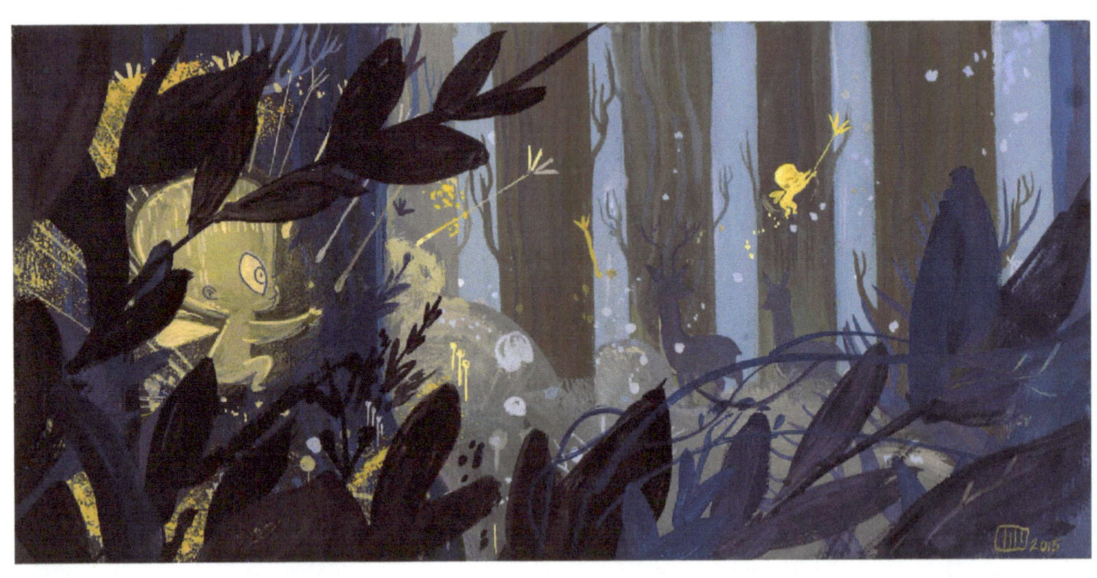

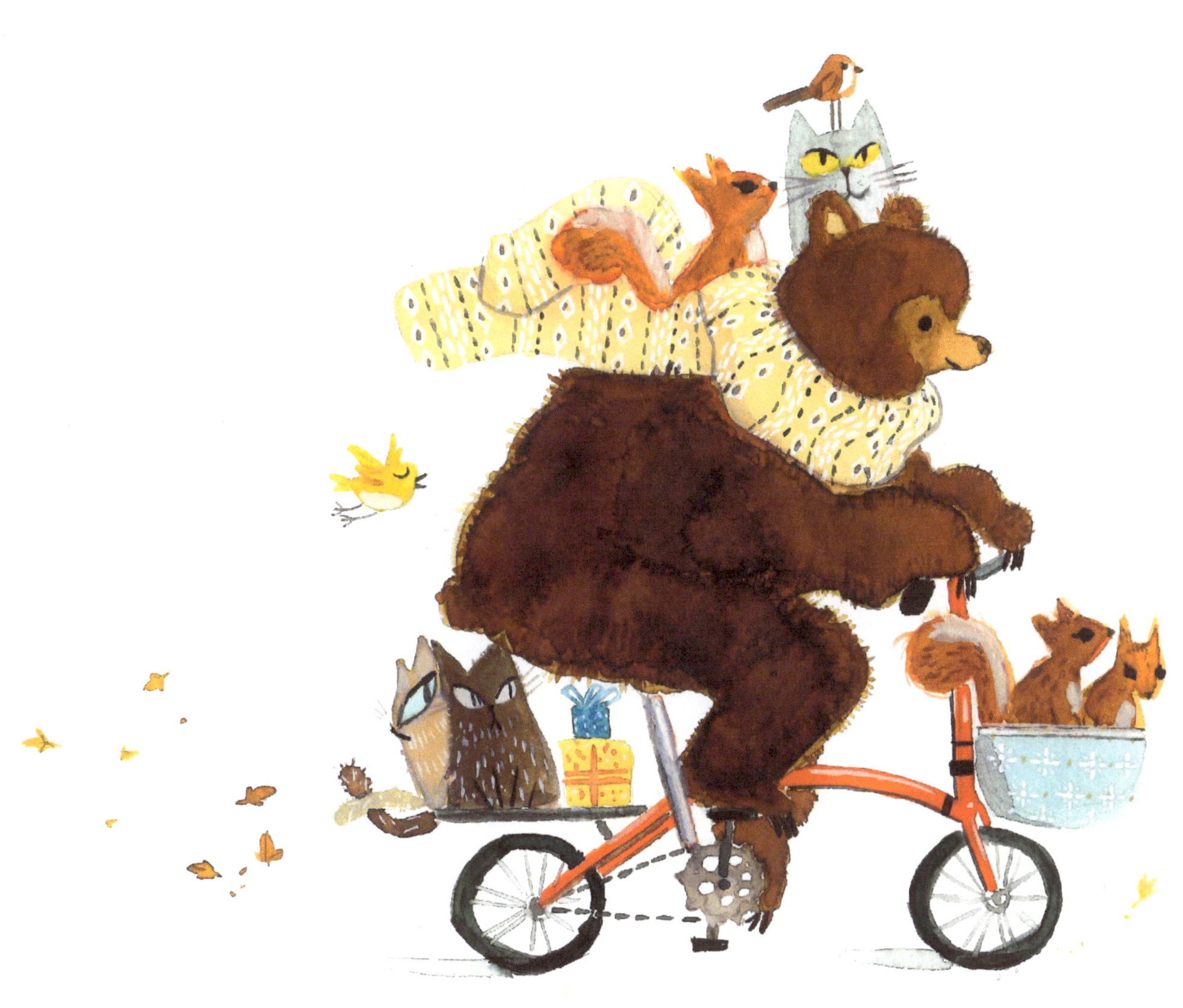

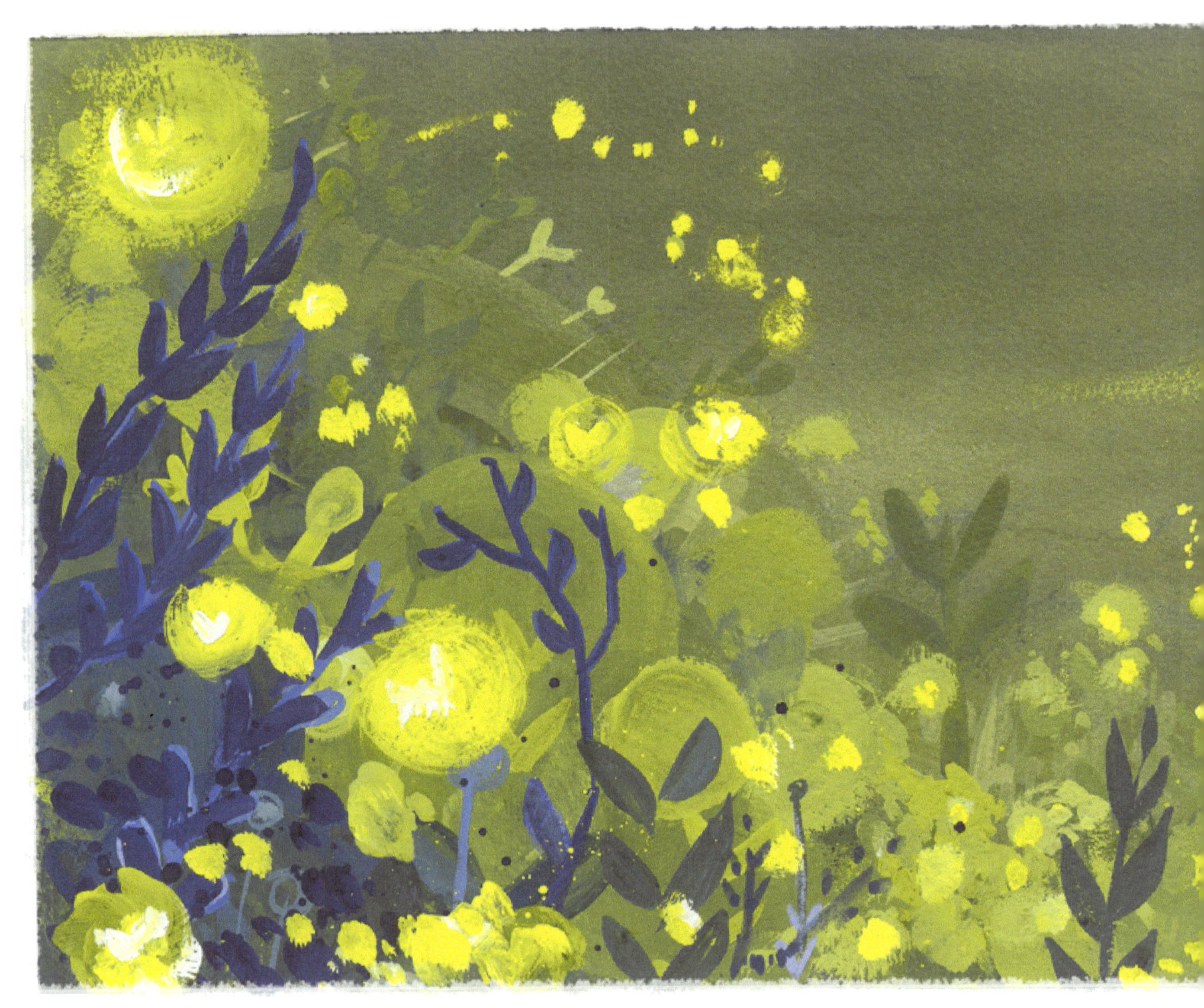

Exhibited and auctioned
at the Animation Art Show 2013

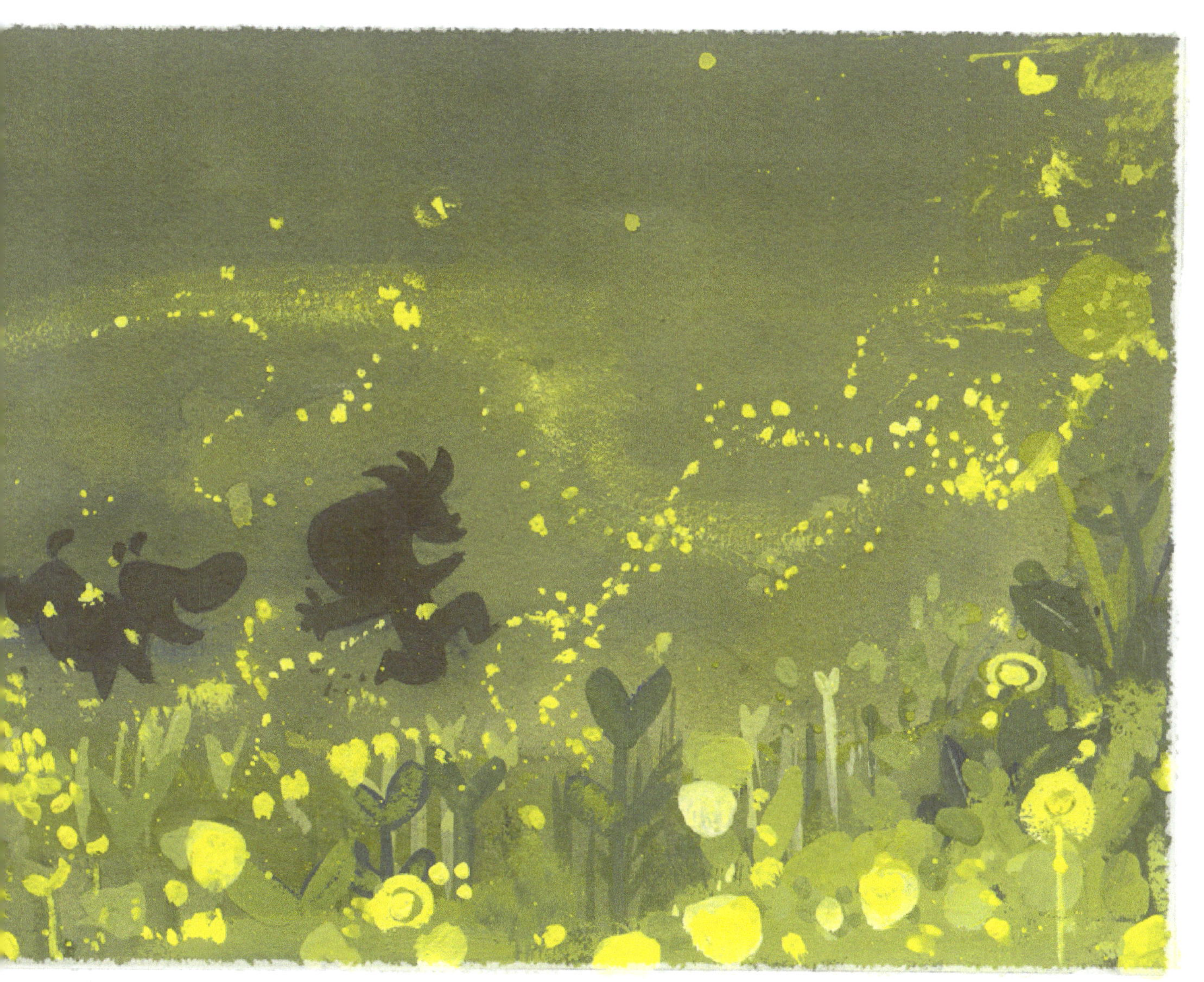

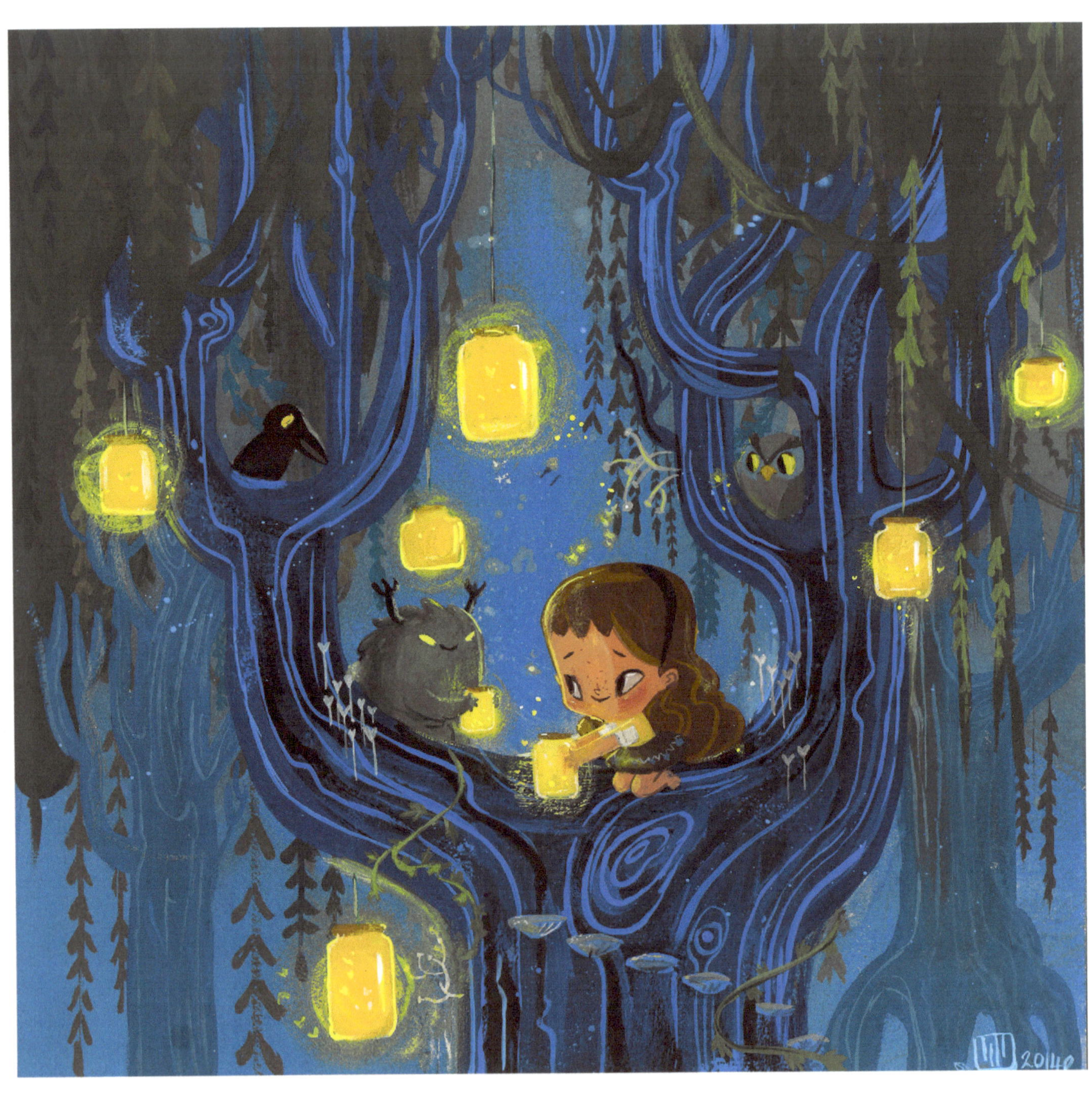

Exhibited and auctioned
at the Animation Art Show 2014

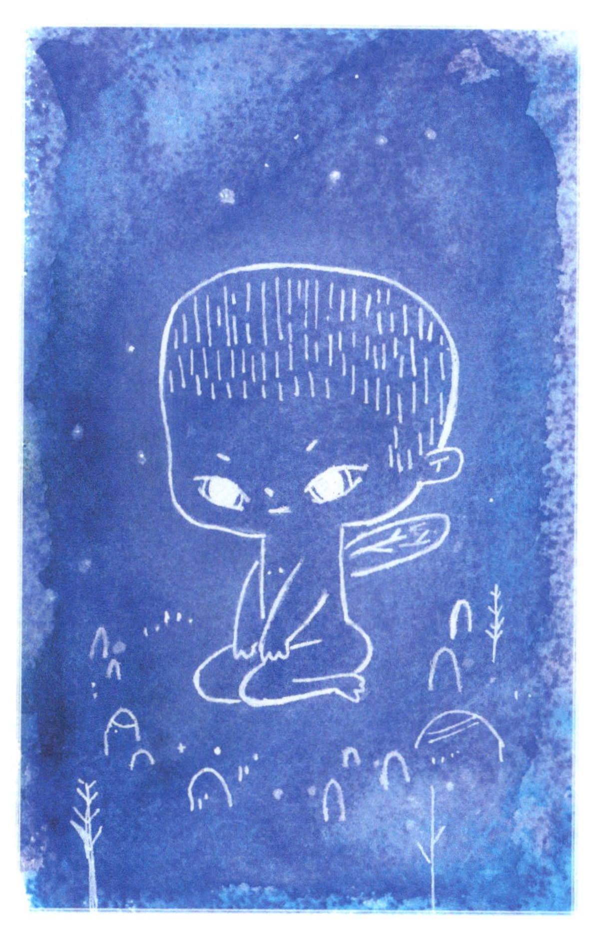

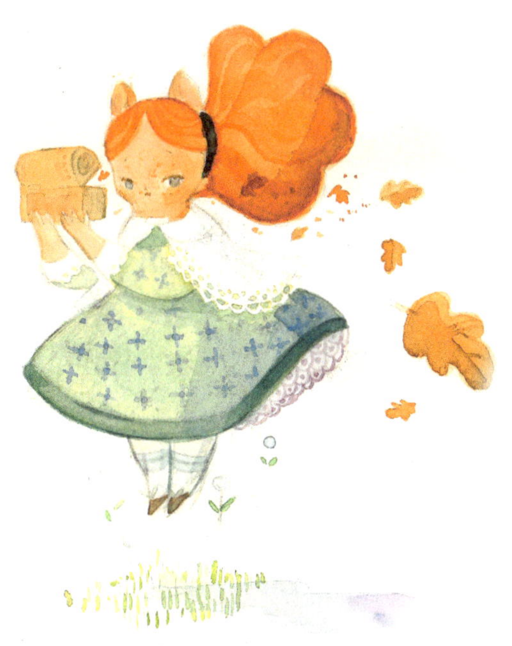

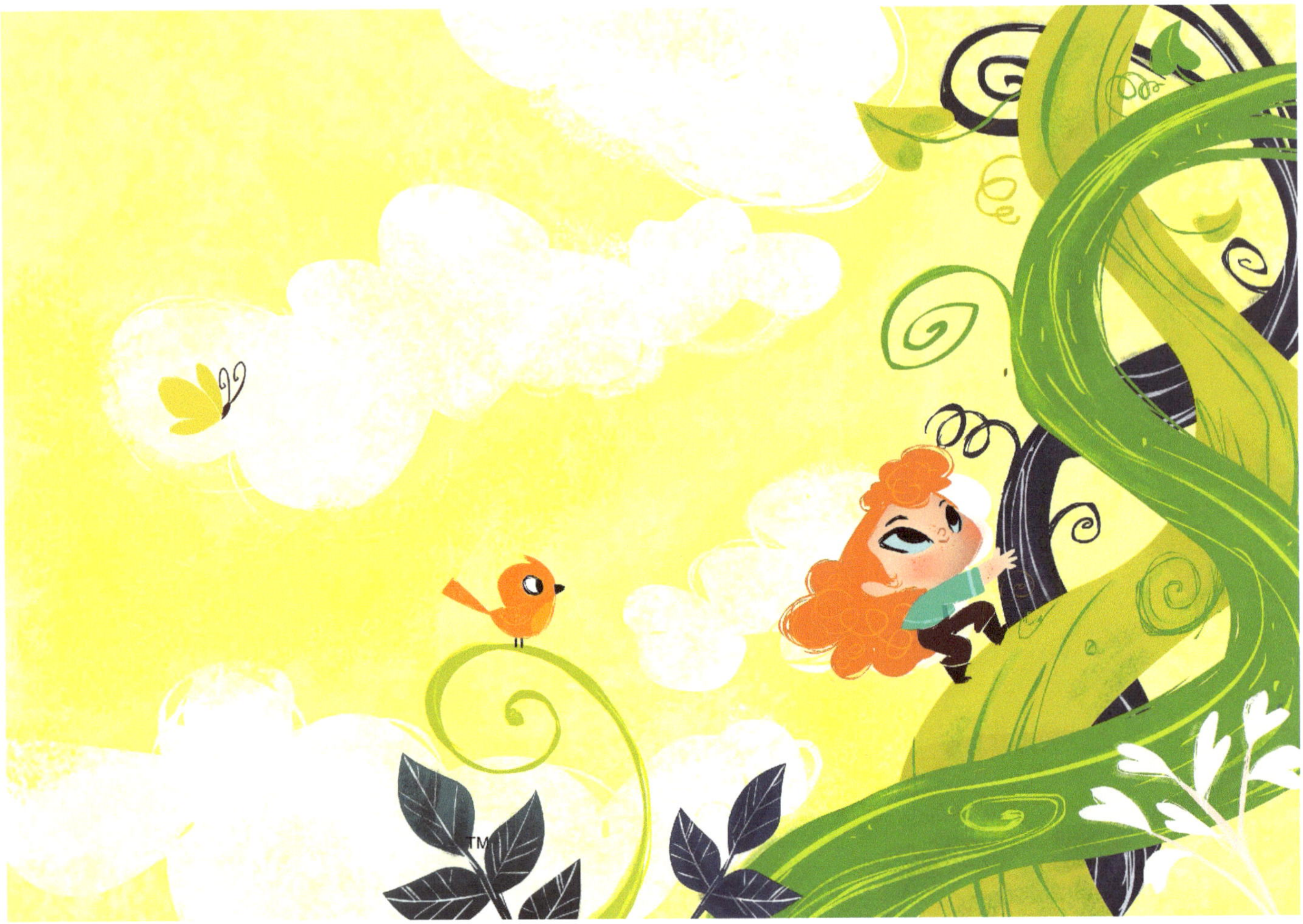

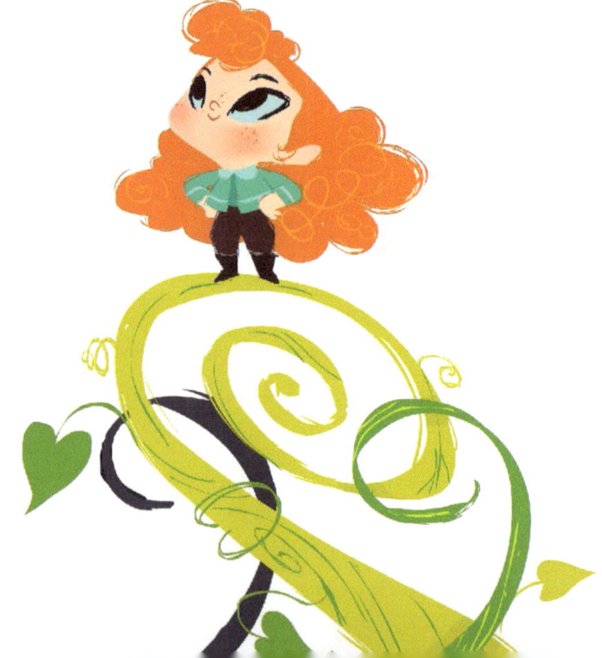

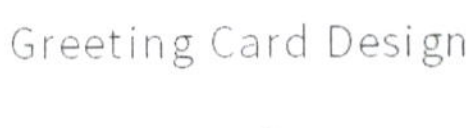

Greeting Card Design

- Huggitos -

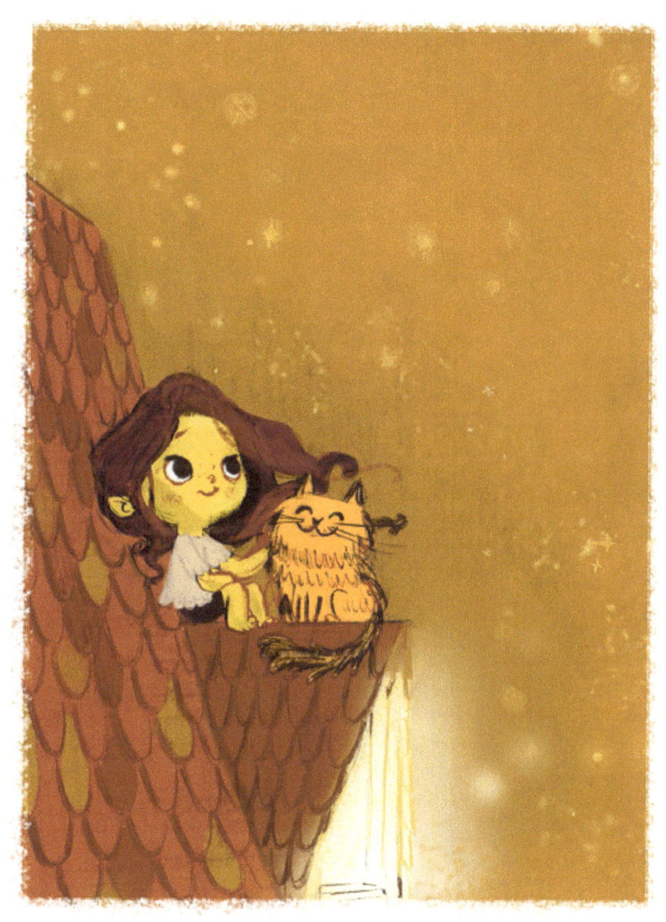

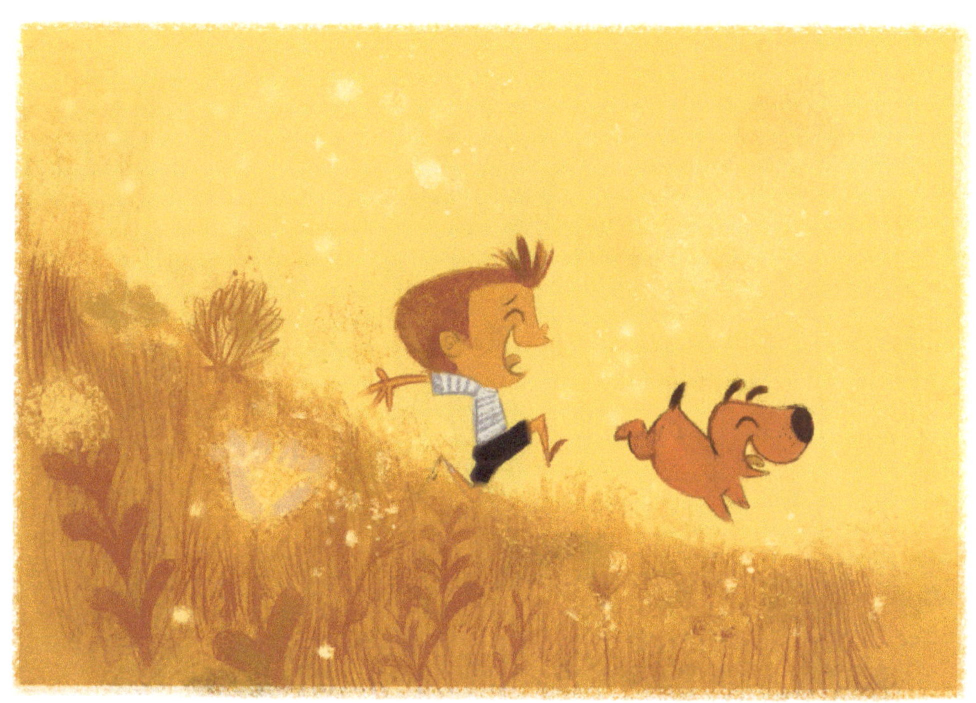

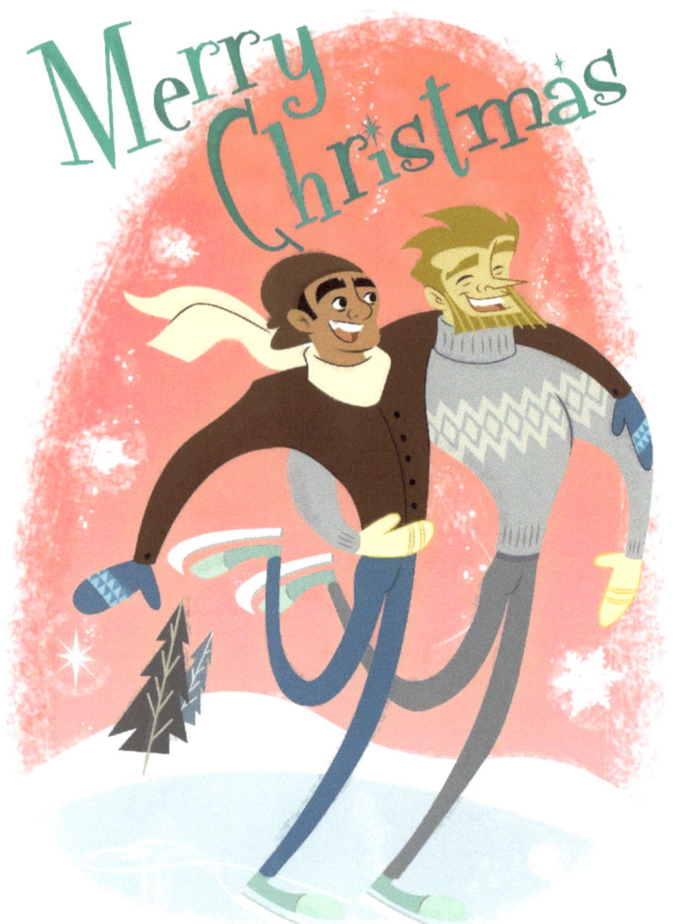

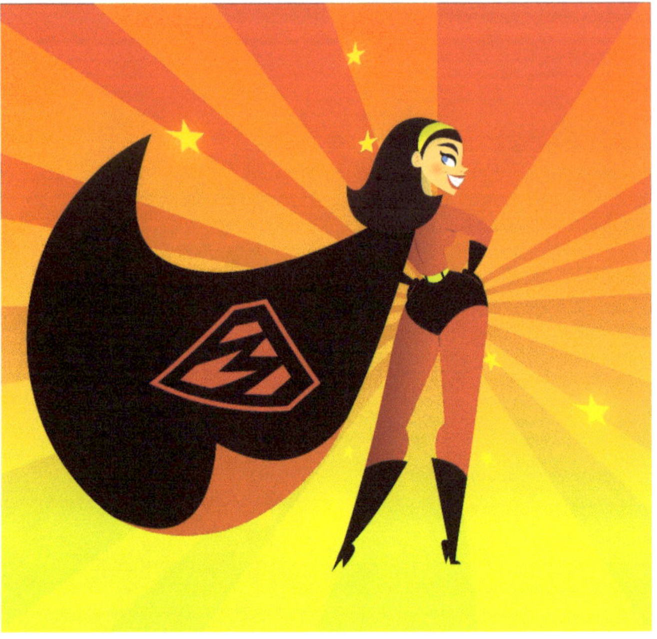

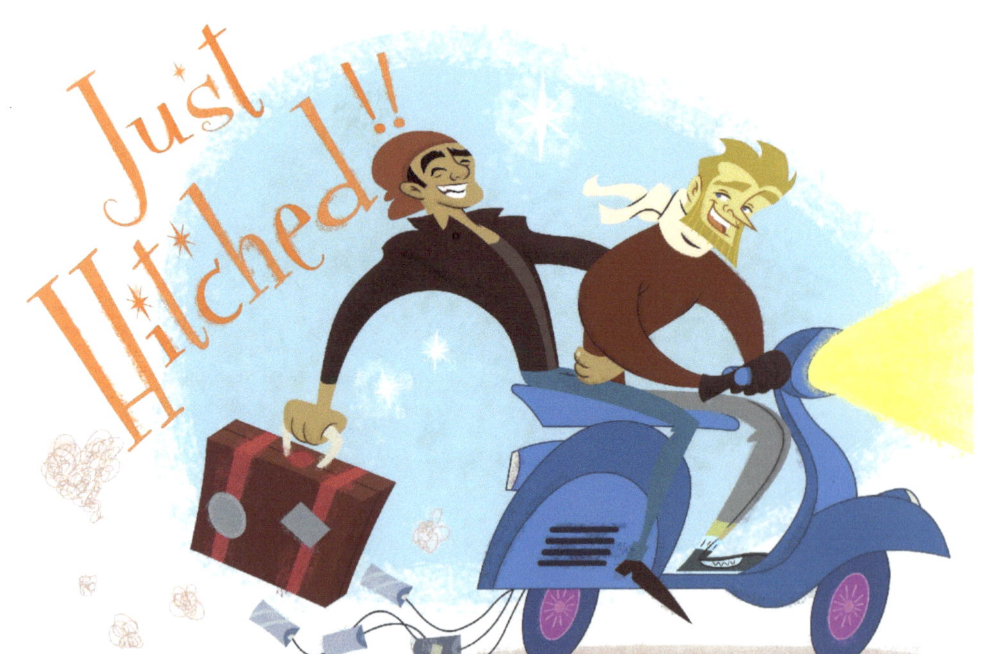

Greeting Card Design

- Huggitos -

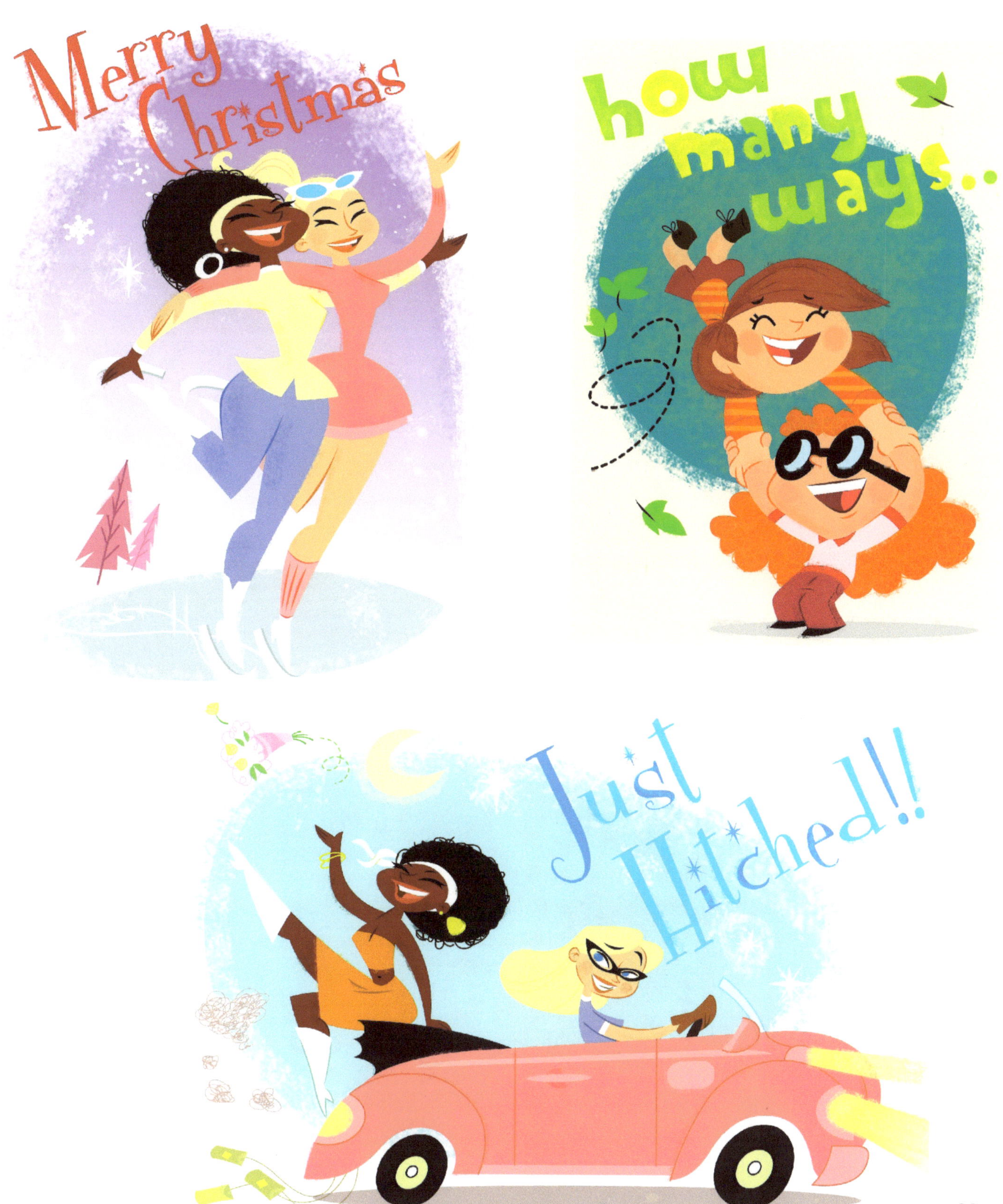
Merry Christmas
how many ways..
Just Hitched!!

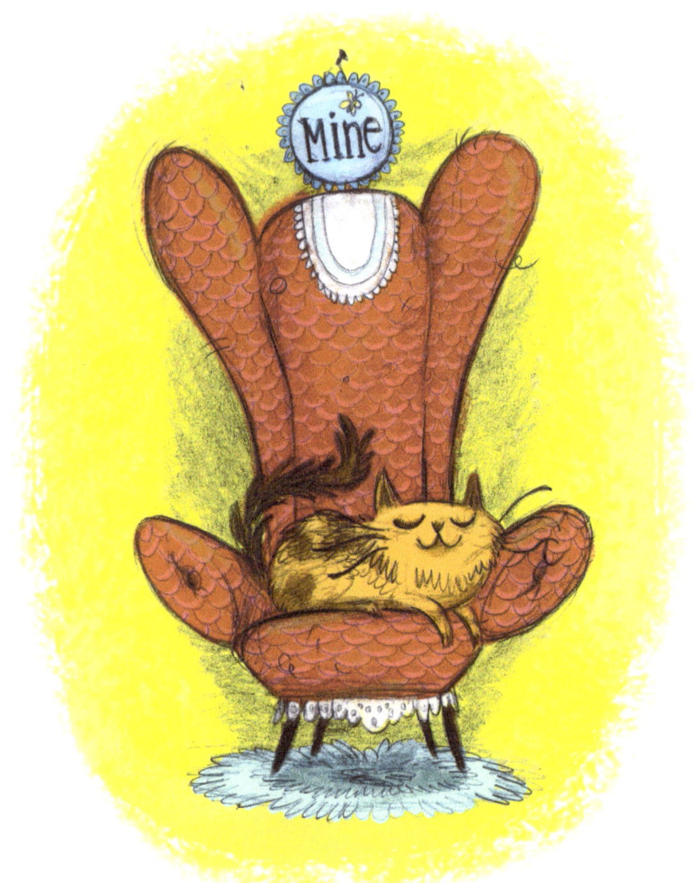

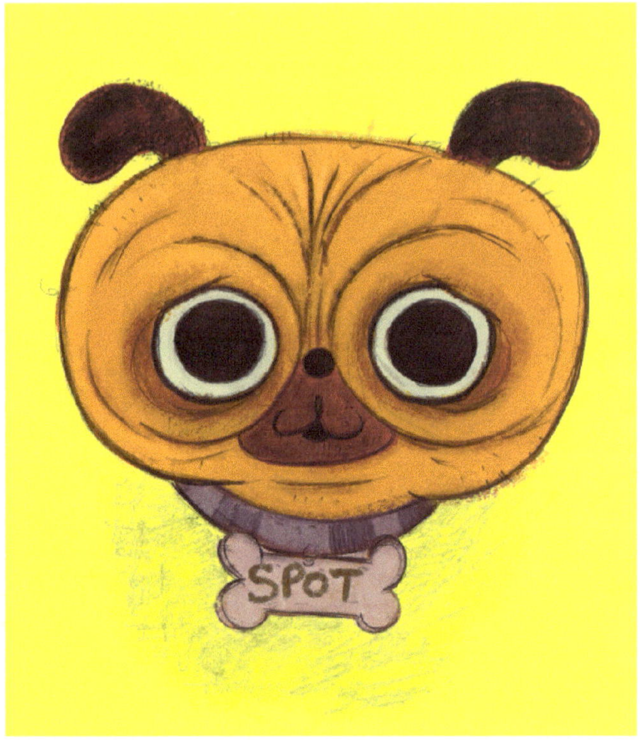

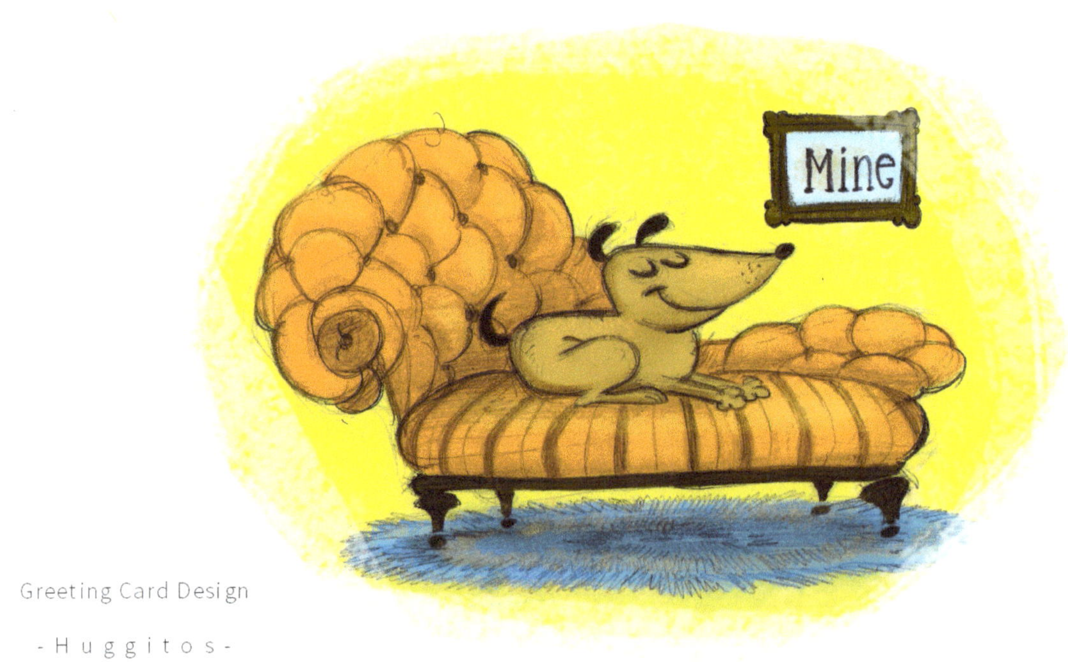

Greeting Card Design

- Huggitos -

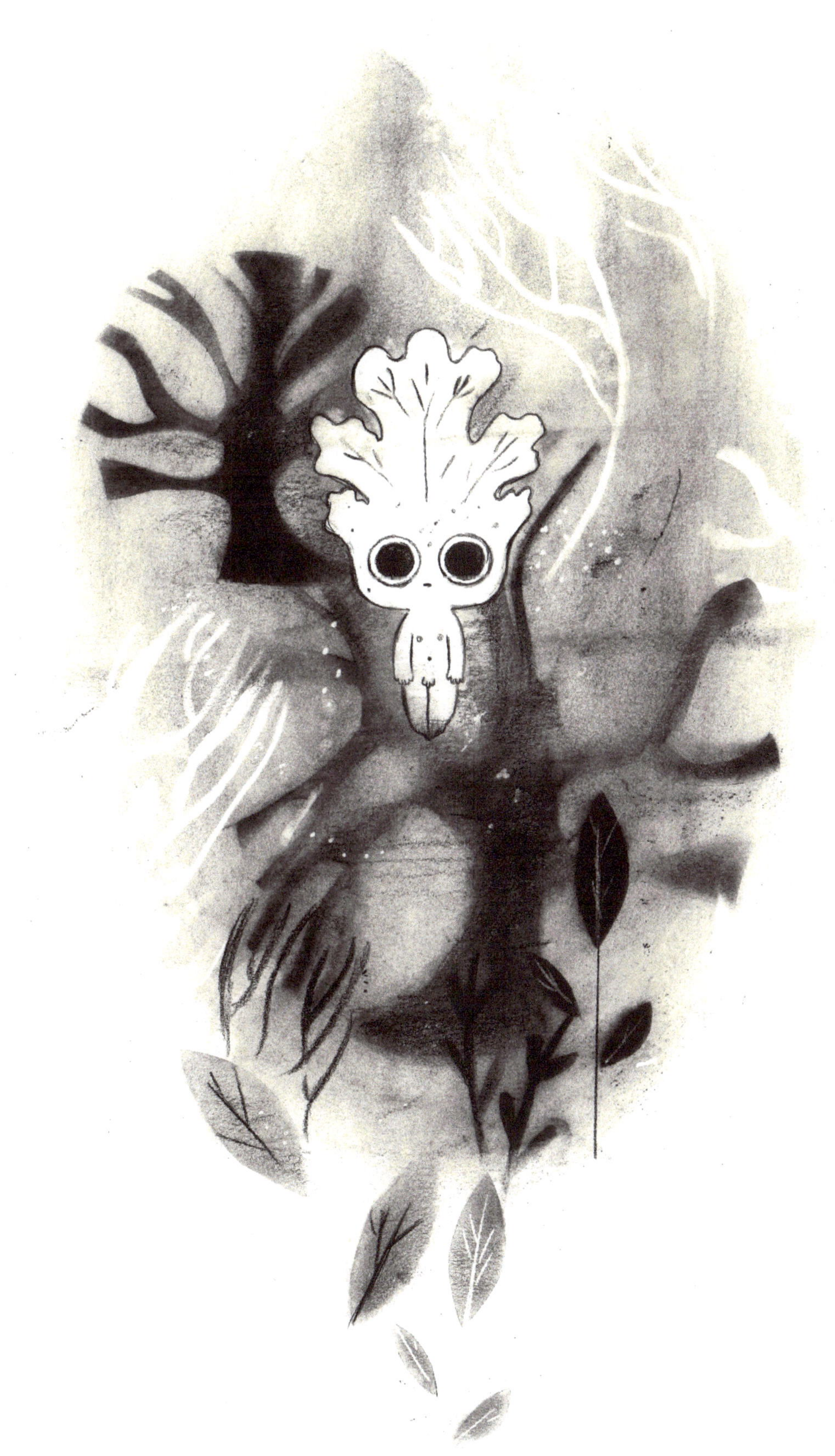

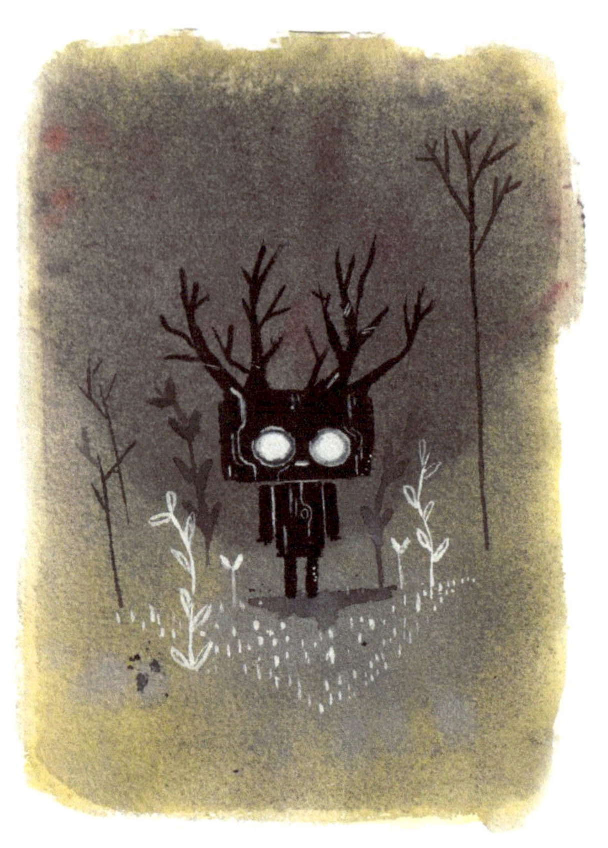

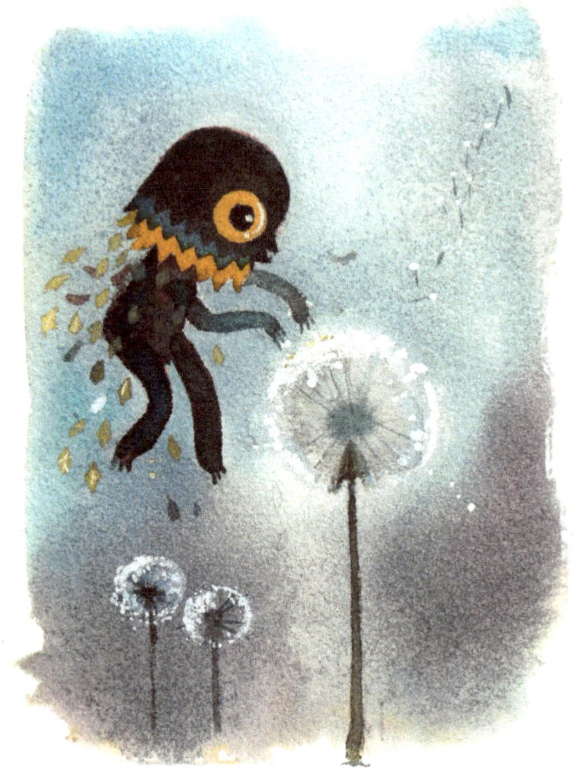

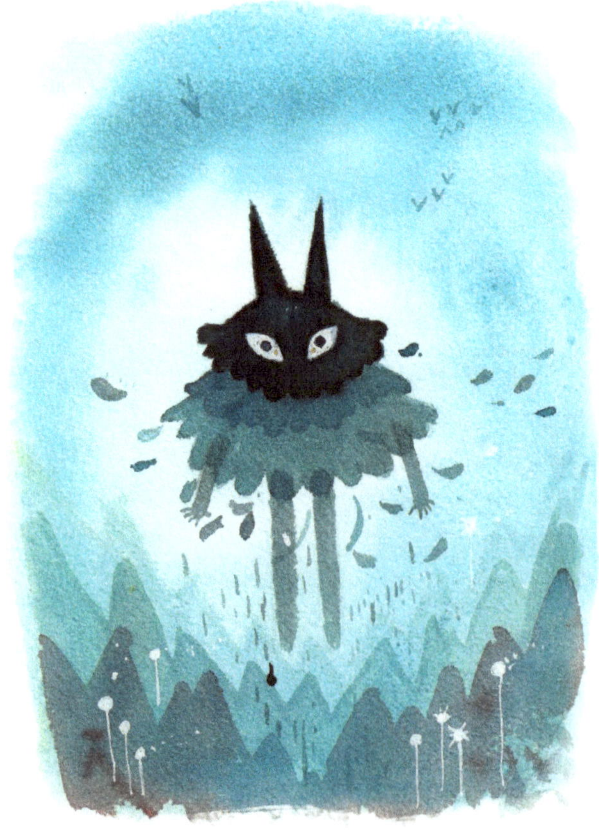

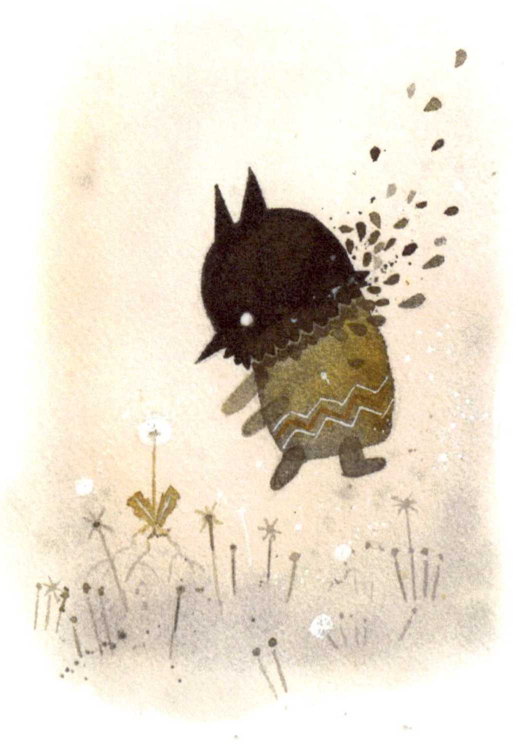

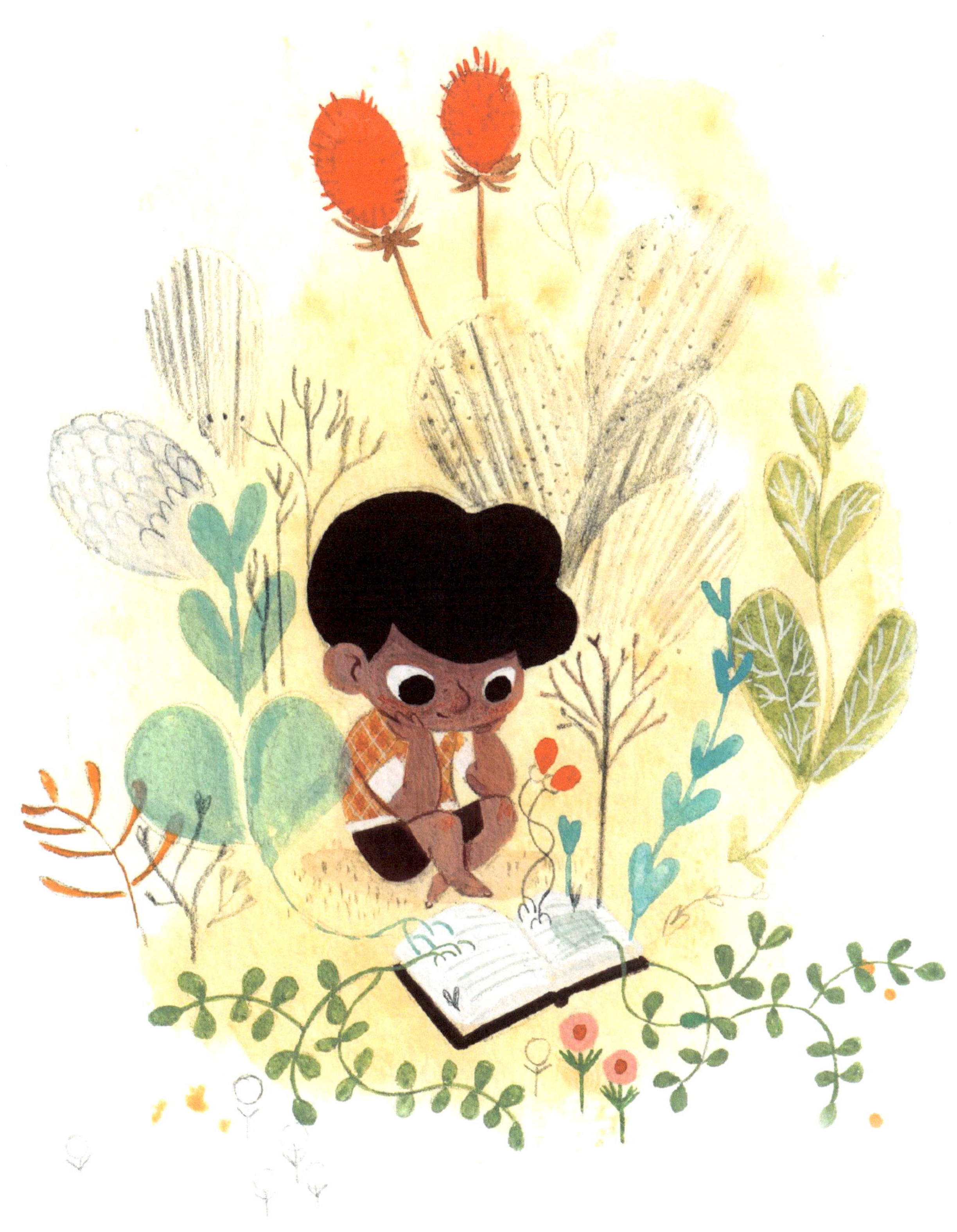

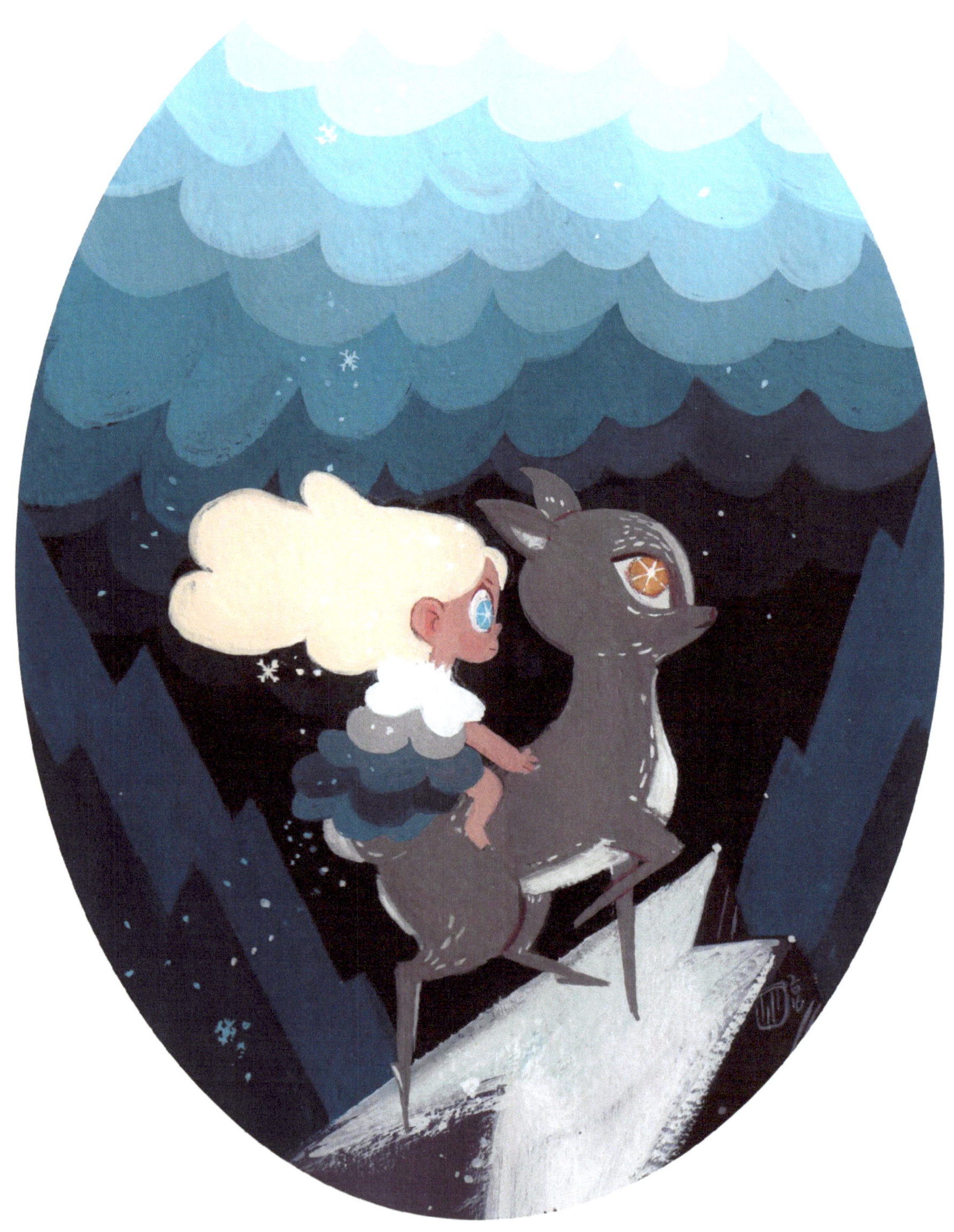

"Snowflake"
Russian Fairytales
Exhibited in St.Petersburg, Russia.

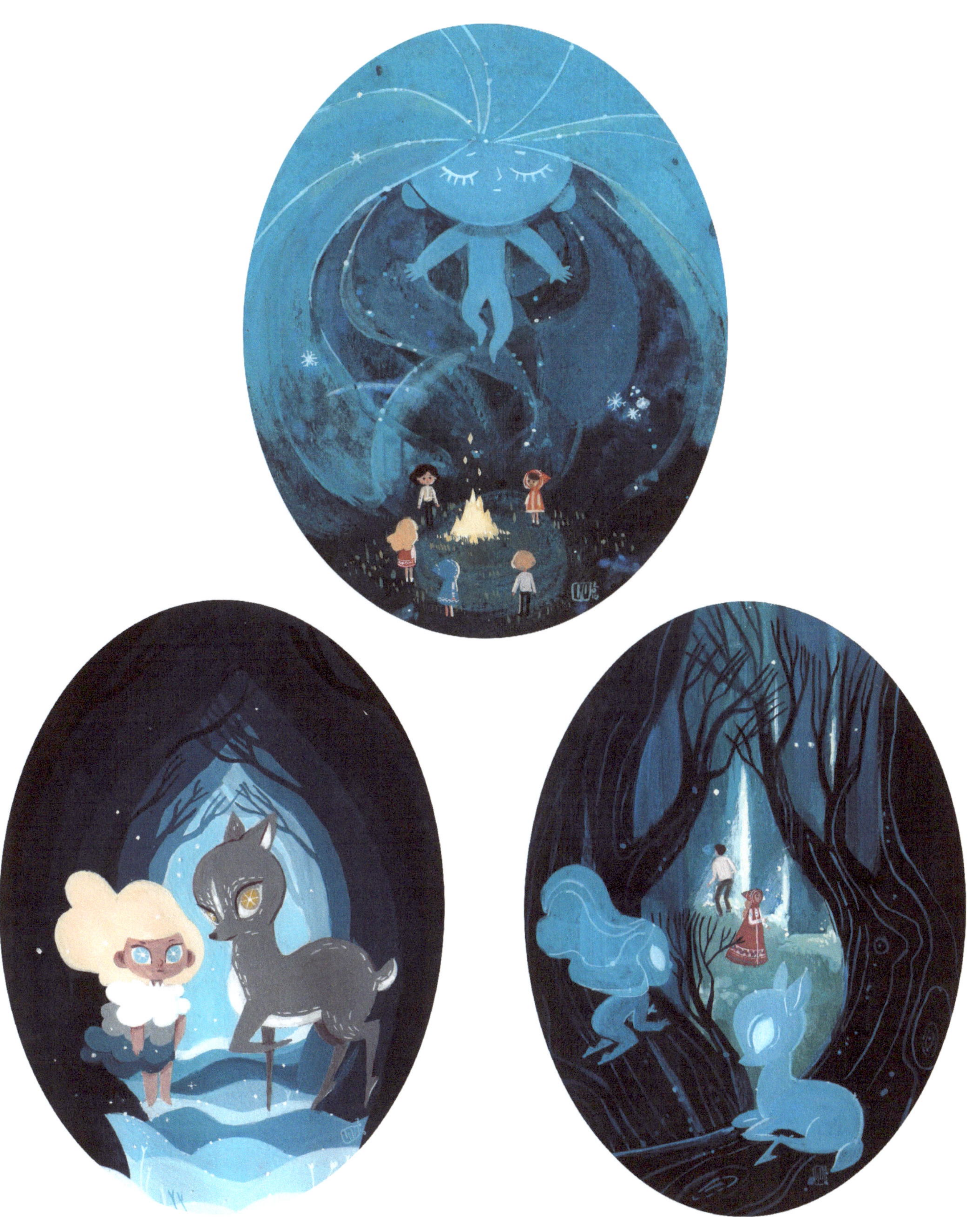

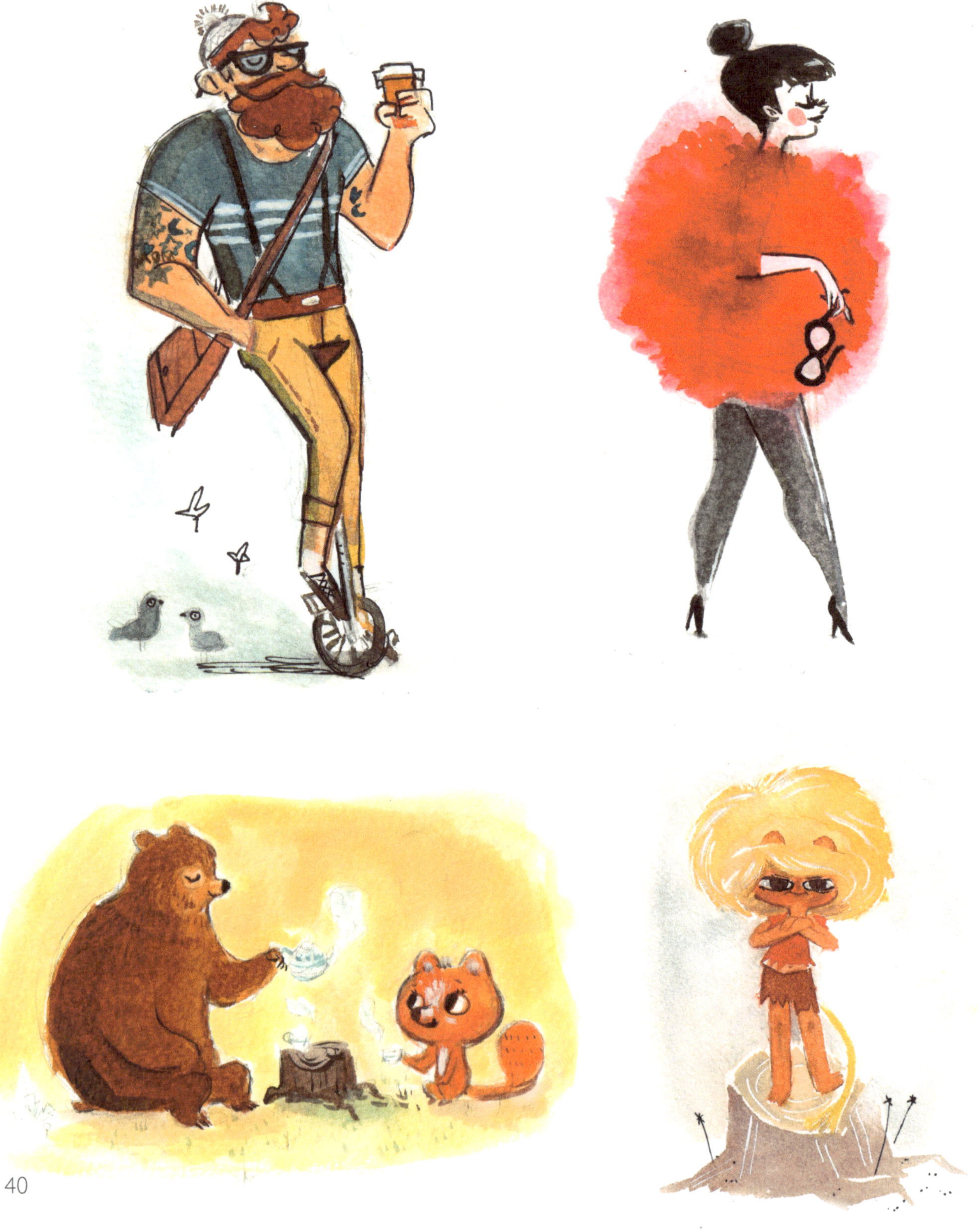

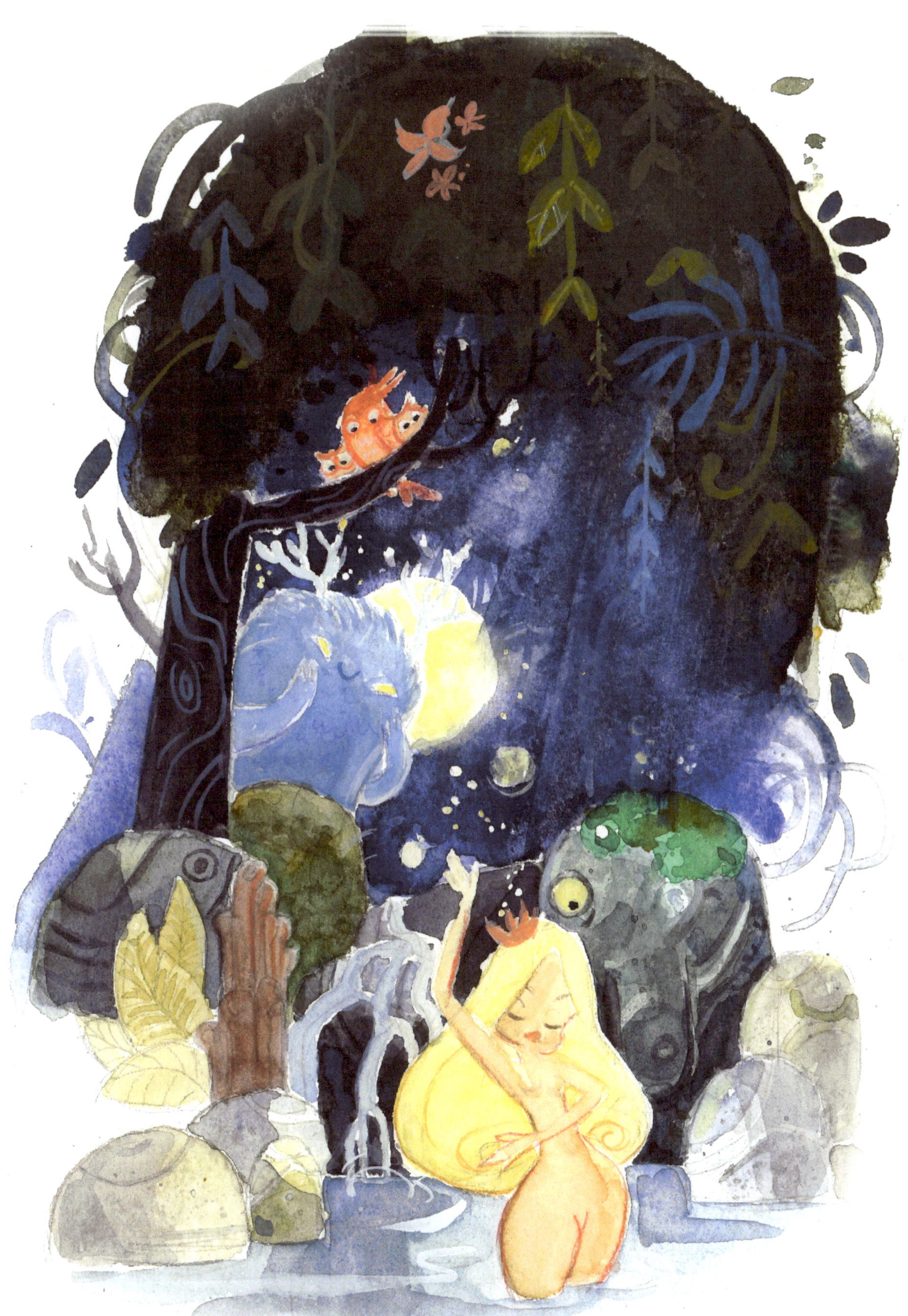

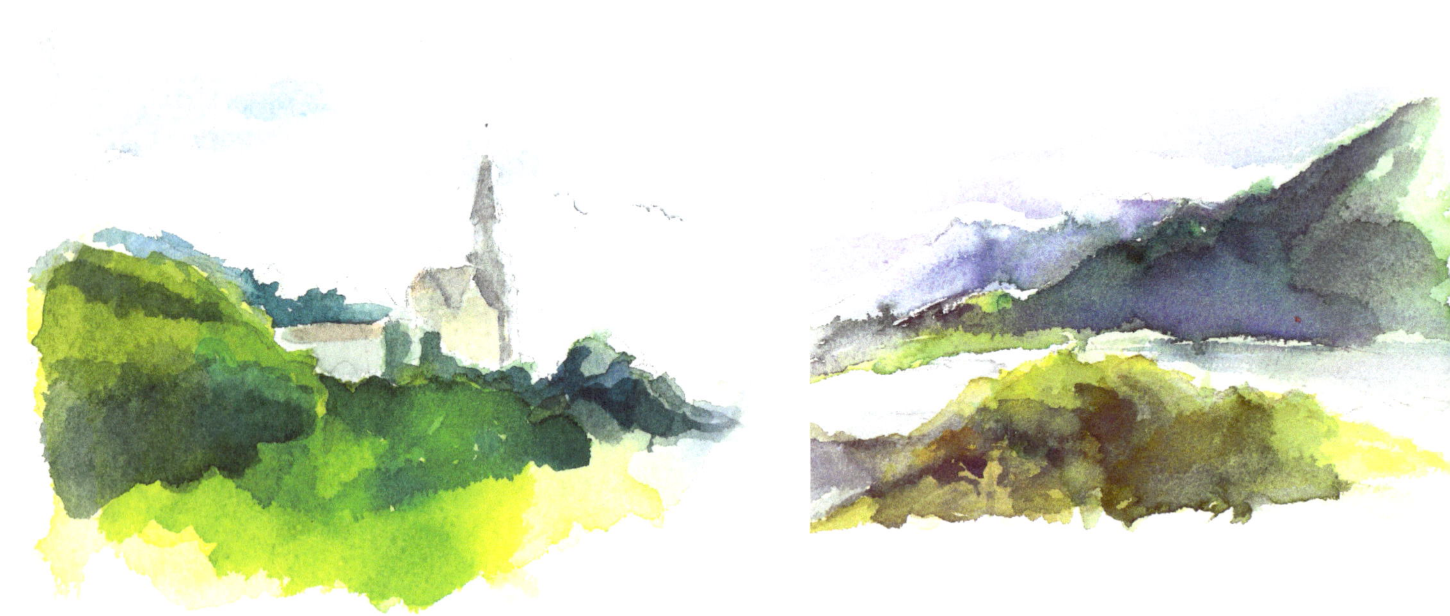

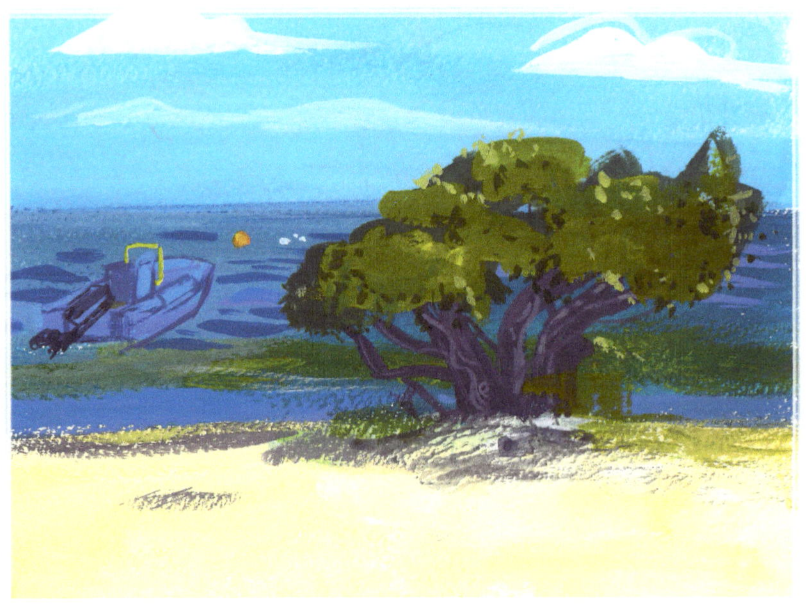

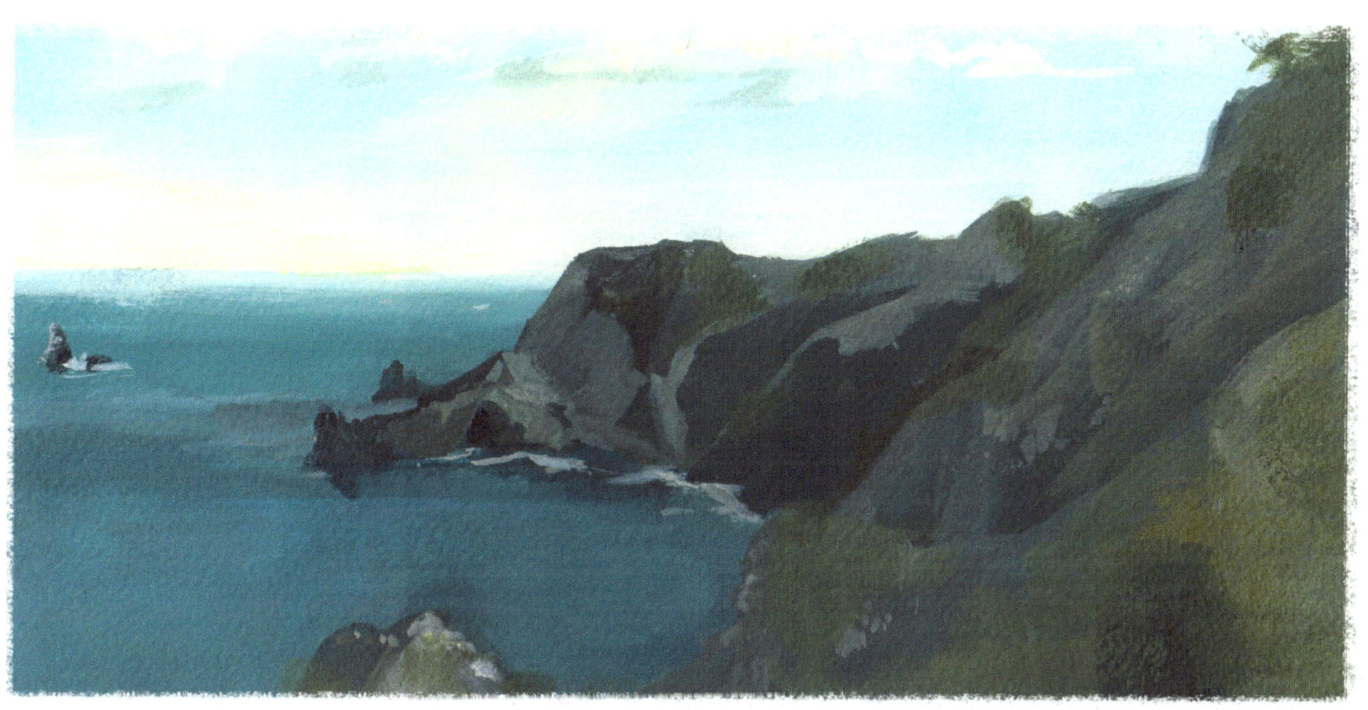

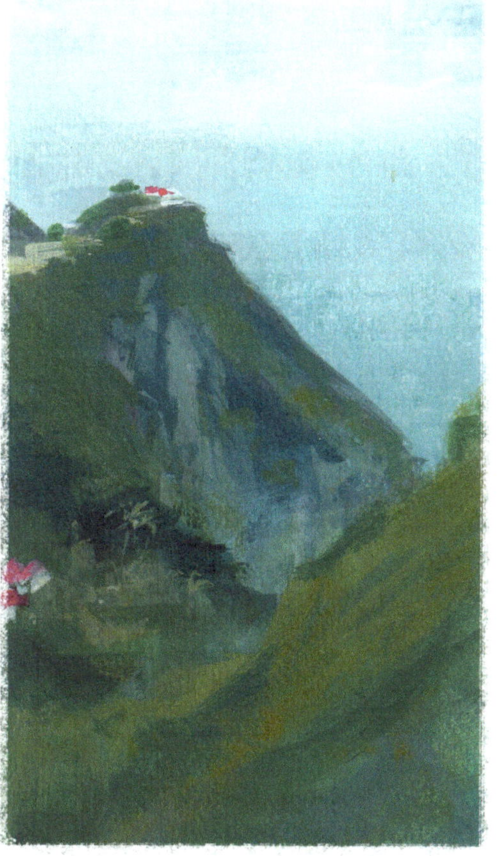

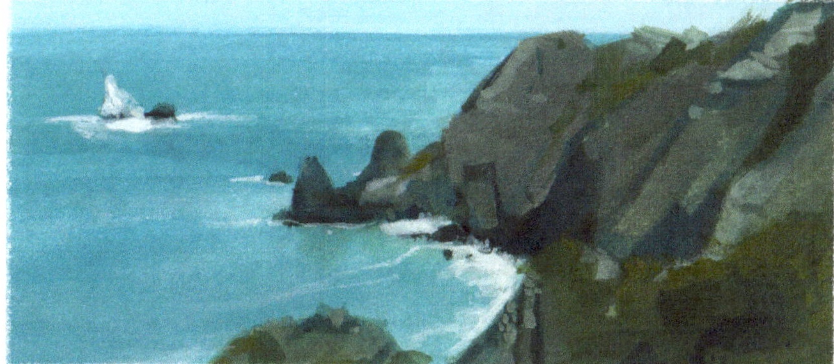

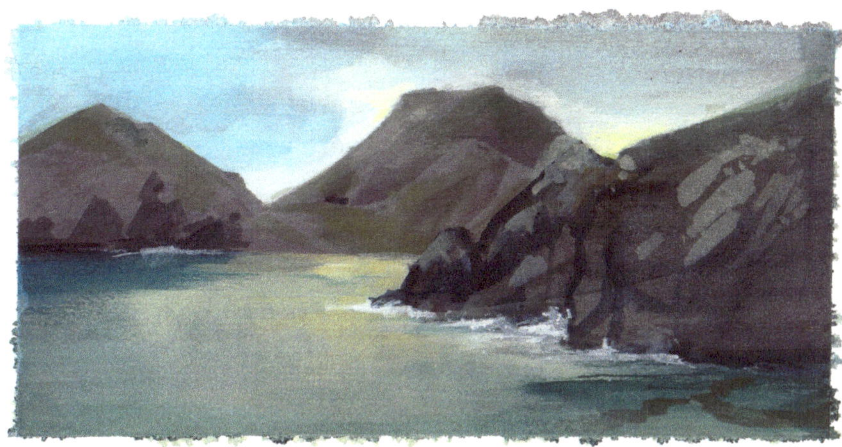

.Life-Drawing.

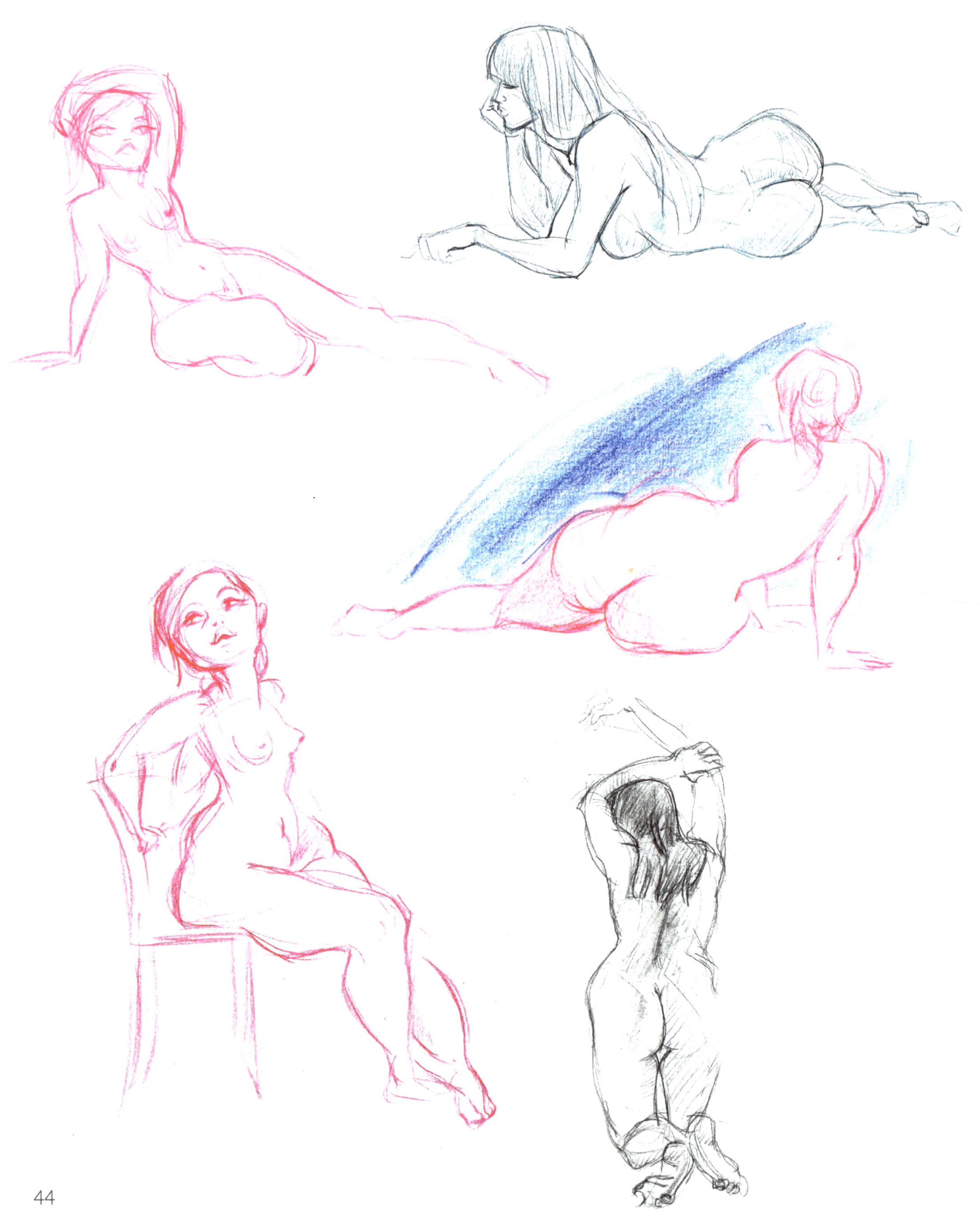

44

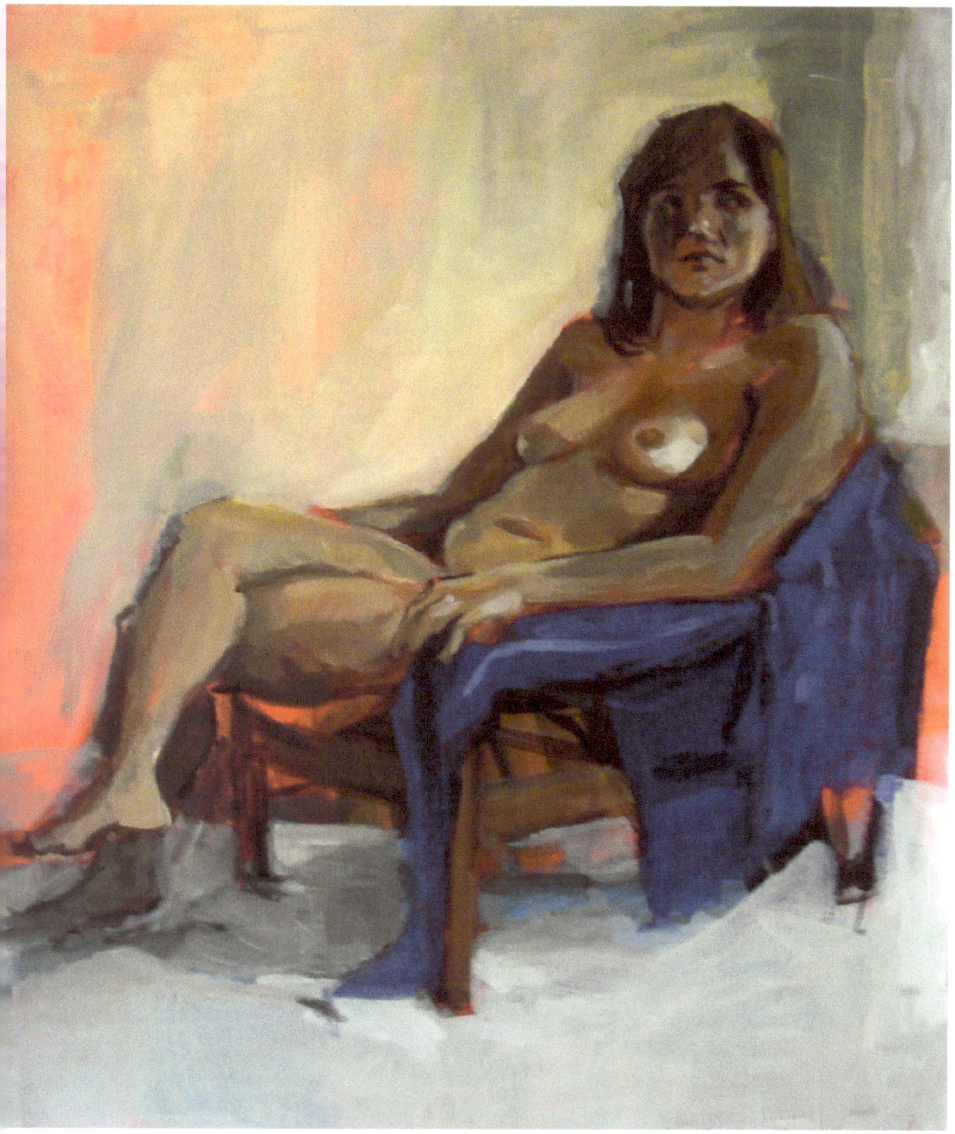

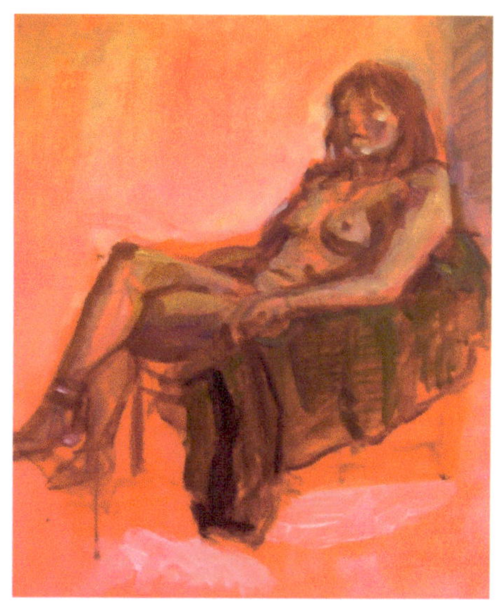

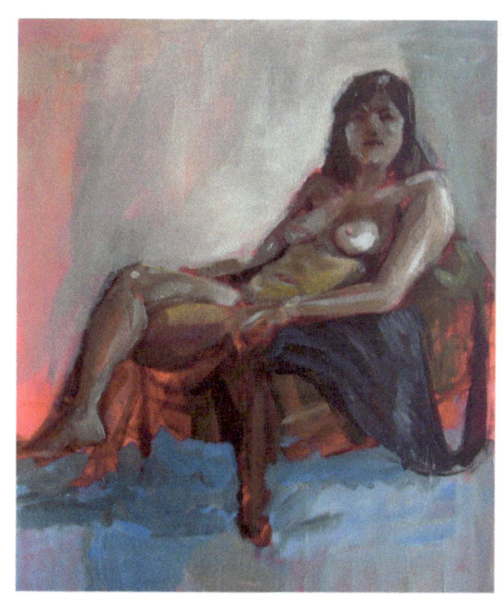

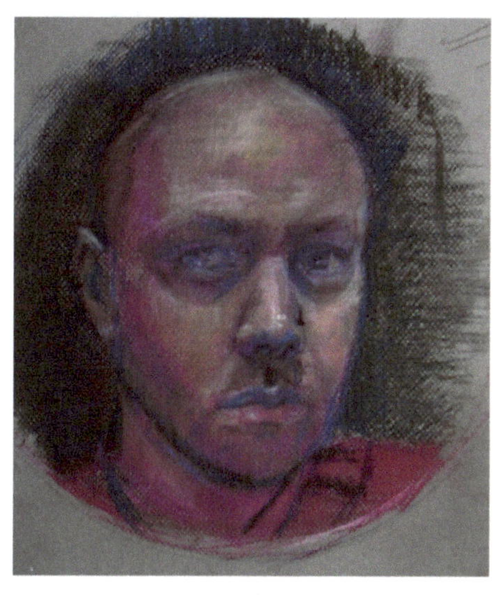

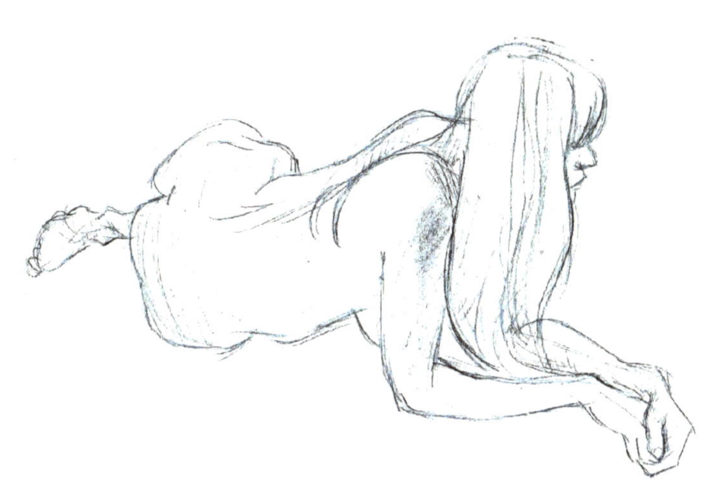

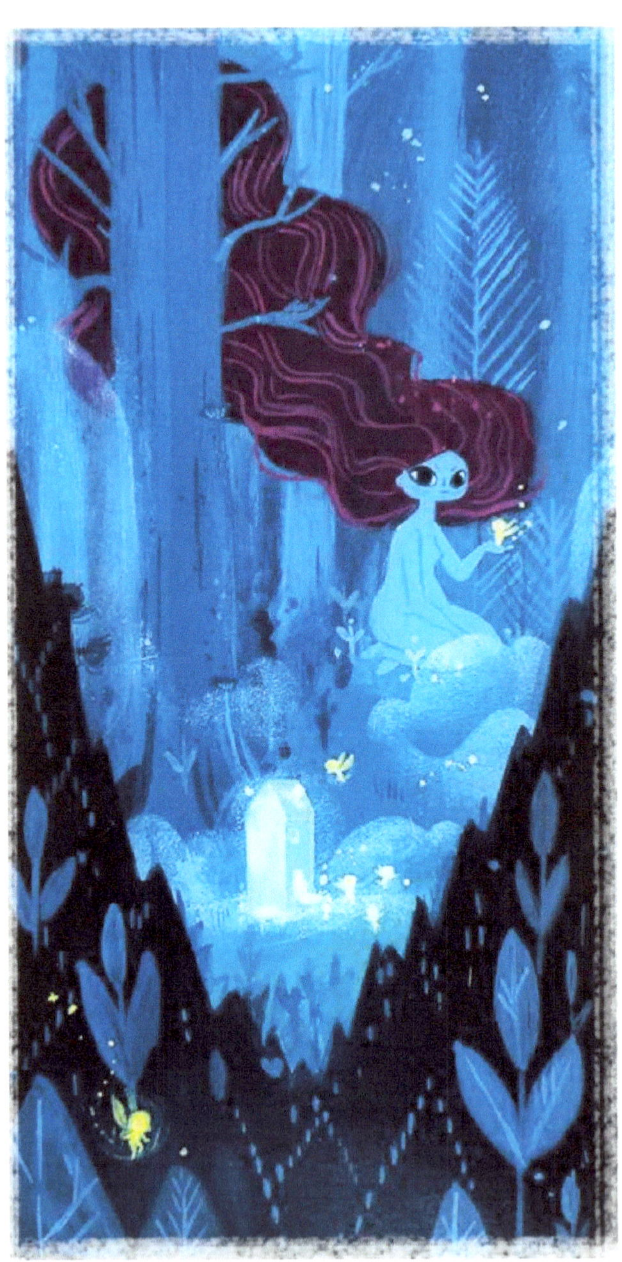

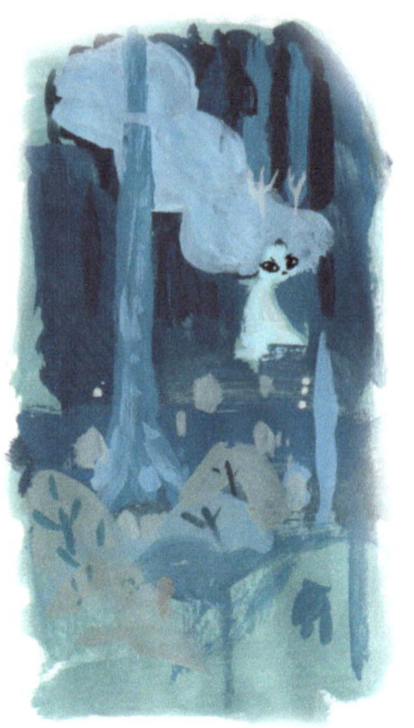

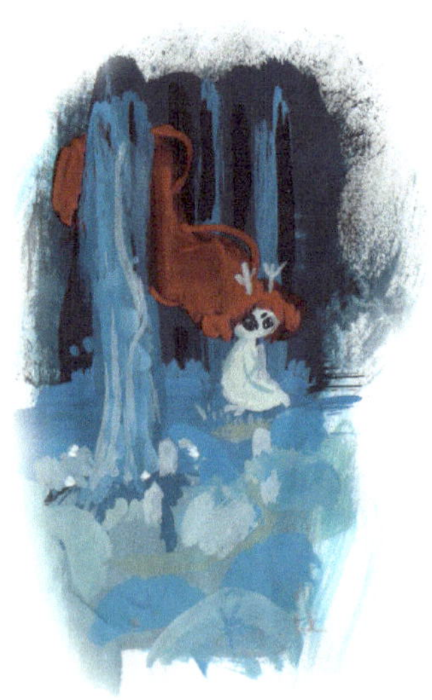

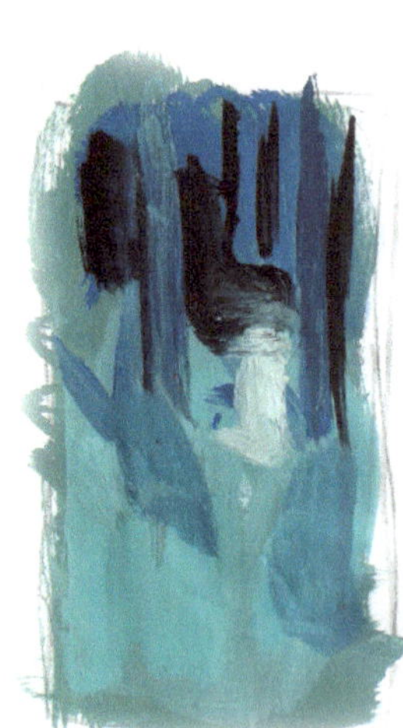

I always make sketches and colour keys before going onto the final stages of painting.

Above are some colour keys I made to help me understand how the colours would look together.
This process is an important one, as it gives me all the information I need at the beginning and
I don't have to start over again and again if the base colours aren't working.

.Process.

I usually do just a few colour keys before I begin painting but sometimes I am not happy with the choices I made. In cases like these, I will make around 10 colour keys and not look at them for a day or two, if I'm still unsure I will make a few others.
This particular one took me a while as you can see.

The final illustration is on the next page.

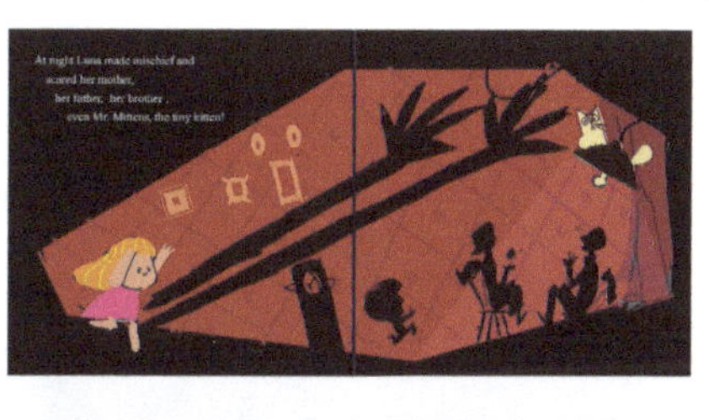 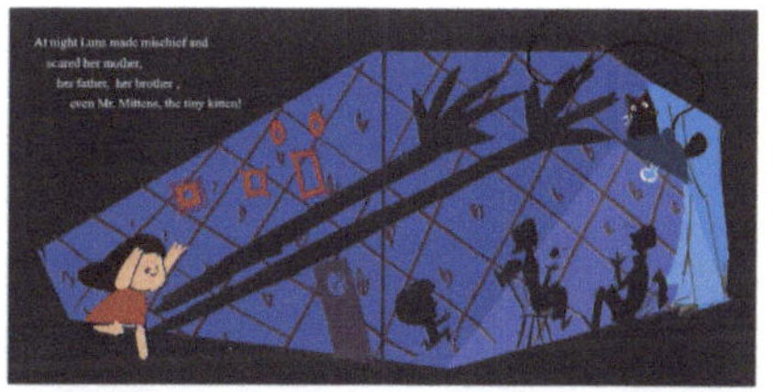 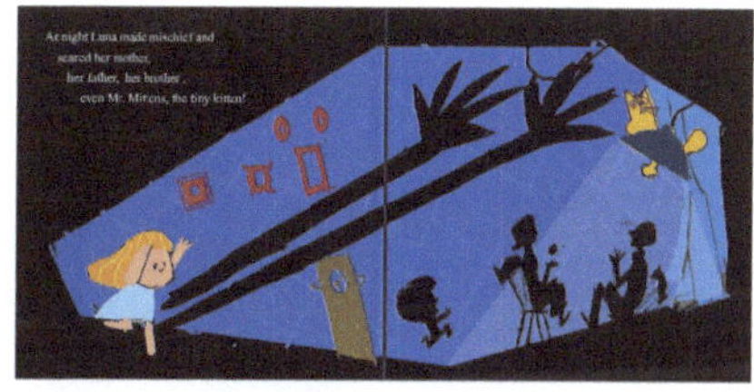
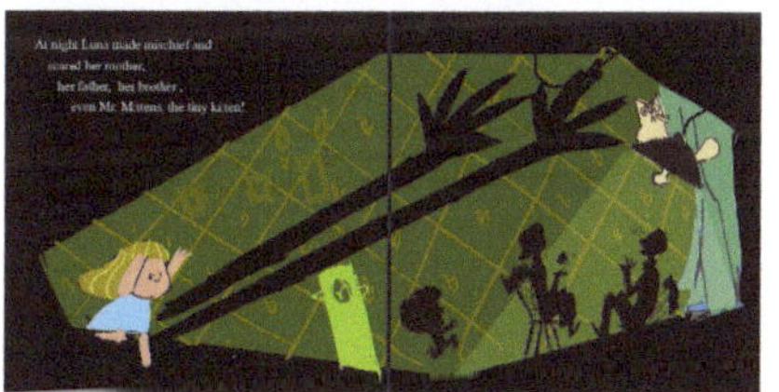 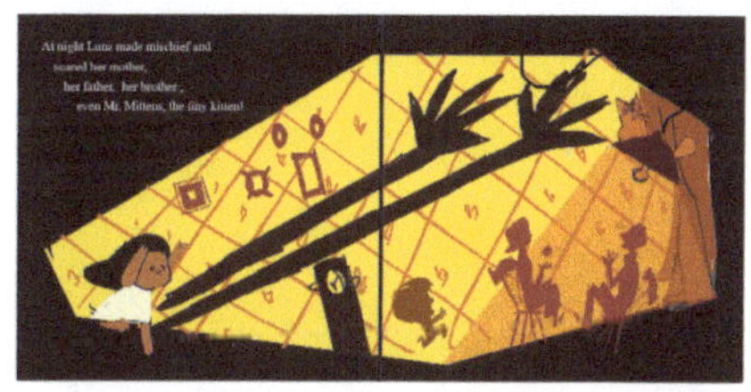 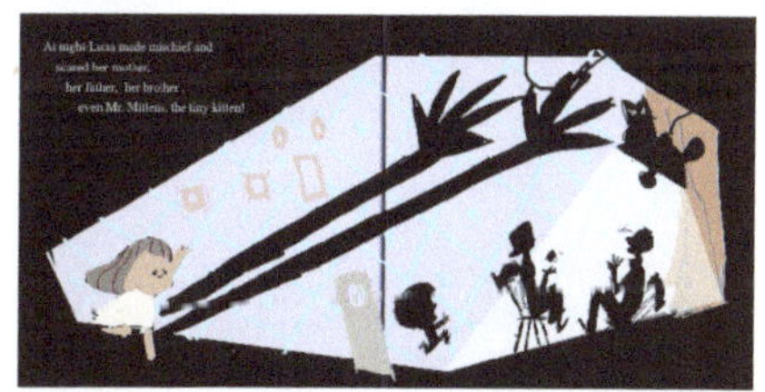
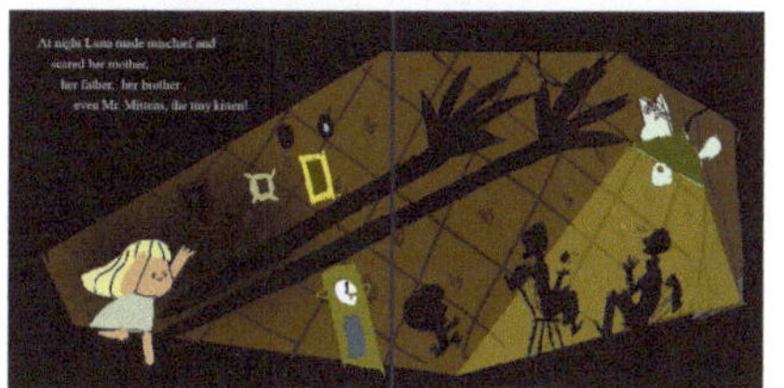 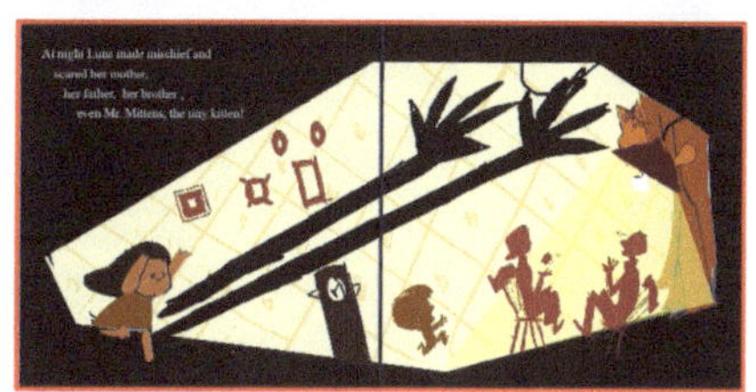 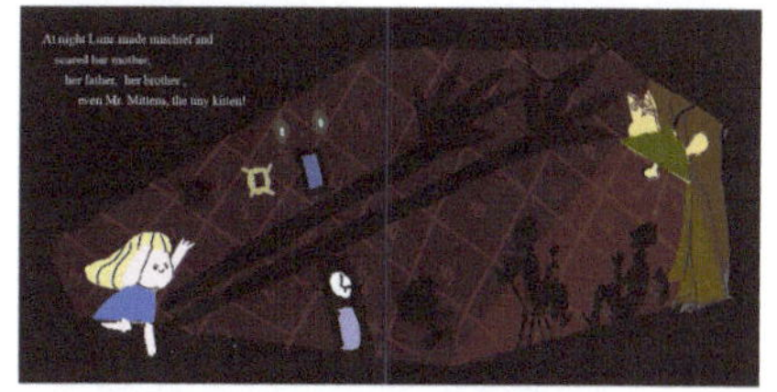
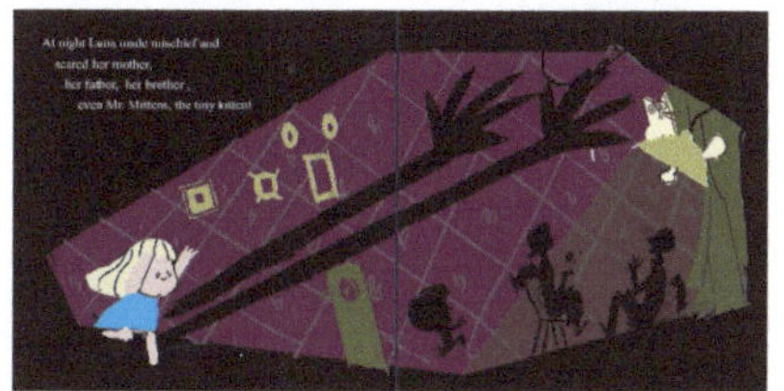 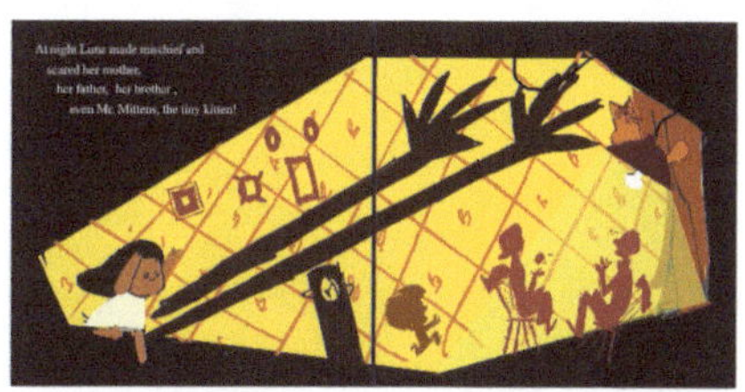 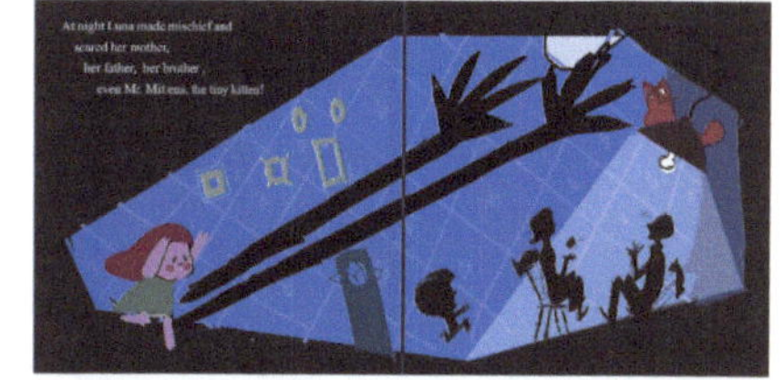
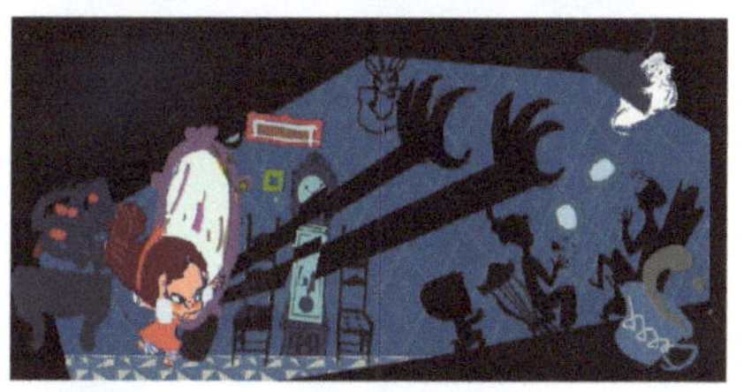 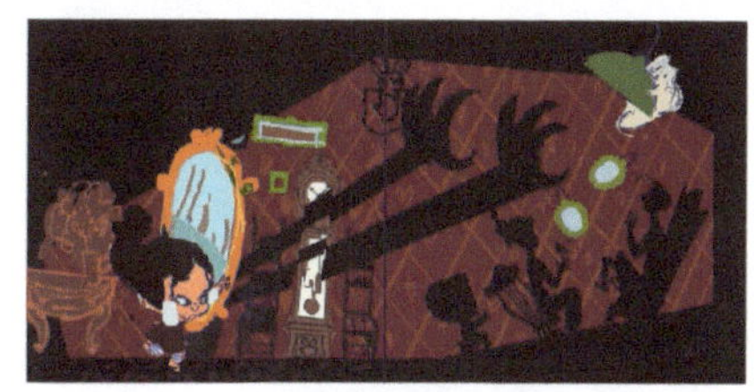 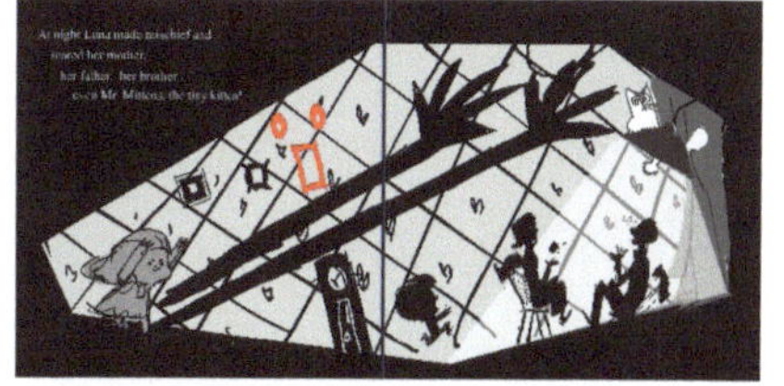
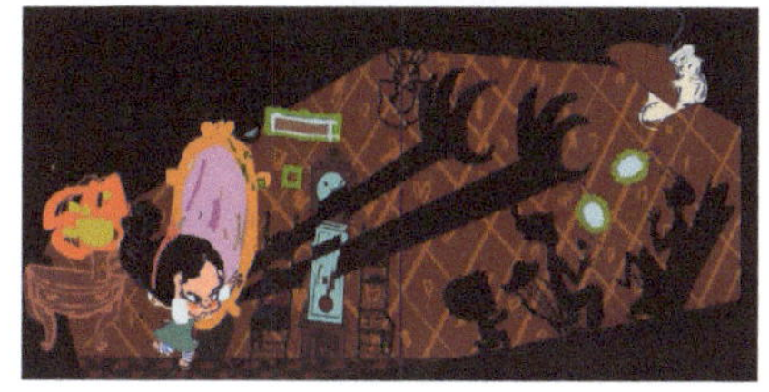 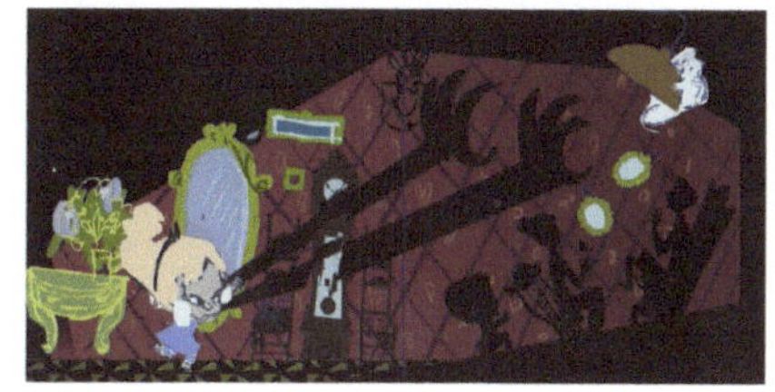 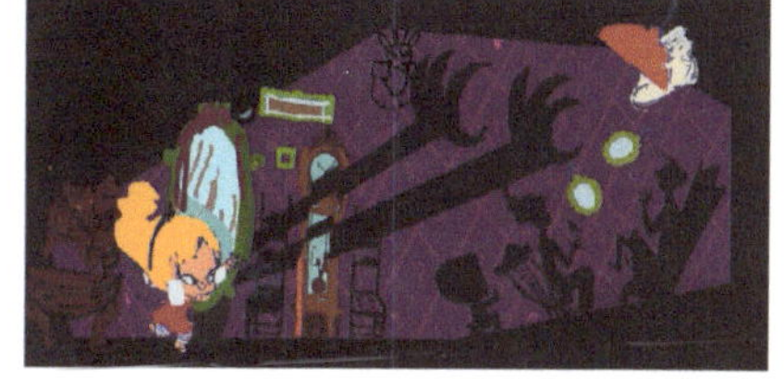

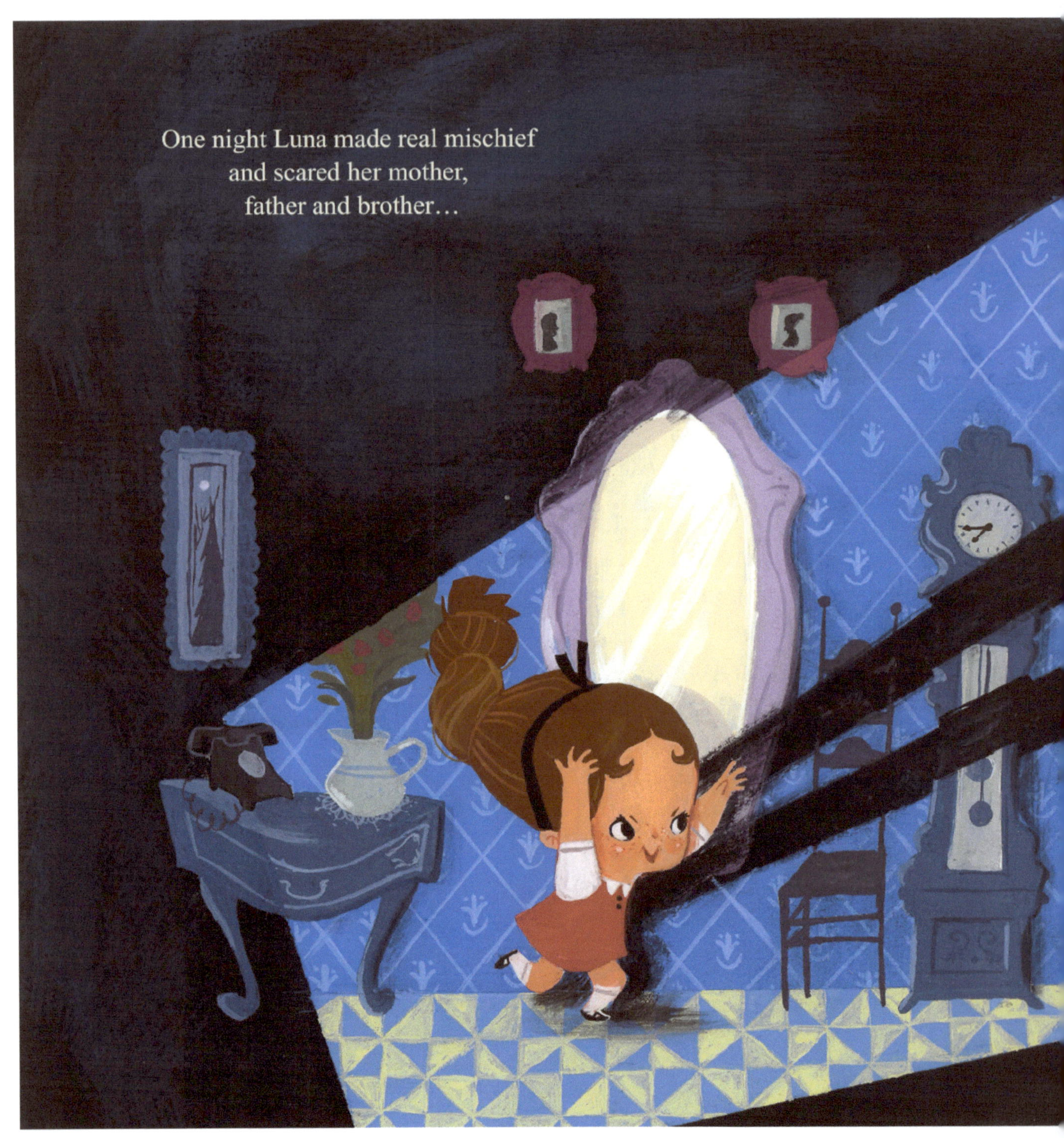

Concept work for my picture book
"The Truth about Monsters"
Inspired by Mary Blair's style

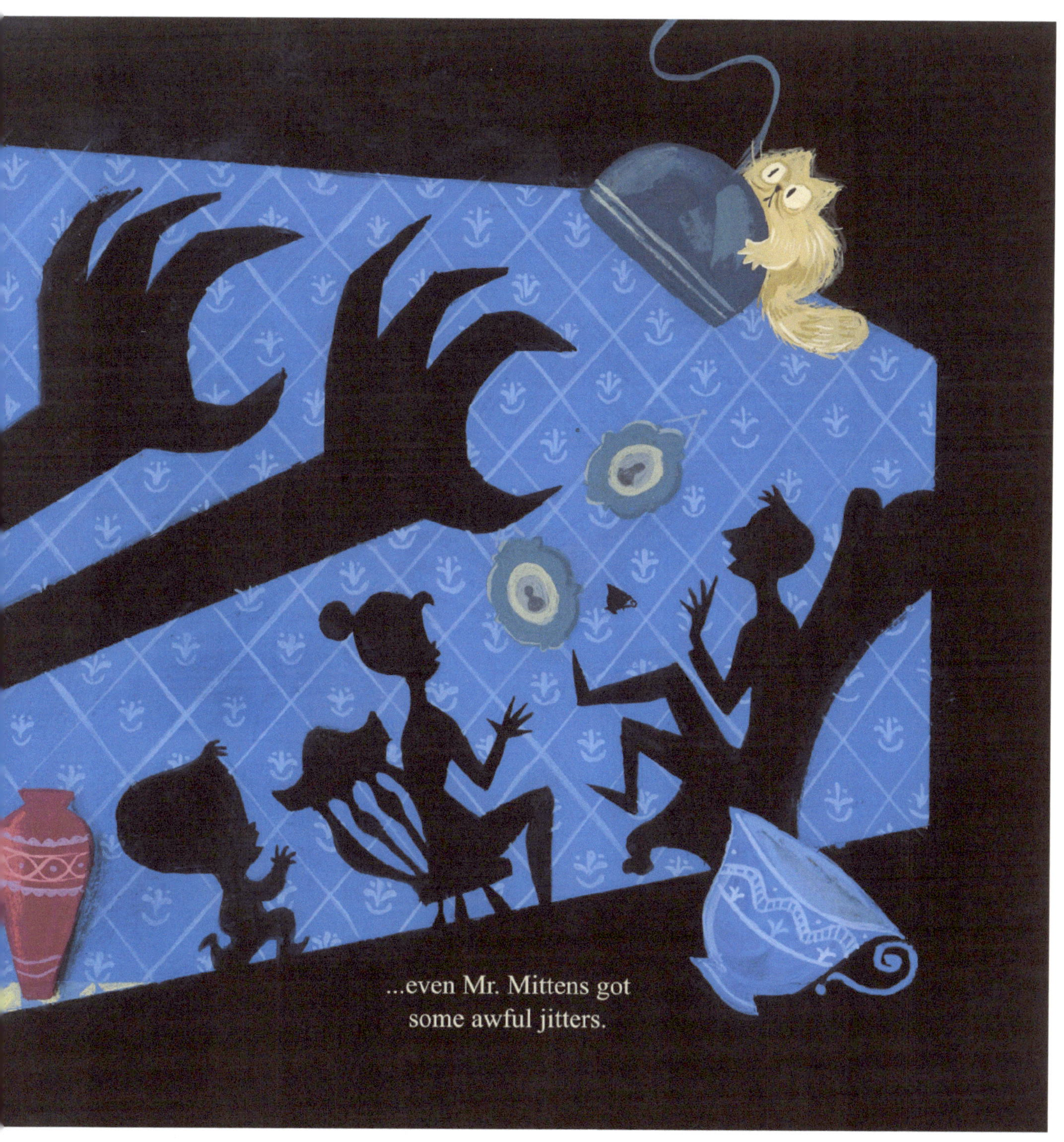

...even Mr. Mittens got
some awful jitters.

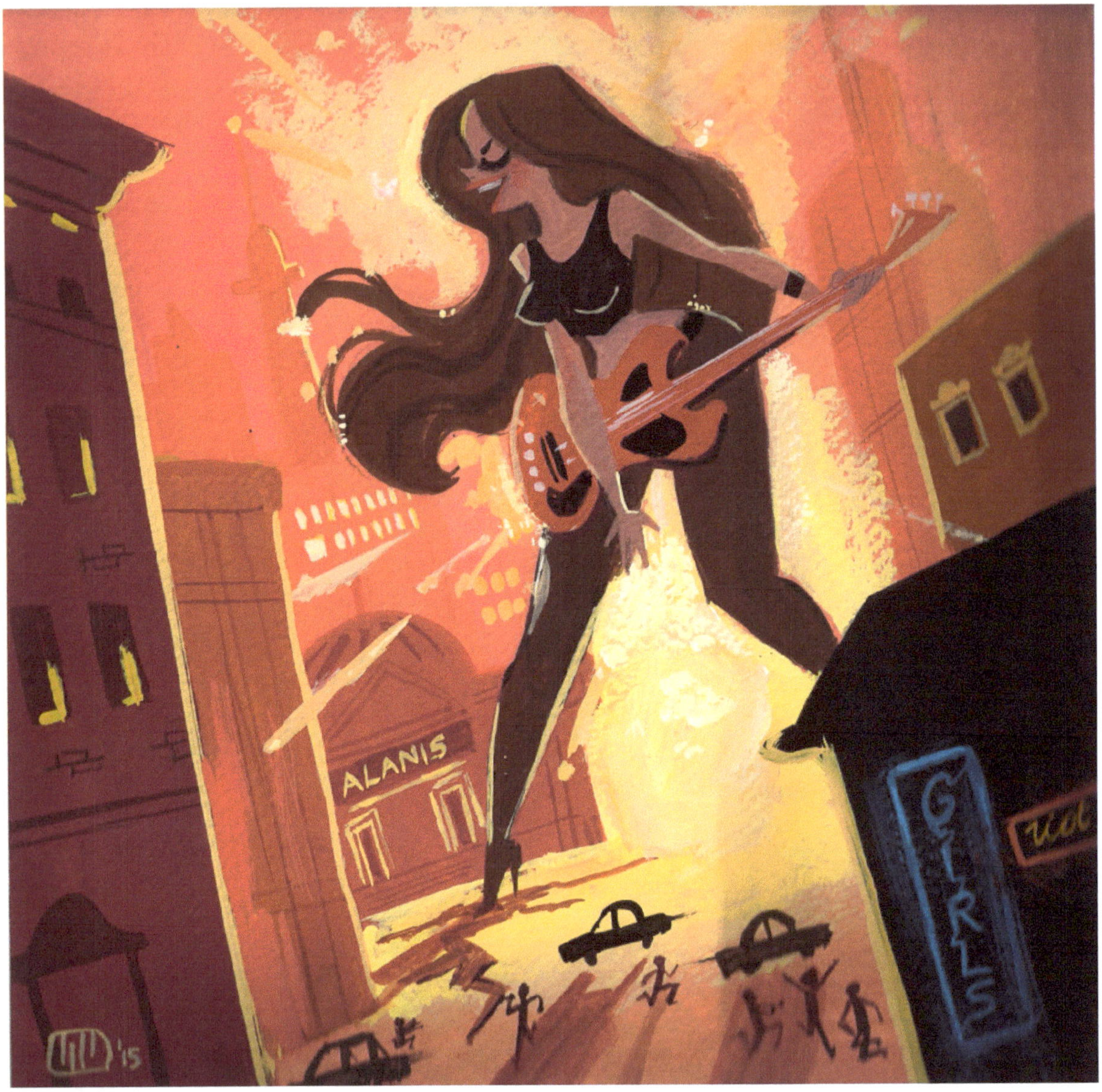

Exhibited in Rome, Italy
at GALLERIA PARIONE9 2015
"Sexy Rock"

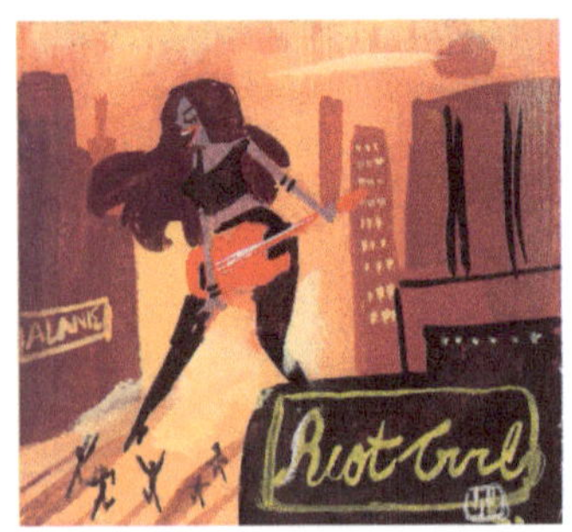
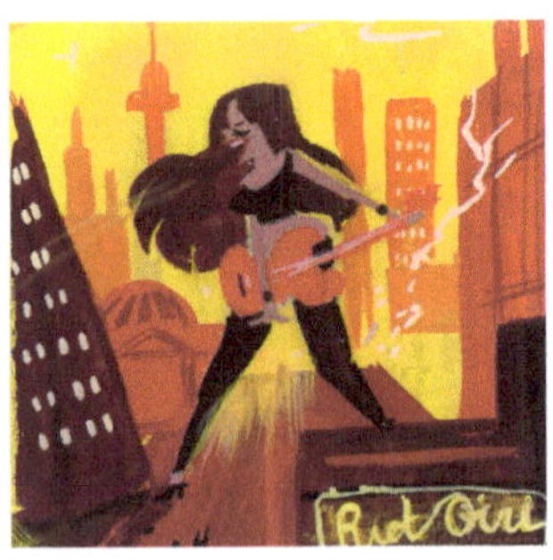
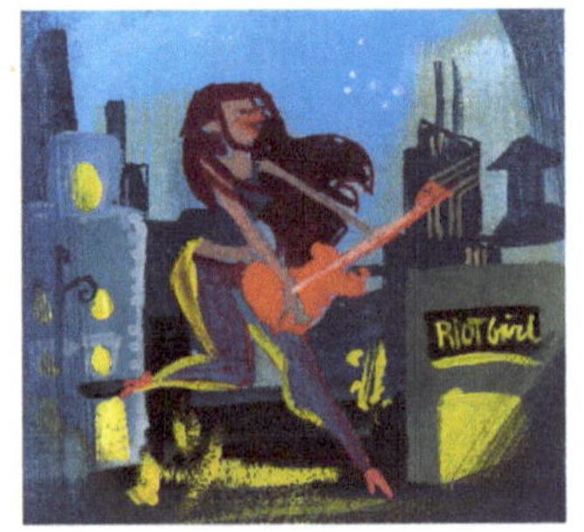
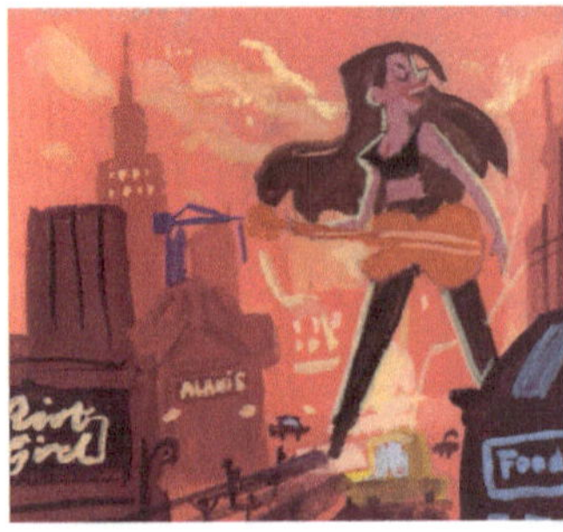

The Colour Keys above helped to decide which scheme worked best.

The Making of:

The Truth about Monsters

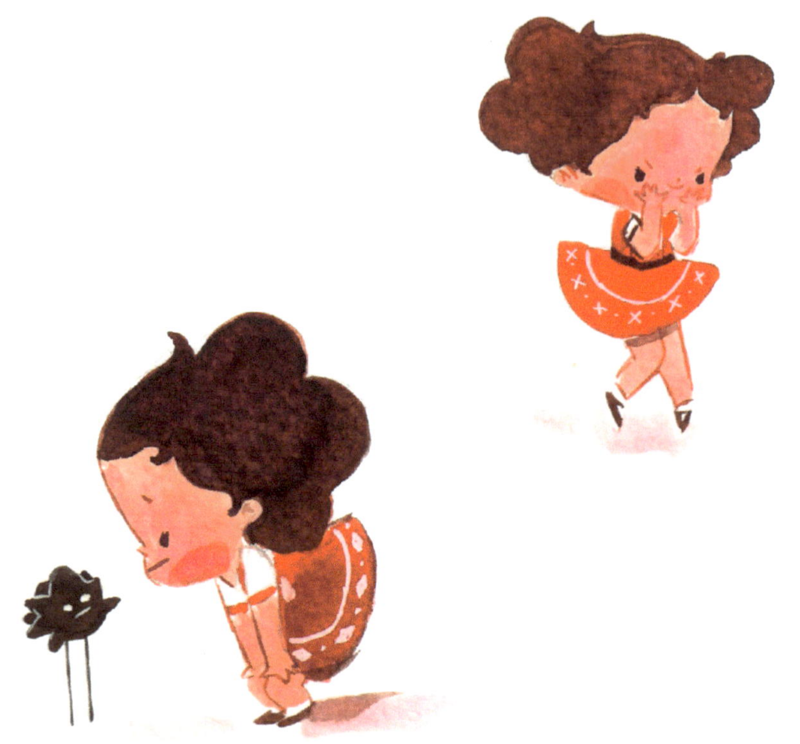
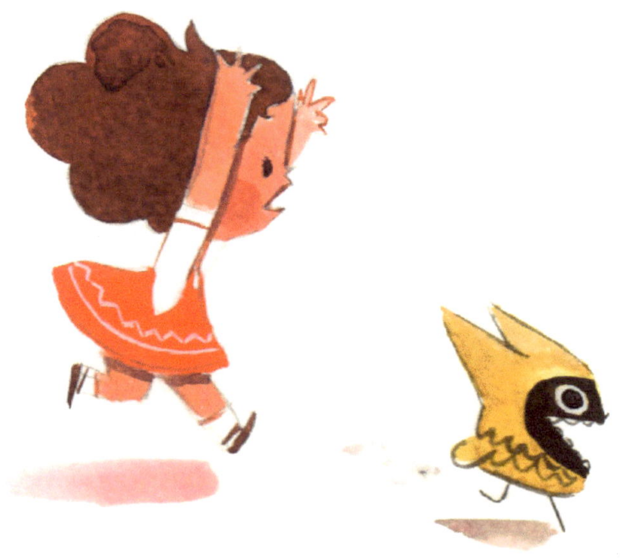

Making a Picture Book

The last part of this book is dedicated to Children's Picture Book Illustration and the making of my book "The Truth about Monsters".

The story is about a little girl, Luna, who is quite naughty, loves to scare and give her family a fright; she's a little monster! On a bright morning she meets some wonderful new creatures who are actually monsters. They whisk her away to a new and exciting place where she discovers what monsters are really about.

Most picture books start with story, but do not neccessarily have to begin there. In my case, as I am more visual, it started with a sketch of a little girl and a monster.
The story was then built around this sketch.
After several drafts, I showed it to a few writer friends which helped me to flesh out the boring parts and give the character more depth and life. It is important (obviously) to know your characters inside and out.

These kind of books go through a gruelling process of editing. I find this process limiting but also freeing because although the text is there to guide you, it doesn't need to describe every single thing. As a reader you do not need to be told what the character looks like, or how he or she is dressed etc. The illustration is there to supply the visual information.
Picture books are done several times, as you will see in the coming pages, that one needs a few drafts to get it just right. I tend to get married to my ideas quite quickly so it's hard for me to see when something doesn't work for the longest time. From storyboard, character design and concept - it is always interesting, even for me, to see how it started to what it looks like when completed.

The process, as you can imagine wasn't linear by any means. Once I had a working story, I proceeded to make art for the book but there were many times I revisited older ideas or designs but for the purpose of clarity I broke this last part into smaller chapters:

Making a Picture Book
Storyboard (Pass 1)
Storyboard (Pass 2)
Chararacter Design (Luna)
Chararacter Design (Monsters)
Concept (Visual Development)
Storyboard (Pencil)
Colour Keys
Finished Book
Painting Process
Covers

Storyboard (Pass 1)

This is the first storyboard I made after the story was nailed down. Some panels were too complicated, quite stiff and at this point I still didn't know what Luna or the monsters even looked like but I wanted to see how thestory flowed visually.

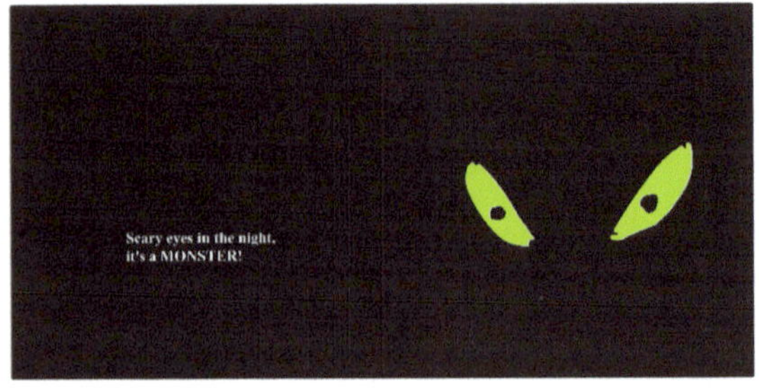

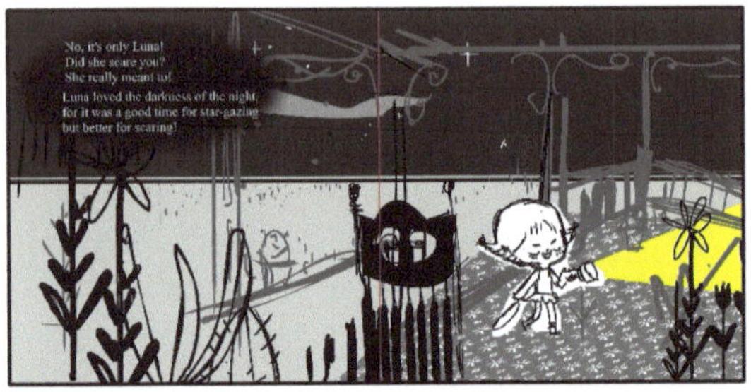

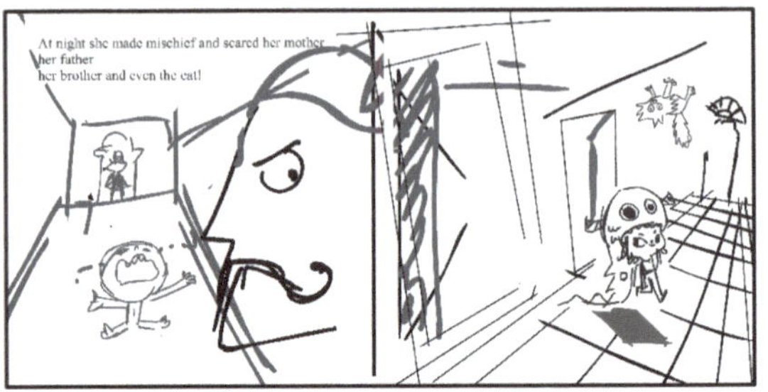

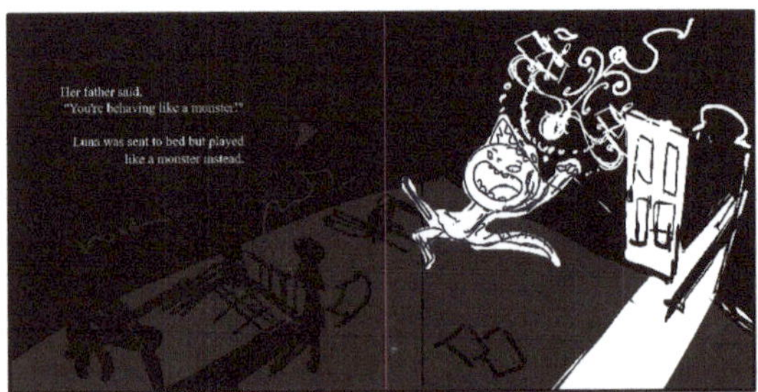

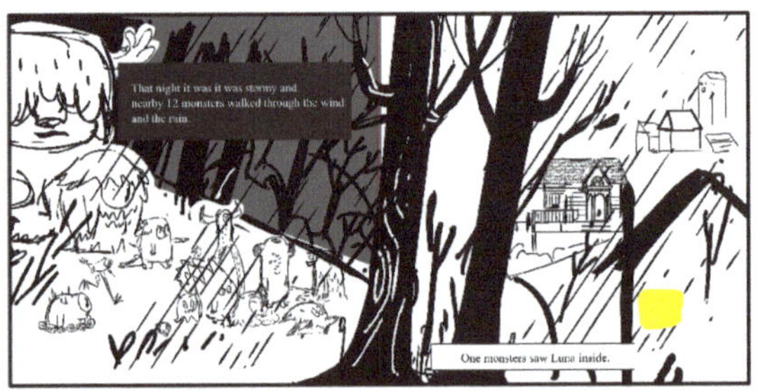

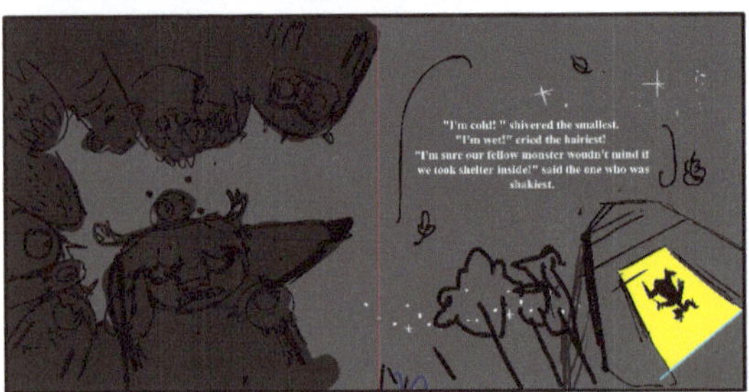

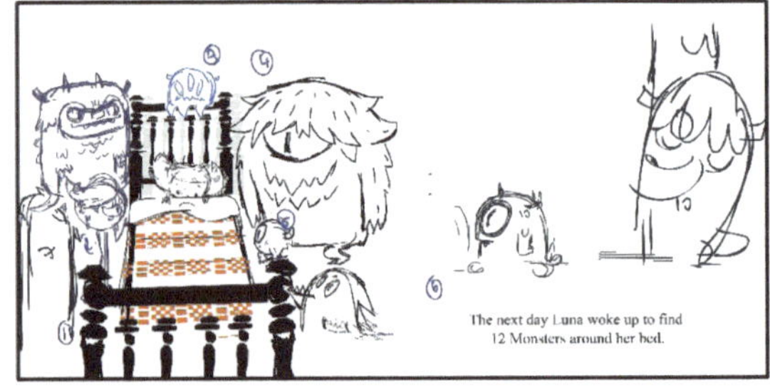

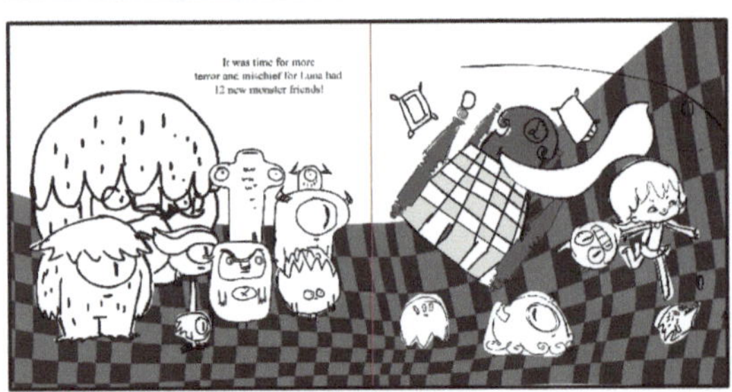

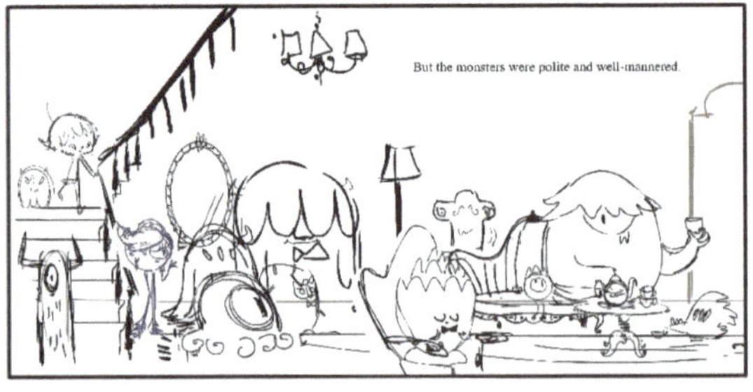

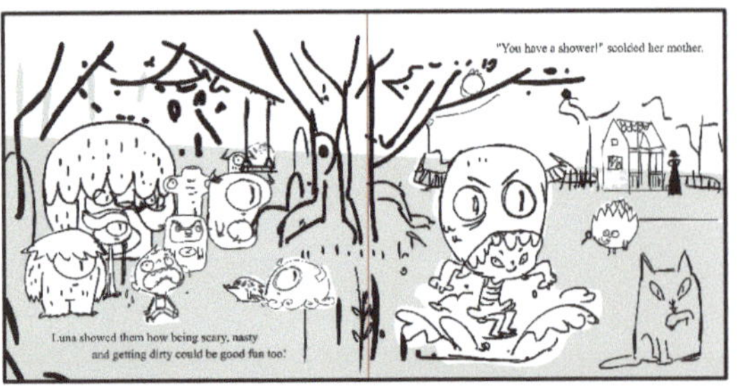

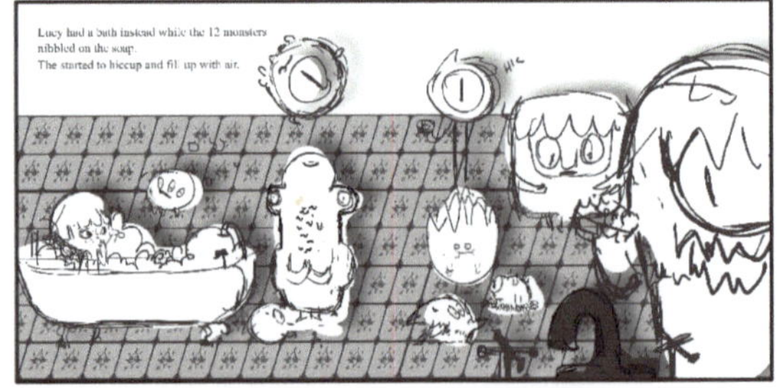

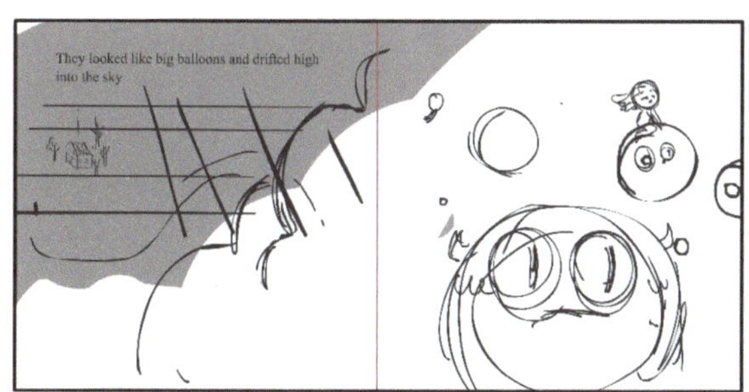

They looked like big balloons and drifted high into the sky

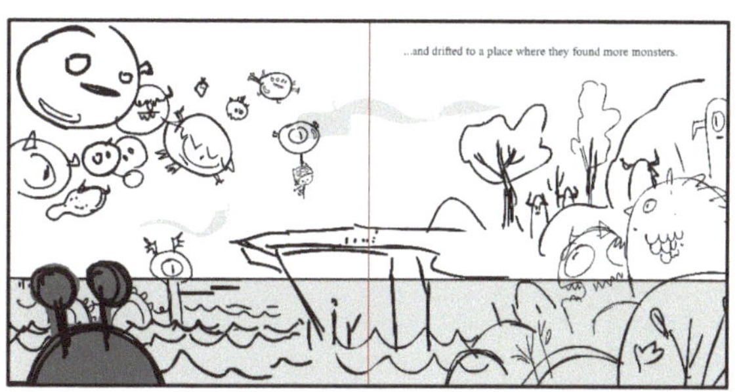

...and drifted to a place where they found more monsters.

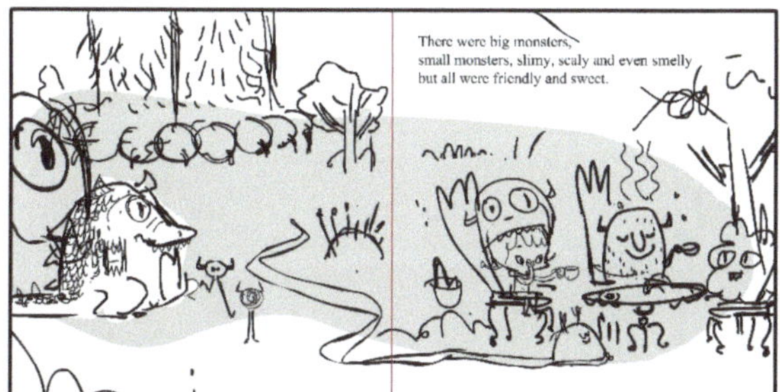

There were big monsters, small monsters, slimy, scaly and even smelly but all were friendly and sweet.

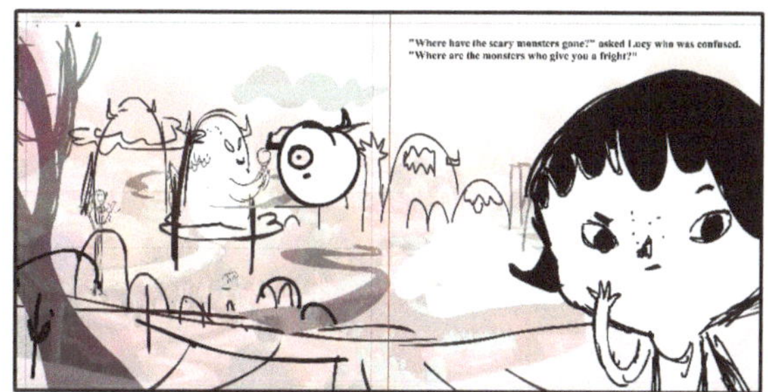

"Where have the scary monsters gone?" asked Lucy who was confused.
"Where are the monsters who give you a fright?"

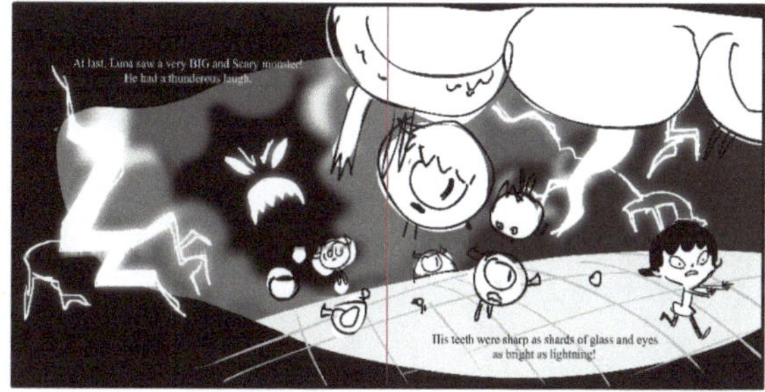

At last, Luna saw a very BIG and Scary monster! He had a thunderous laugh.
His teeth were sharp as shards of glass and eyes as bright as lightning!

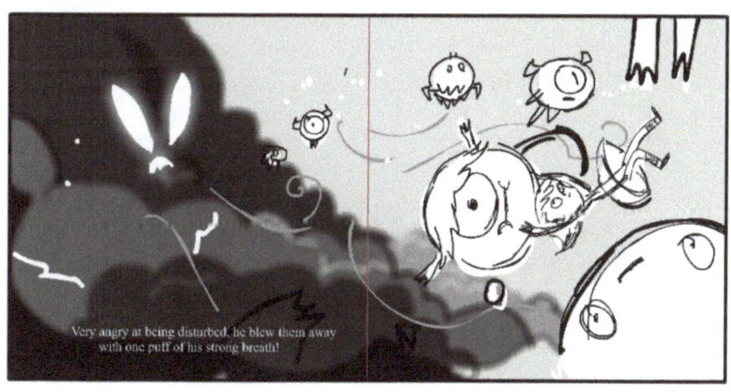

Very angry at being disturbed, he blew them away with one puff of his strong breath!

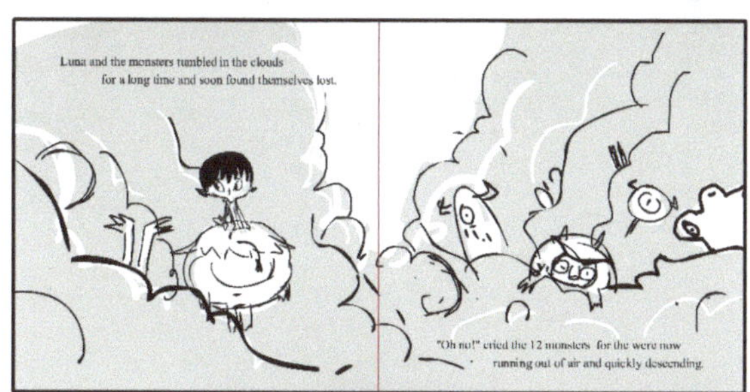

Luna and the monsters tumbled in the clouds for a long time and soon found themselves lost.
"Oh no!" cried the 12 monsters for the were now running out of air and quickly descending.

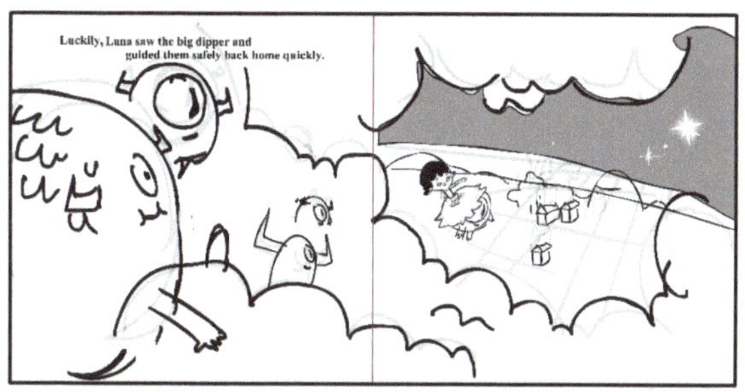

Luckily, Luna saw the big dipper and guided them safely back home quickly.

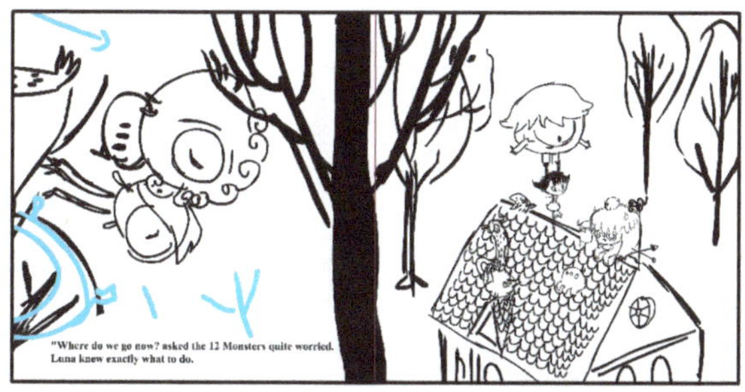

"Where do we go now? asked the 12 Monsters quite worried. Luna knew exactly what to do.

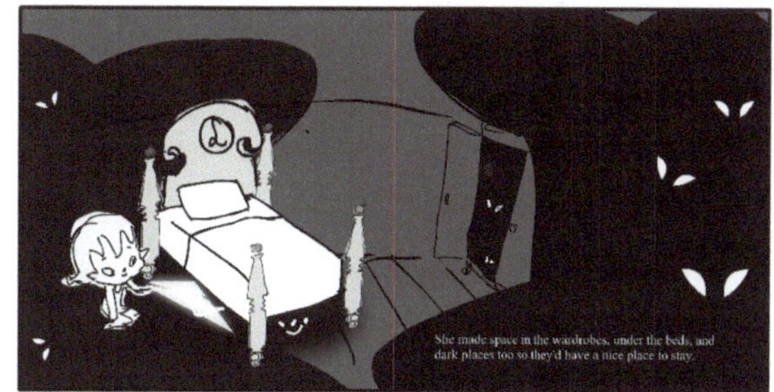

She made space in the wardrobes, under the beds, and dark places too so they'd have a nice place to stay.

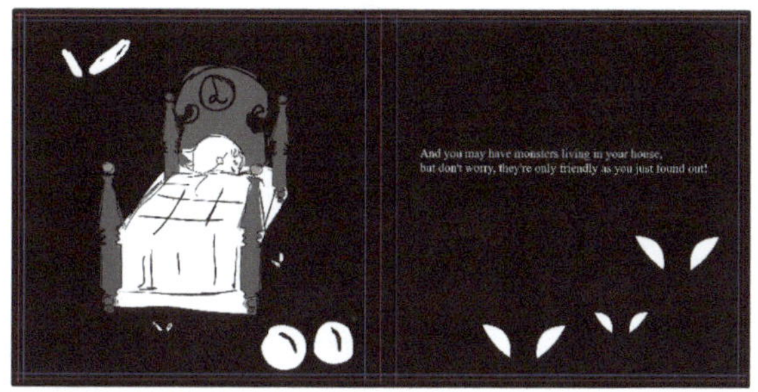

And you may have monsters living in your house, but don't worry, they're only friendly as you just found out!

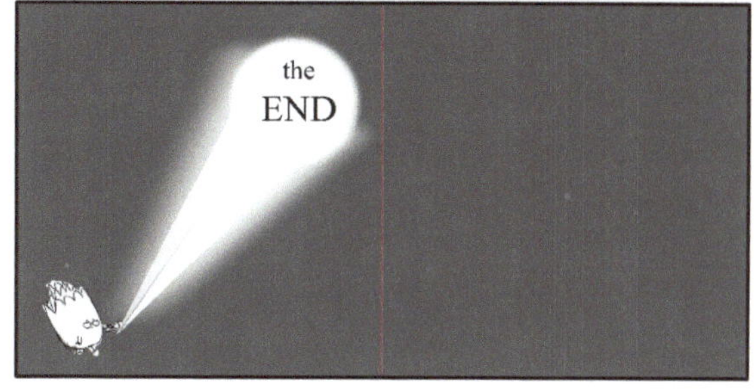

the
END

Storyboard (Pass 2)

At this point I had to drop some panels because some were either too boring, repetitive or literal. I was happy with the second pass but now I needed to design Luna and the monsters.

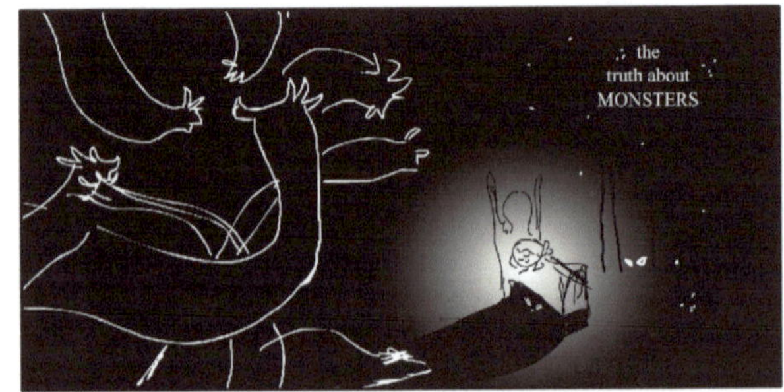

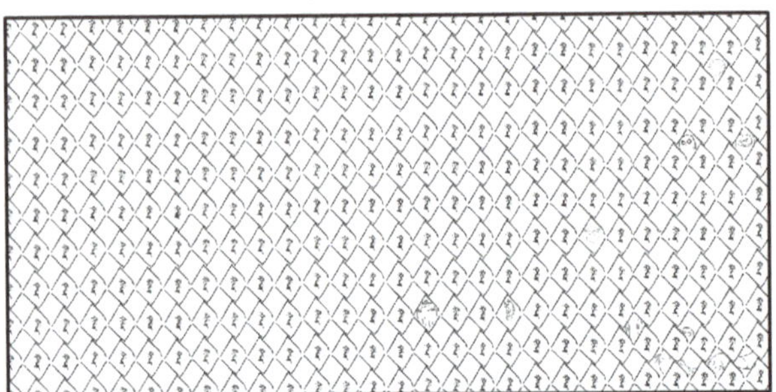

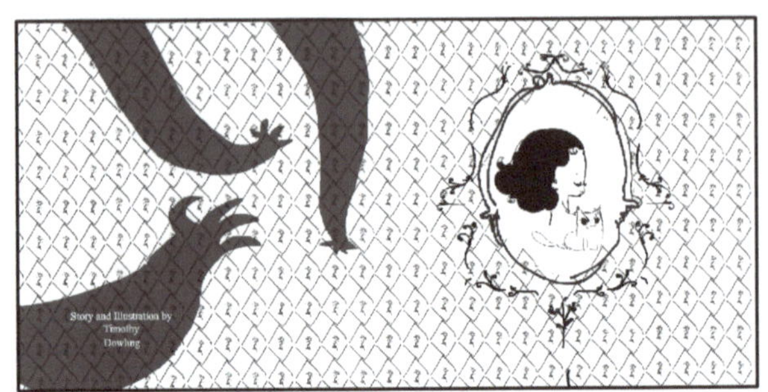

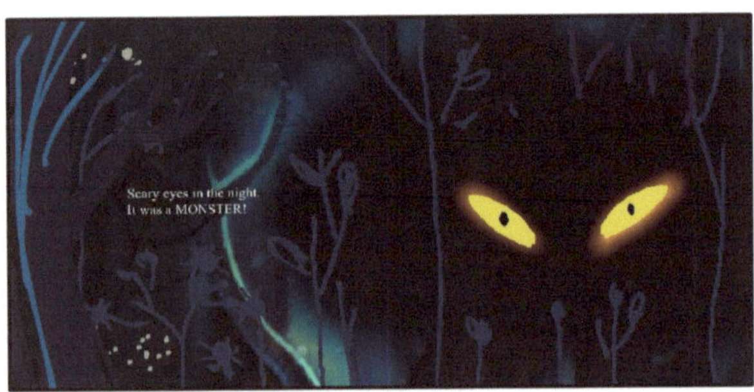

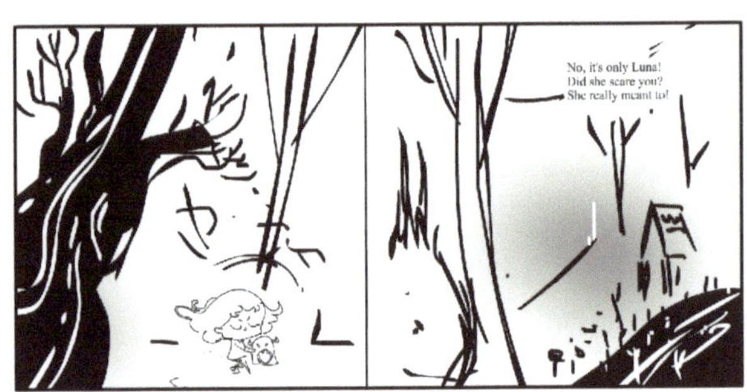

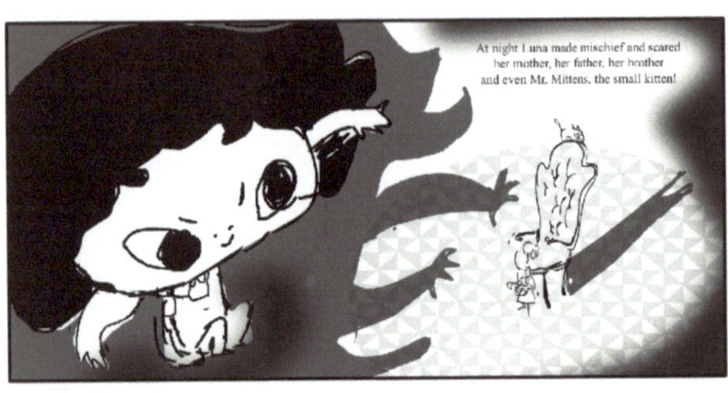

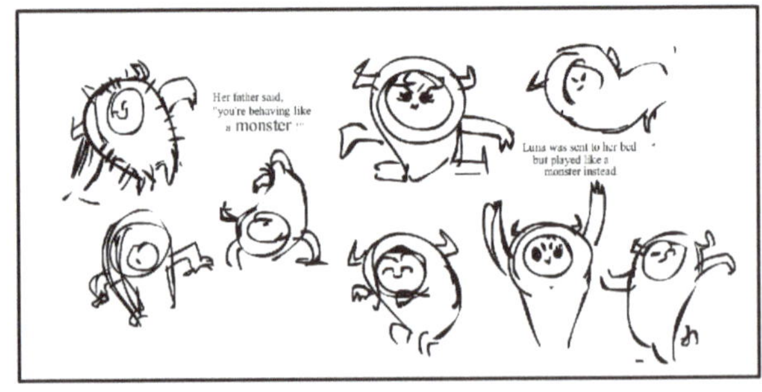

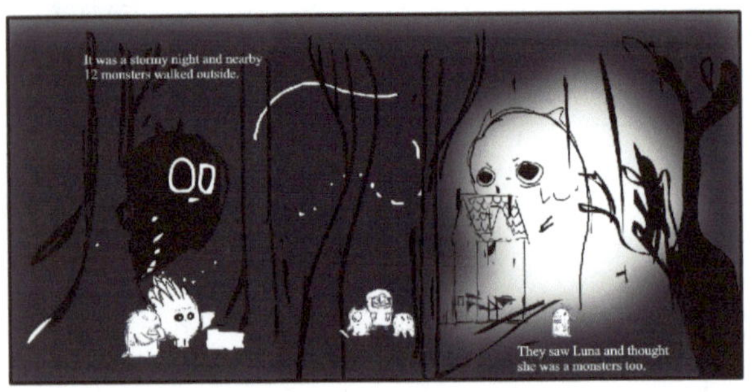

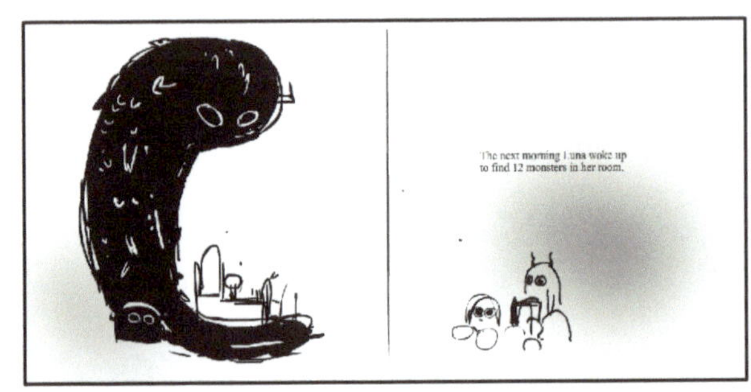

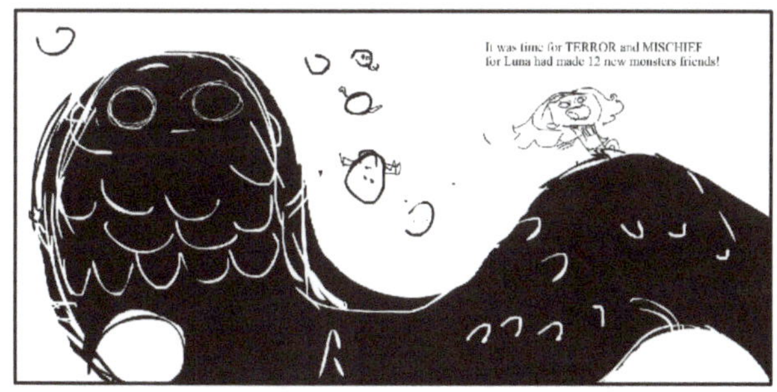

It was time for TERROR and MISCHIEF
for Luna had made 12 new monsters friends!

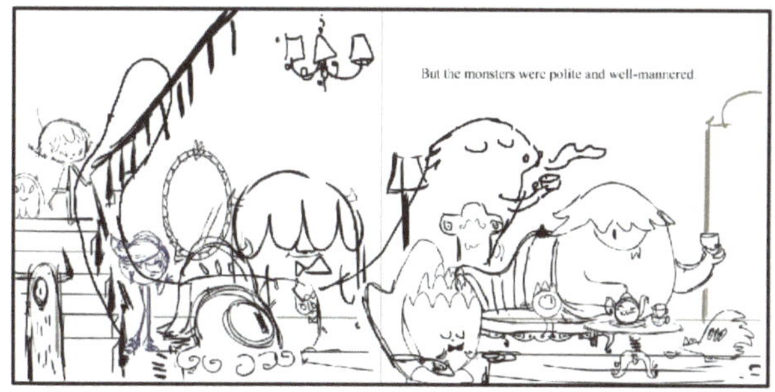

But the monsters were polite and well-mannered.

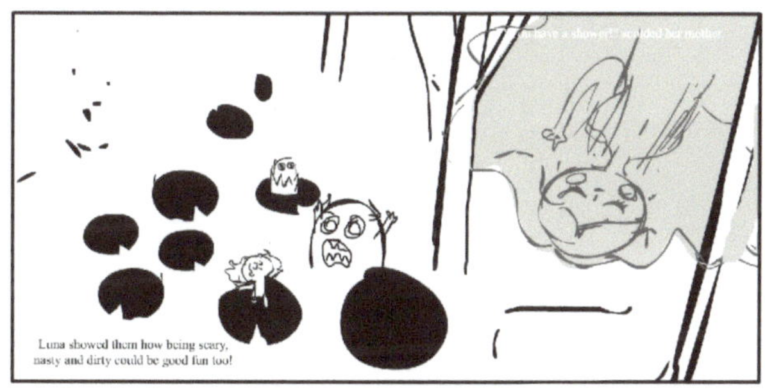

"...have a shower!" scolded her mother.
Luna showed them how being scary,
nasty and dirty could be good fun too!

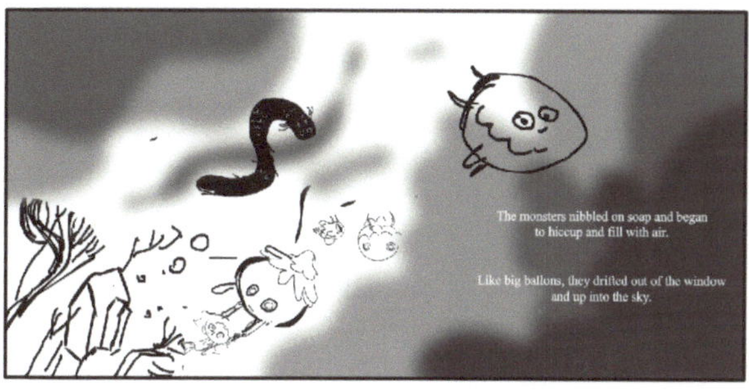

The monsters nibbled on soap and began
to hiccup and fill with air.

Like big balloons, they drifted out of the window
and up into the sky.

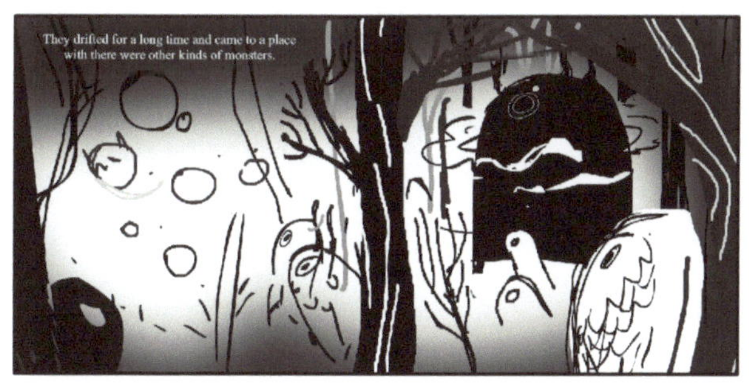

They drifted for a long time and came to a place
with there were other kinds of monsters.

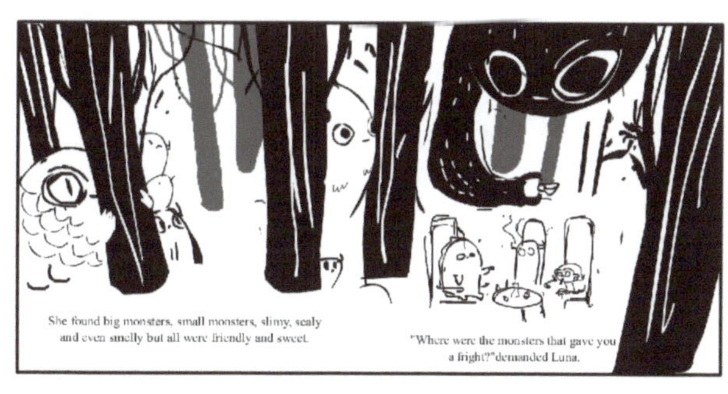

She found big monsters, small monsters, slimy, scaly
and even smelly but all were friendly and sweet.

"Where were the monsters that gave you
a fright?" demanded Luna.

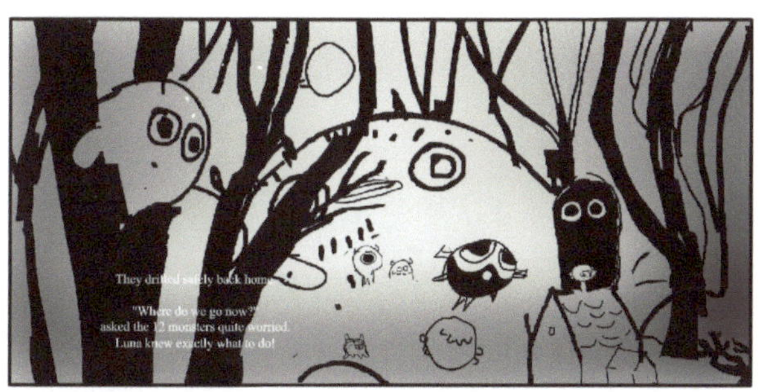

They drifted safely back home.

"Where do we go now?"
asked the 12 monsters quite worried.
Luna knew exactly what to do!

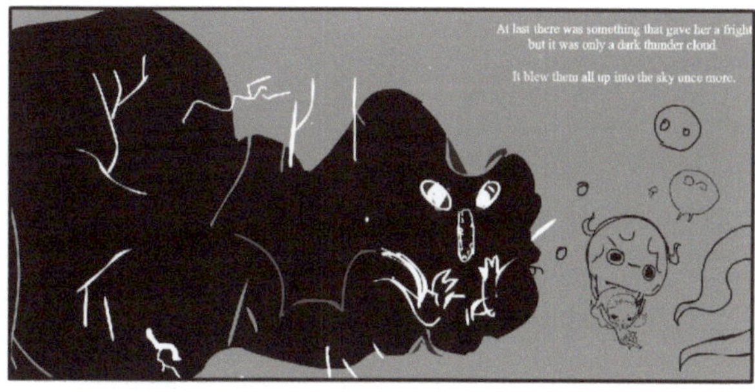

At last there was something that gave her a fright
but it was only a dark thunder cloud.

It blew them all up into the sky once more.

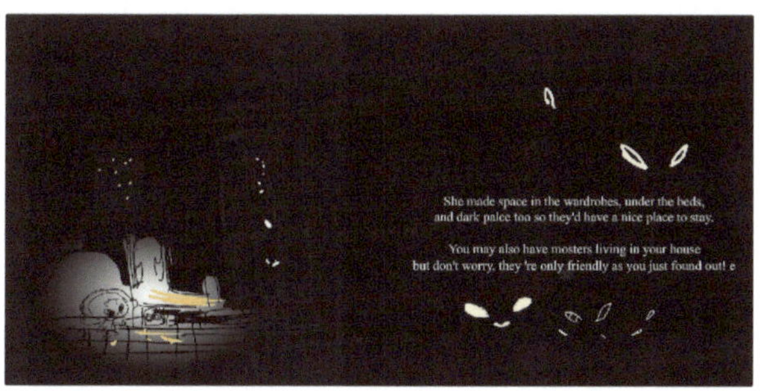

She made space in the wardrobes, under the beds,
and dark palce too so they'd have a nice place to stay.

You may also have mosters living in your house
but don't worry, they're only friendly as you just found out! e

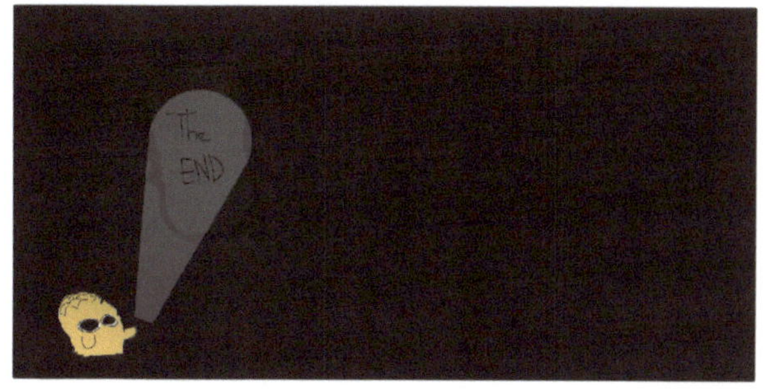

The
END

Character Design (Luna)

Character design in children's books are important for several
reasons, the most being that the design should respresent the
character and also the story, time and place.
Finding the character of "Luna" wasn't easy and took a while
to find her. Before I start to draw, I usually make a list of what
I want the character to look like. In Luna's case, because of her
name which means "moon" I tried putting a design of a moon
into her hair, at least a half-moon.

This design was a little unusual but I liked that about it, however
it did not work and I needed to continue playing with the design.

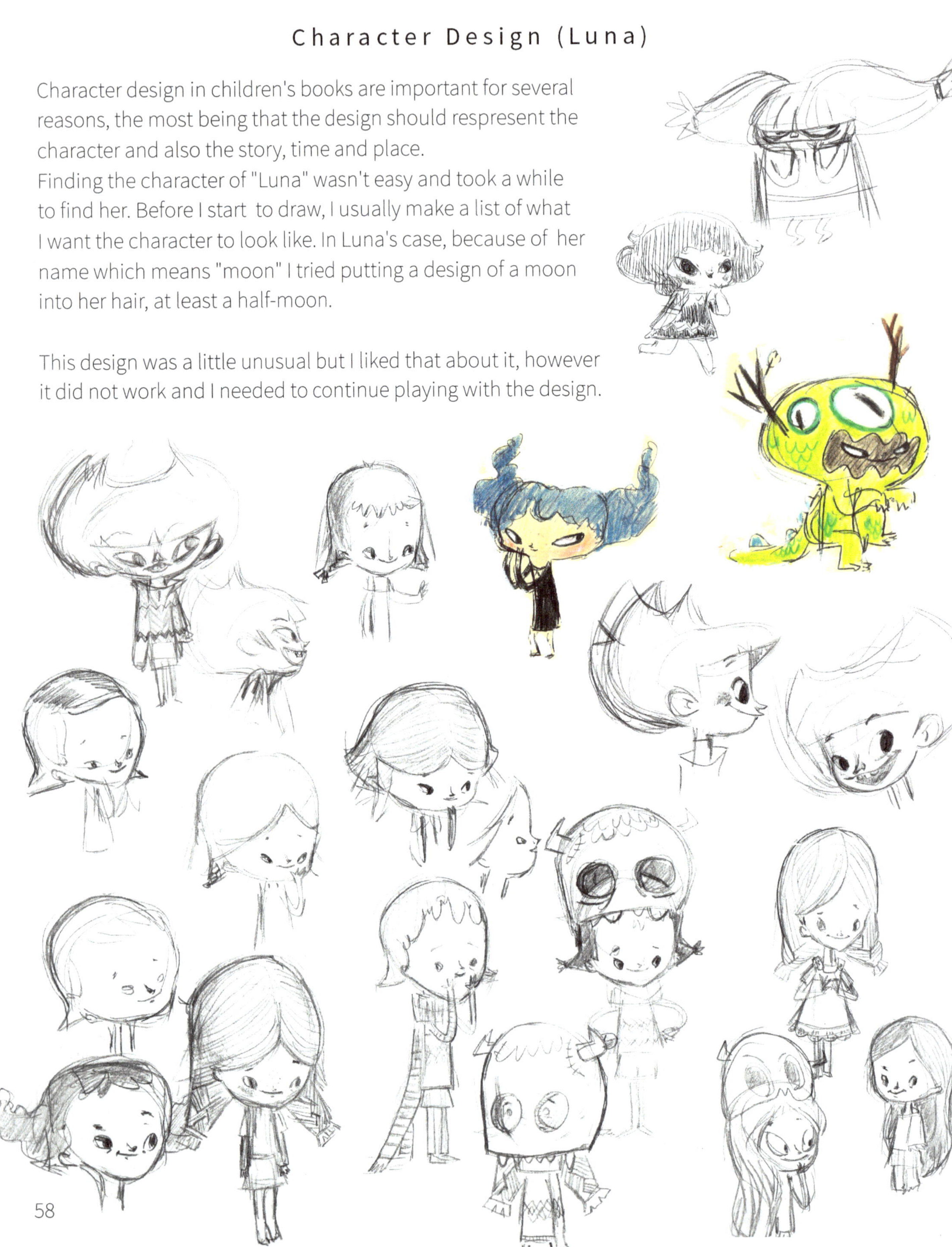

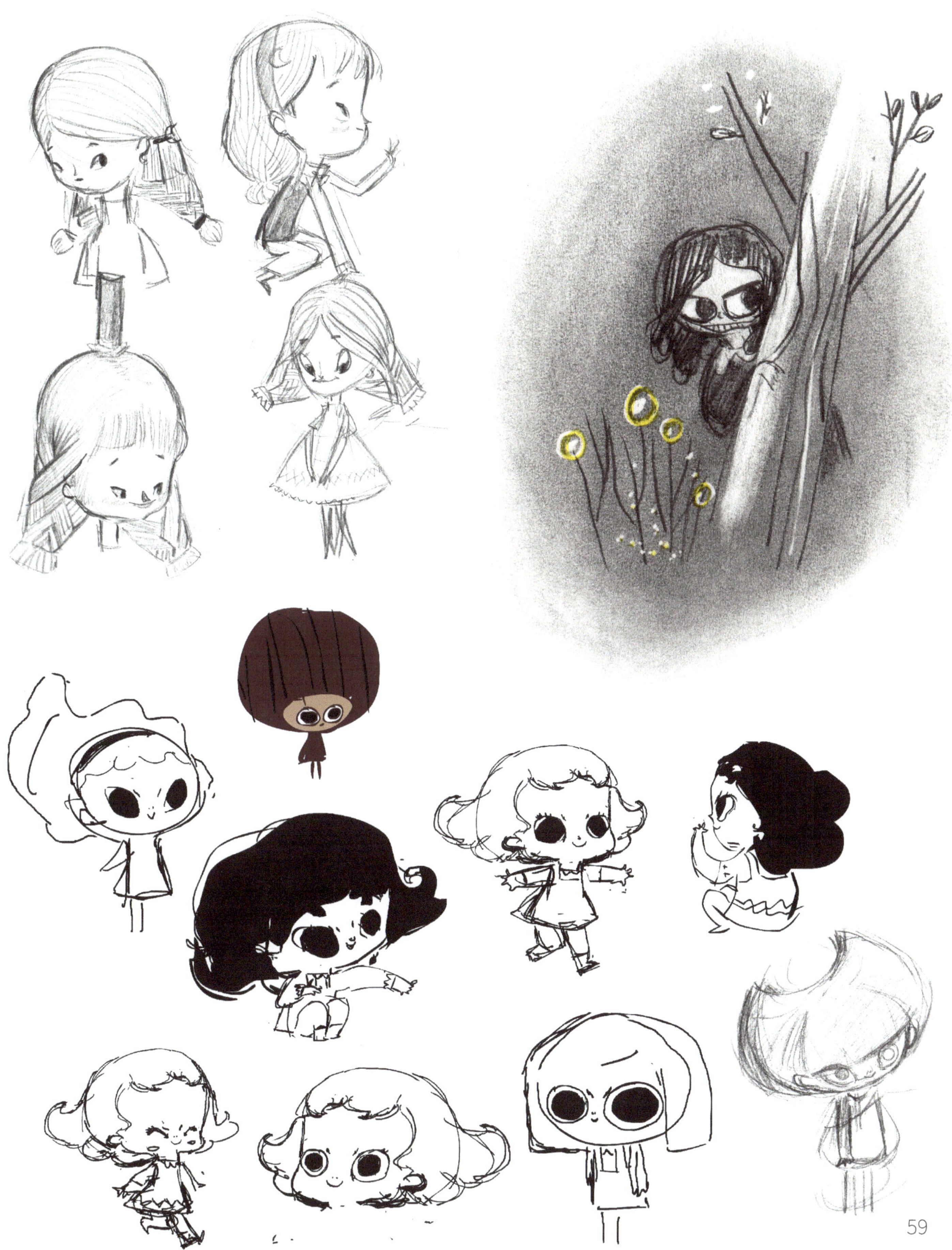

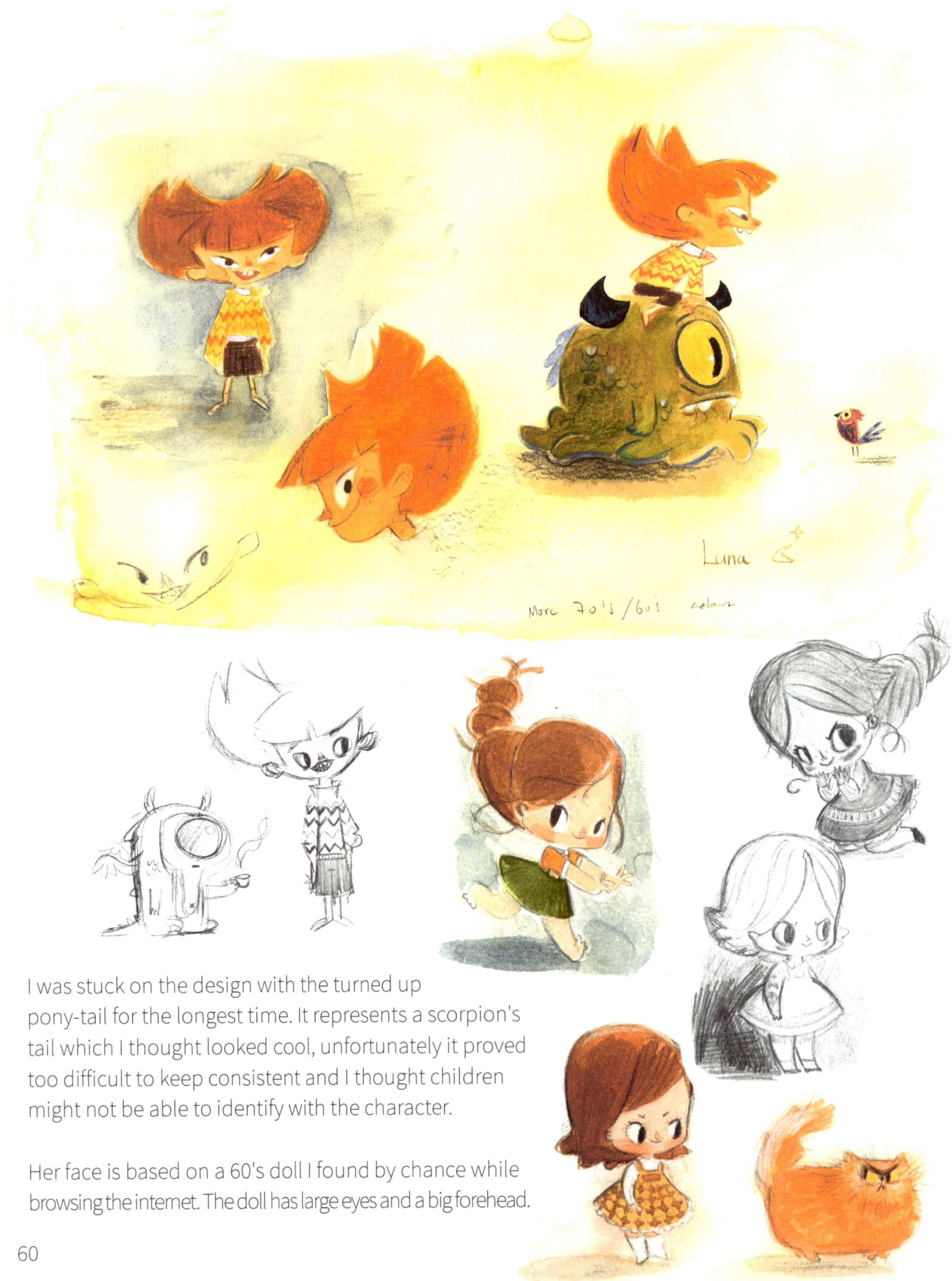

I was stuck on the design with the turned up
pony-tail for the longest time. It represents a scorpion's
tail which I thought looked cool, unfortunately it proved
too difficult to keep consistent and I thought children
might not be able to identify with the character.

Her face is based on a 60's doll I found by chance while
browsing the internet. The doll has large eyes and a big forehead.

60

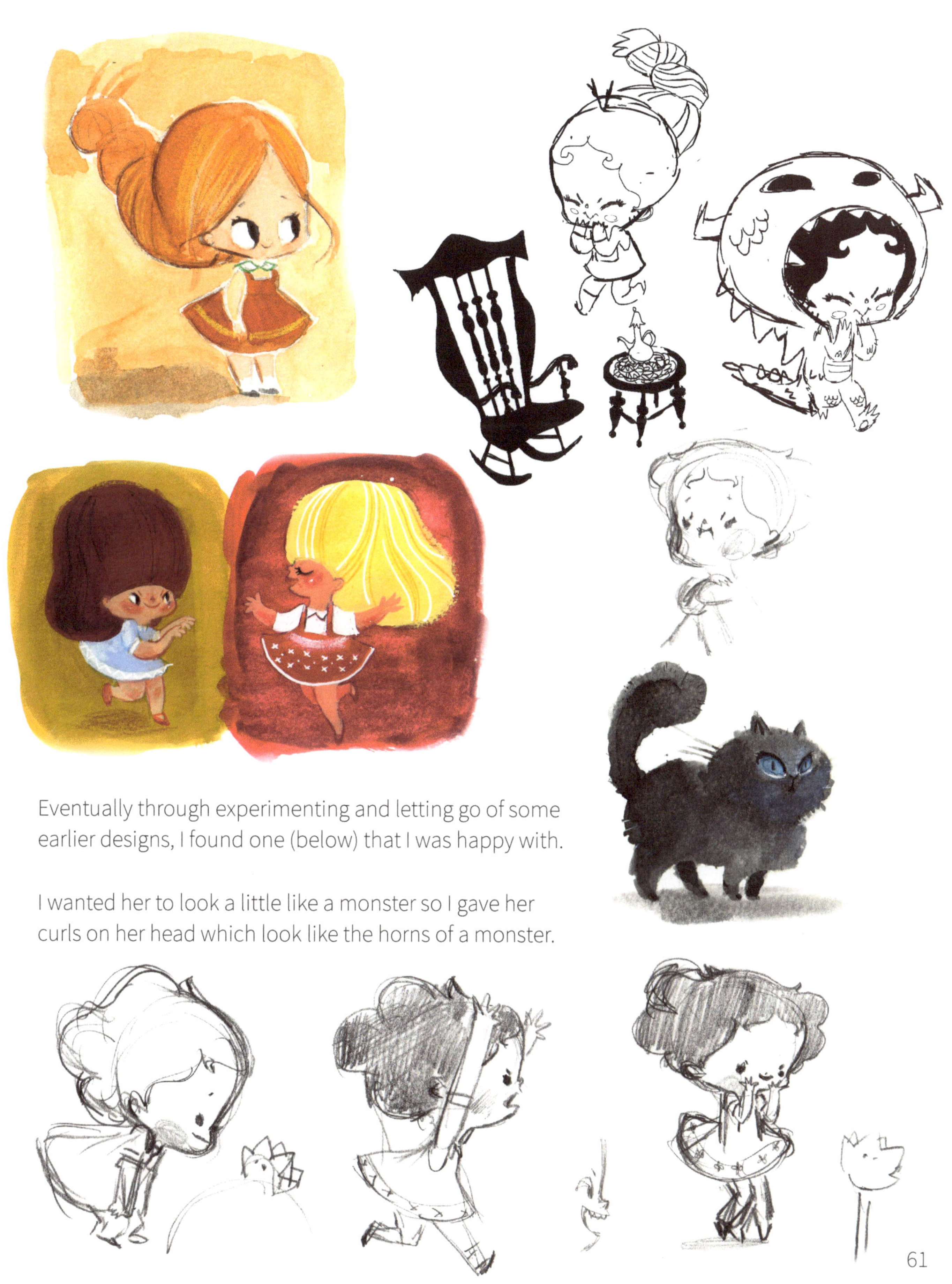

Eventually through experimenting and letting go of some earlier designs, I found one (below) that I was happy with.

I wanted her to look a little like a monster so I gave her curls on her head which look like the horns of a monster.

Character Design (Monsters)

The monster characters set another challenge for me, I did not want them to look like your stereotypical monster character. I played around with different shapes and sizes and looked at many different references, however I settled on a design that looked a little less Western and more Japanese.

As with Luna, I experimented a lot with the designs of the monsters.

There are 12 monsters in this story and I based them on people I know in my life, this helped to narrow down the ones I decided on in the end.

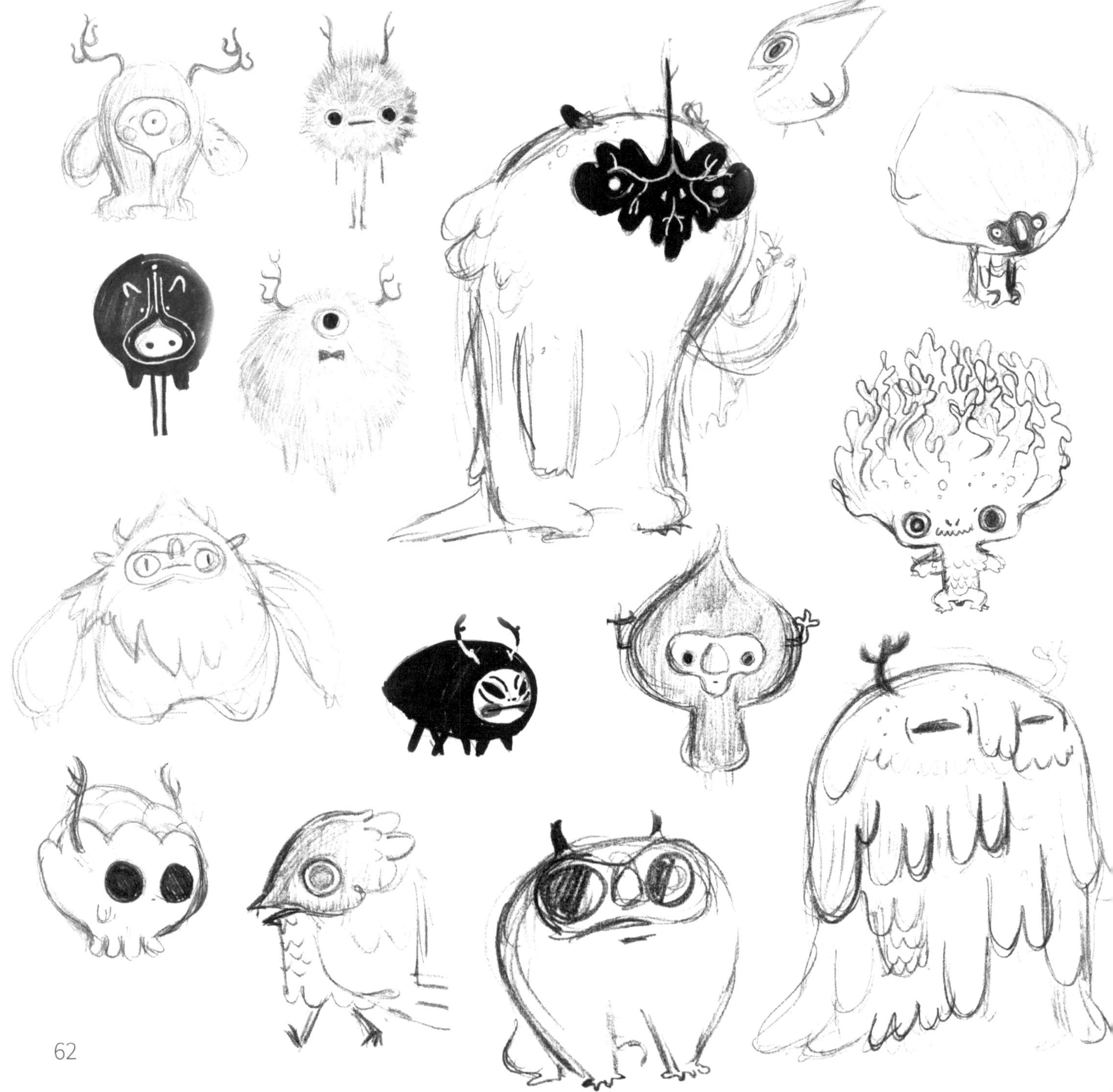

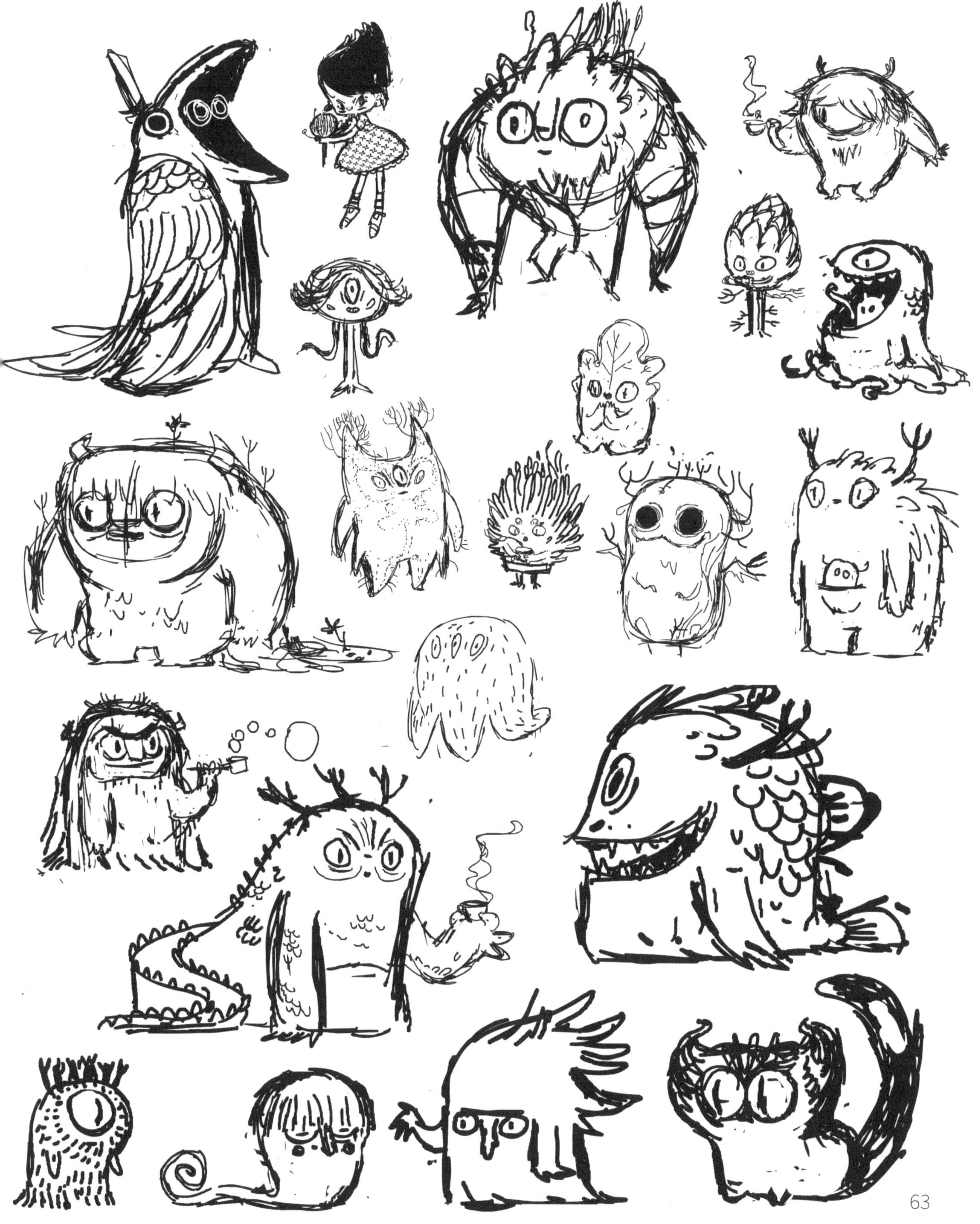

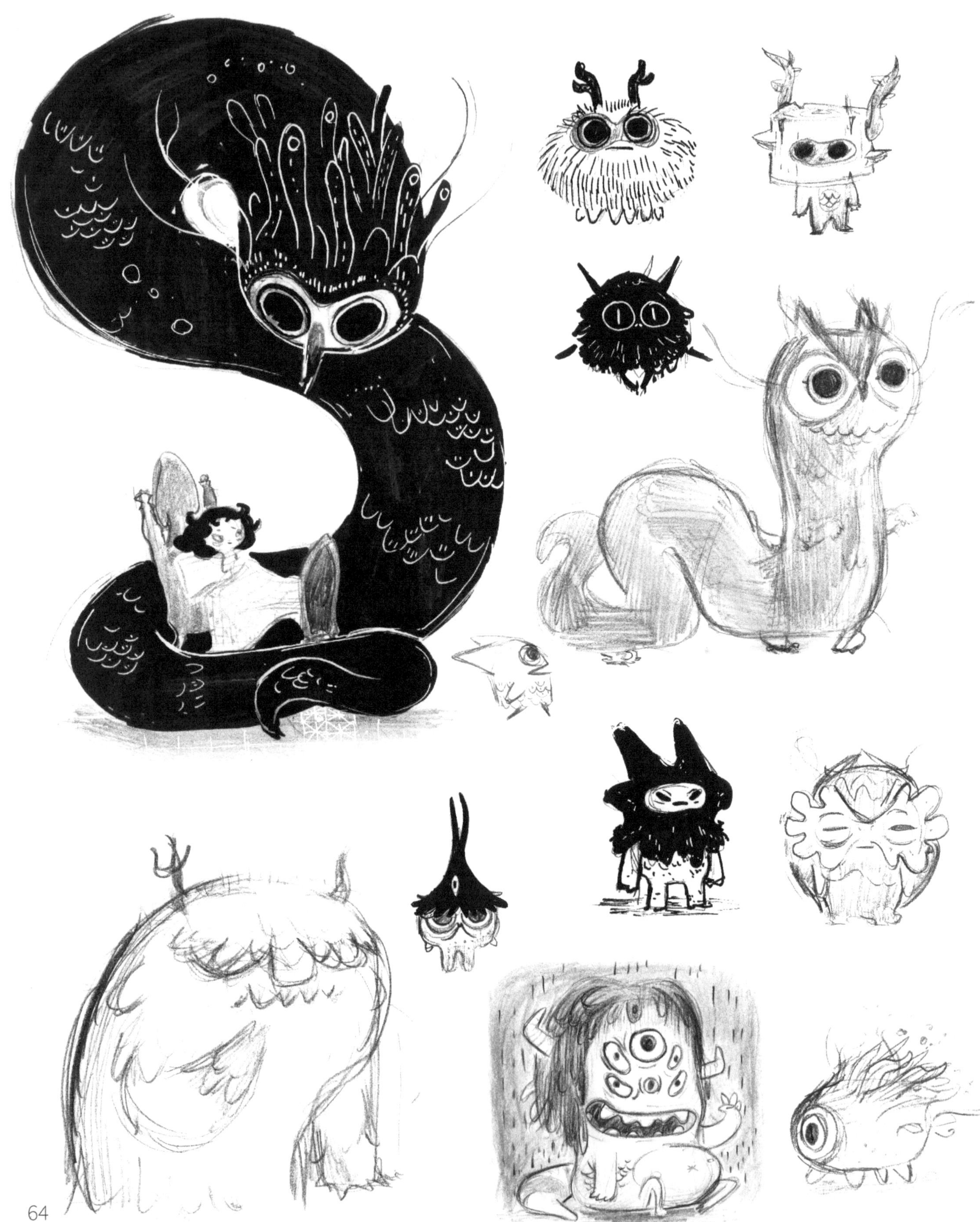

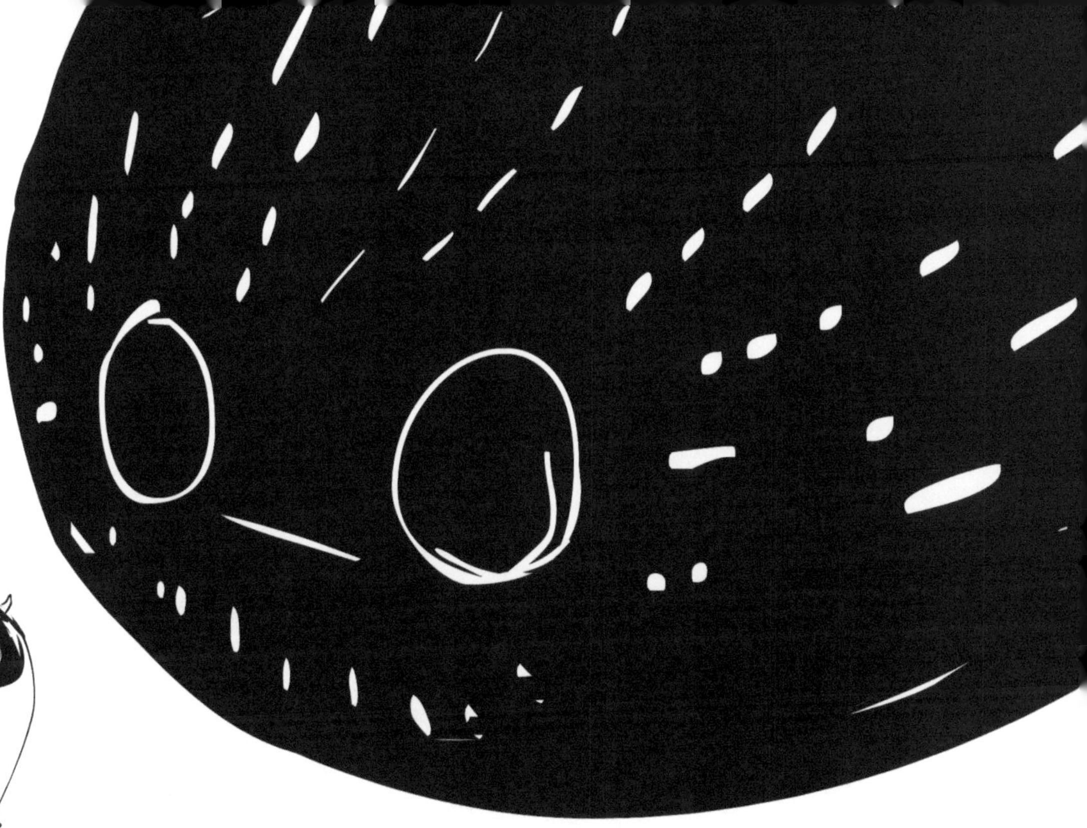

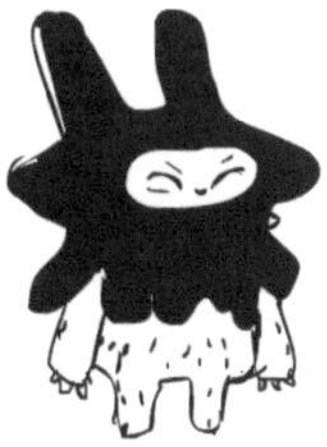

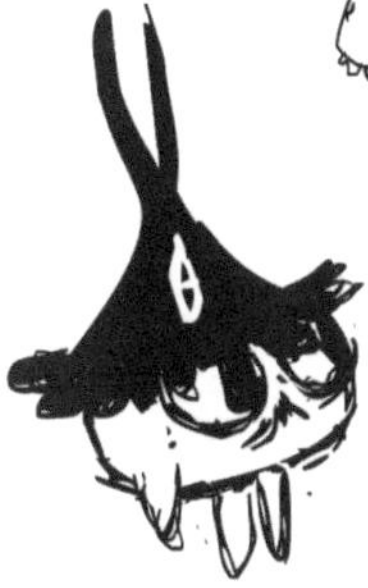

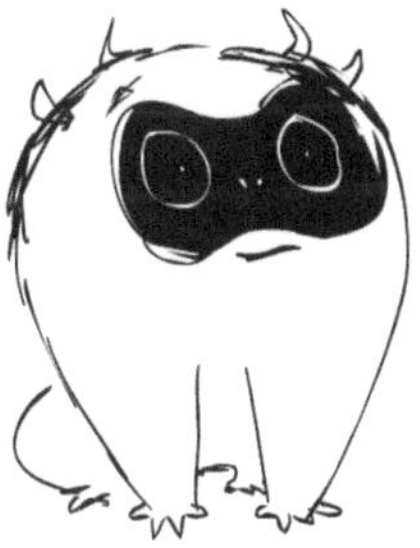

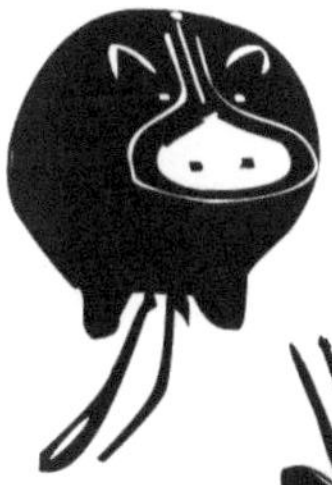

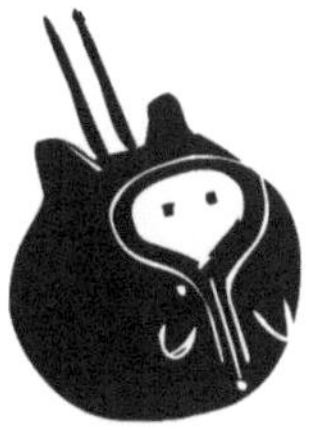

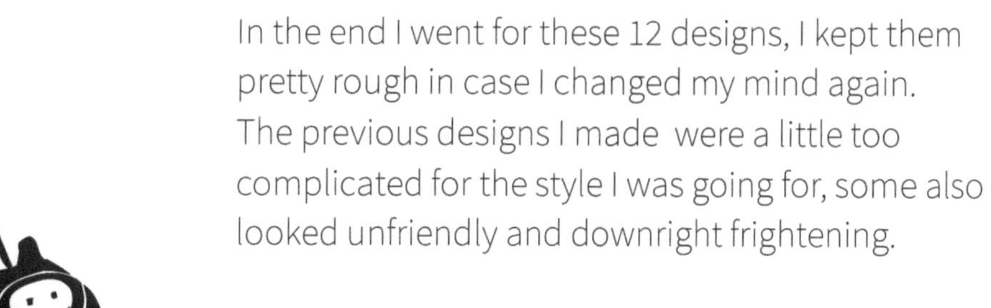

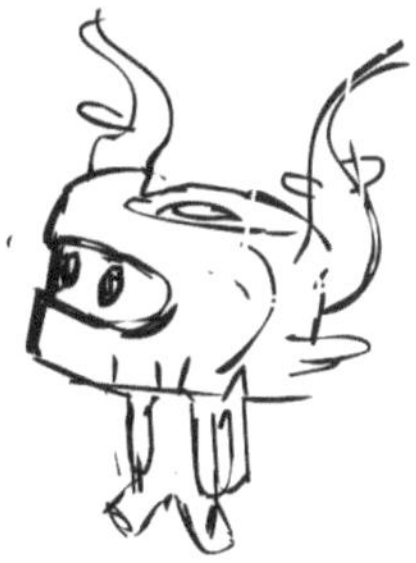

In the end I went for these 12 designs, I kept them pretty rough in case I changed my mind again. The previous designs I made were a little too complicated for the style I was going for, some also looked unfriendly and downright frightening.

The last monster that came about was the biggest one. I wanted a monster that couldn't fit anywhere and could block an entire spread by itself.

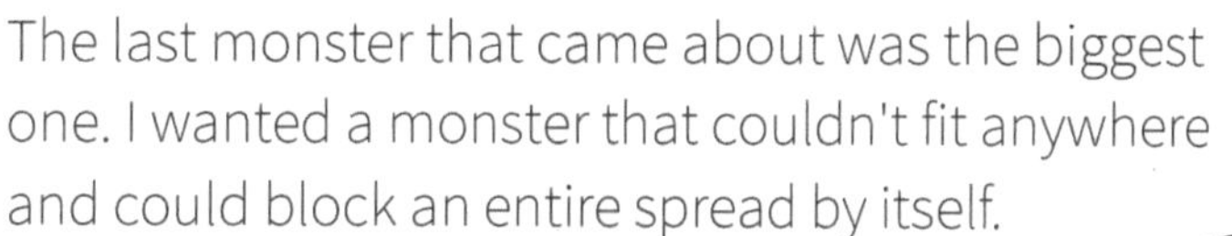

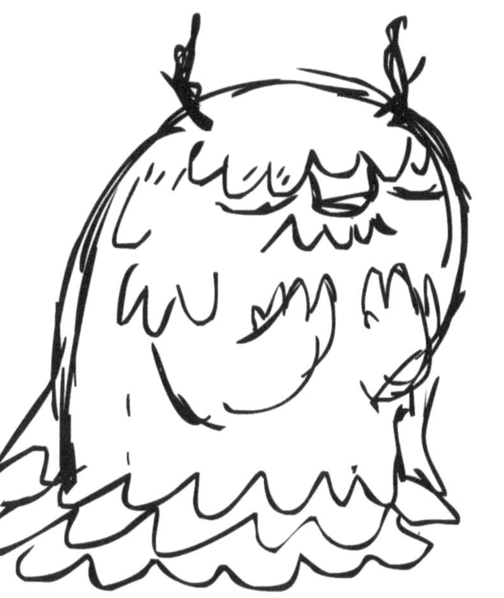

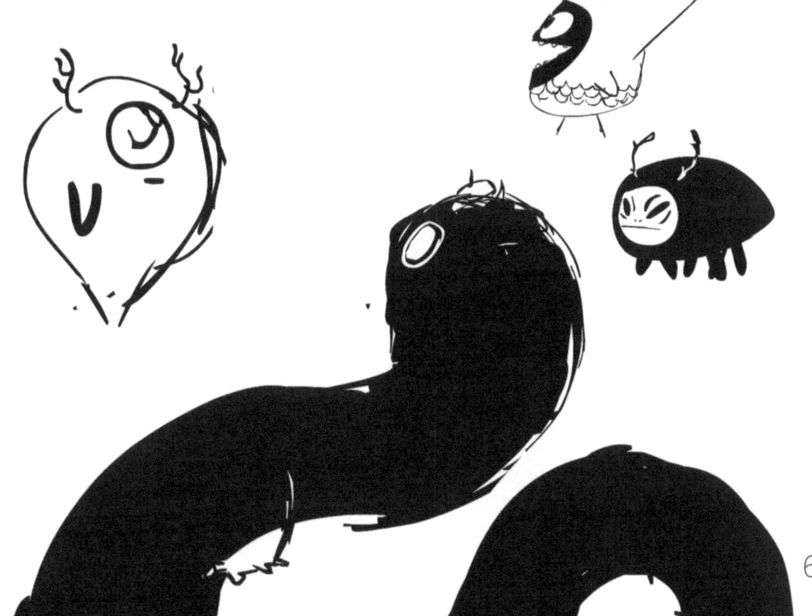

Concept

Just as I played with character designs for the main character and the monsters, I applied the same principle for the entire of the story. I experimented with different styles of looks or concepts before deciding which would work best.

I mainly experimented digitally for speed and not wasting expensive material (good water-colour paper can be really pricey!) I use Flash or Photoshop for drawing digitally but I prefer using real material but the examples below are drawn in Flash.
It's a good idea not to look at your work for a few days to get a fresh eye on it and in this case I thought it looked stiff and the colours could be more subtle.

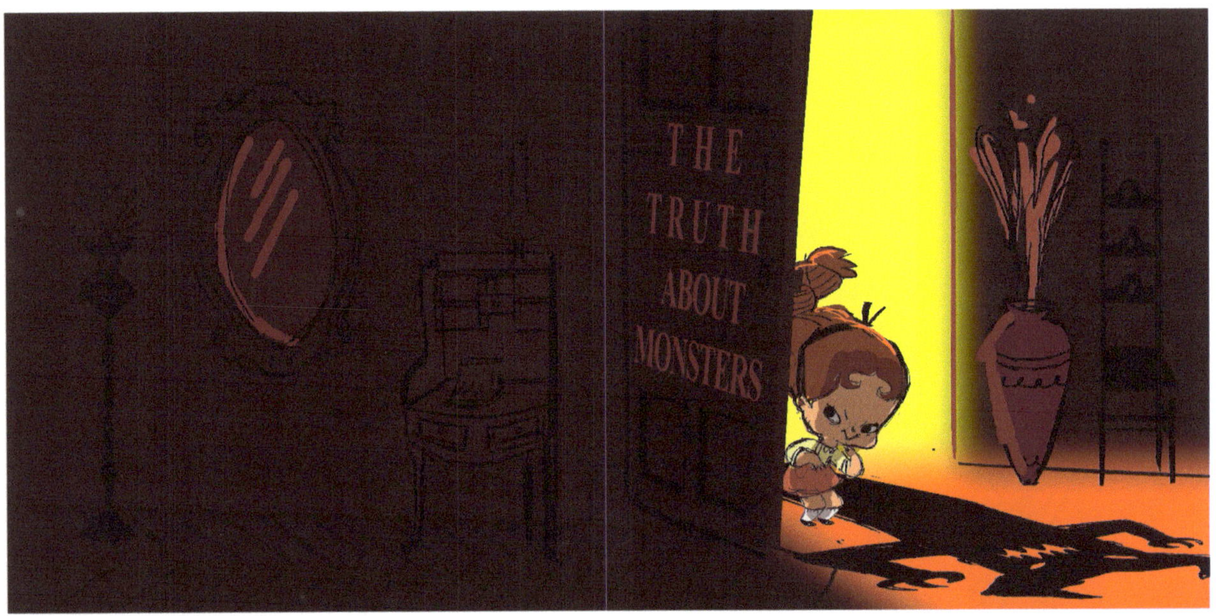

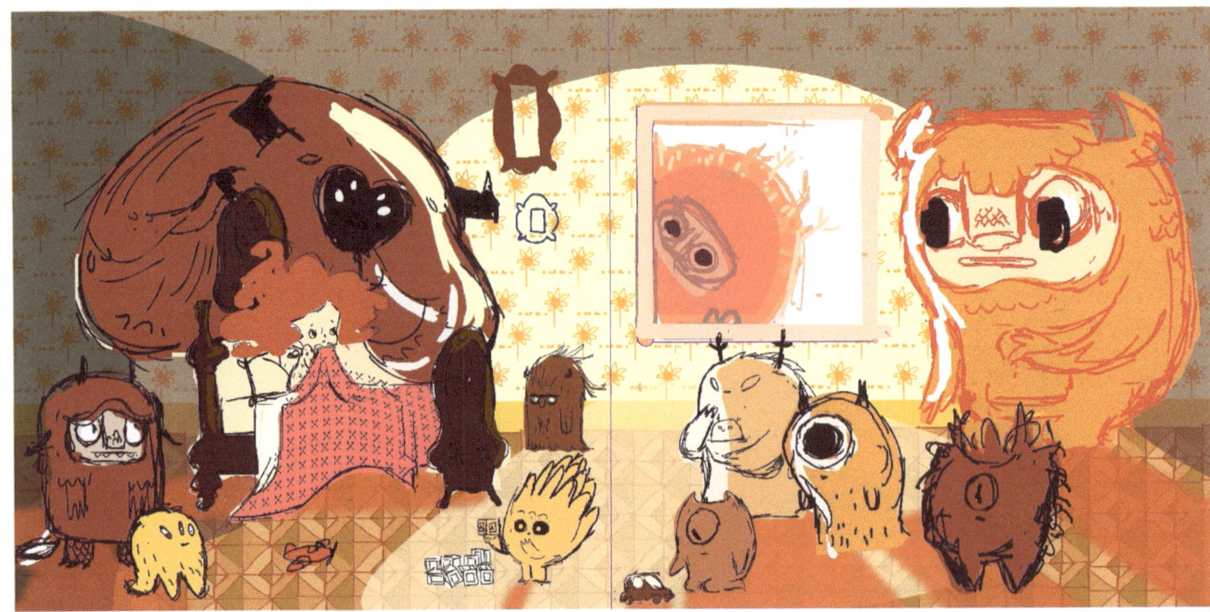

This piece is actually not related to the book but I thought it reflected a sense of direction of where I wanted to go with the style of the book. I like that the colours aren't bold, bright or primary. This one was done with gouache on water colour paper and really thinning down the gouache so it behaved like water colour, eventually though I ended having to use the gouache thicker and thicker to build on the layers below it instead.

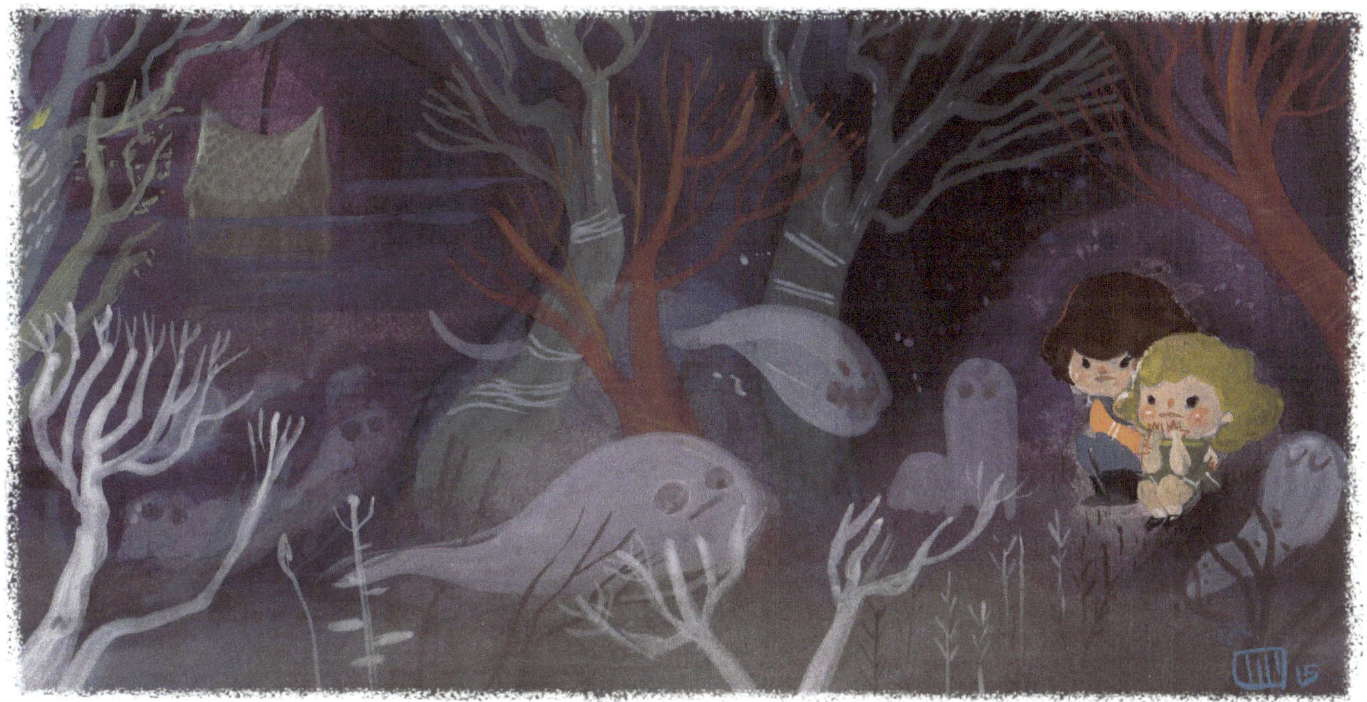

I tried using ink as well (below) and while I liked the result of this one, I found that it was similar to watercolour and I liked working with opague mediums a little more.

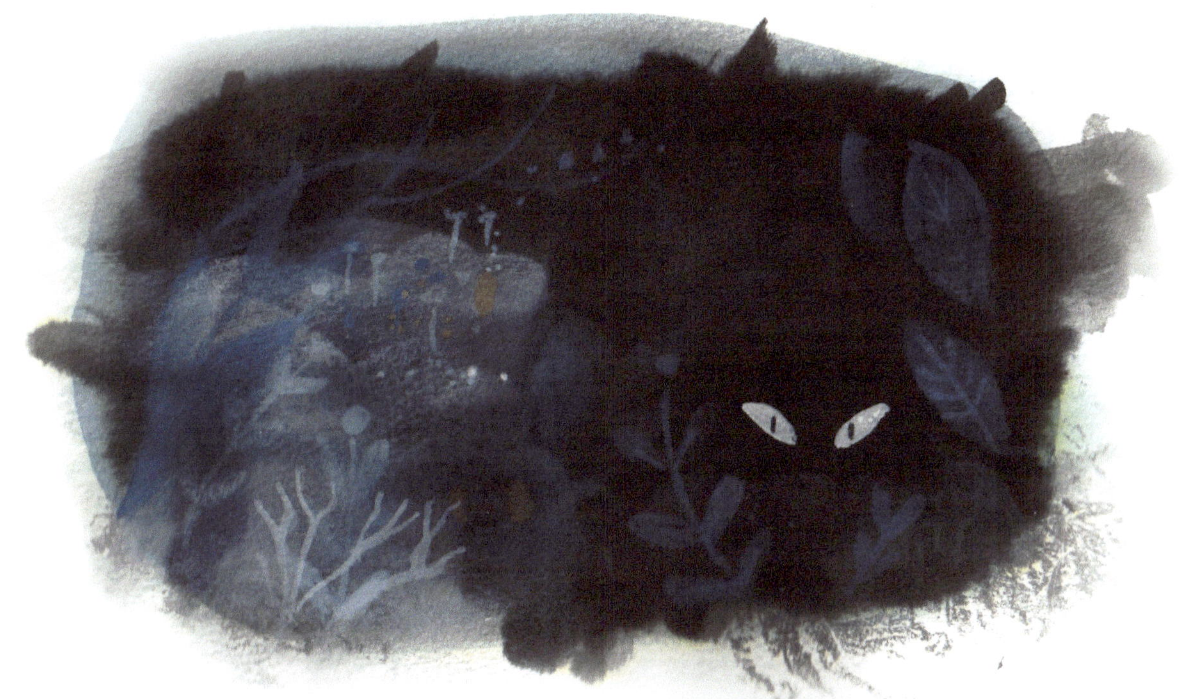

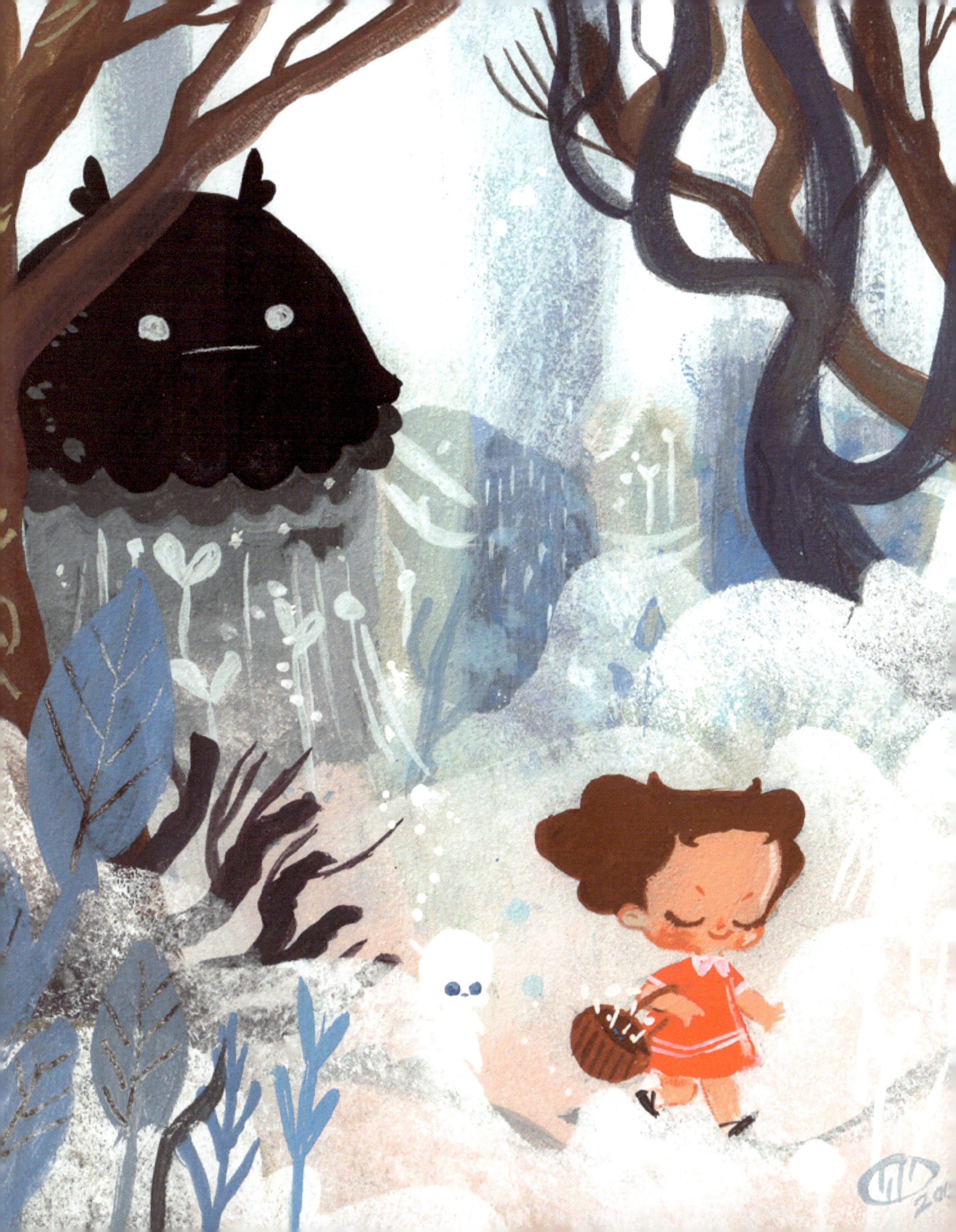

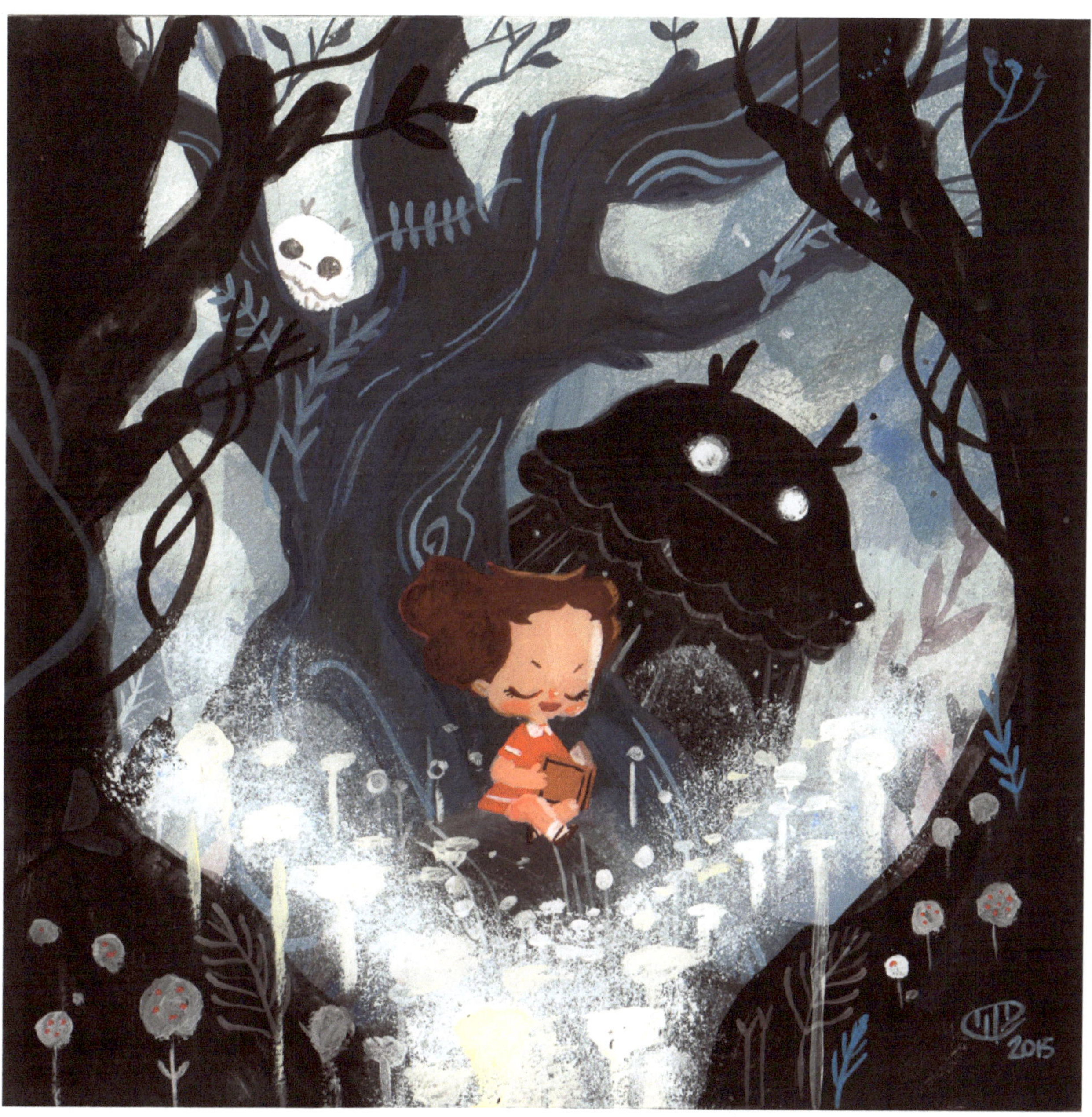

These two gouache paintings helped me to decide and understand the colour scheme and style for the entire book. Children's picture books which I enjoy most use colour sparingly. The best ones, in my opinion, use 3 to 4 colours max and keep designs simple and story uncomplicated.

Now that I have decided on the character design of Luna and the monsters, I wanted to have a cleaner storyboard. I referenced my older boards but did not stick to them firmly. The pencil version of the book served me greatly to check the rhythm and flow of the story.

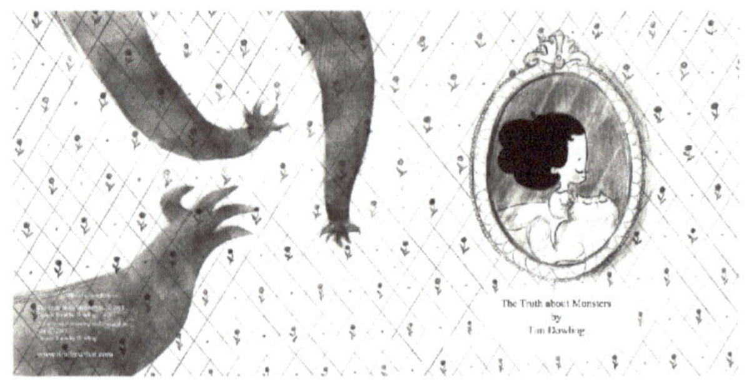

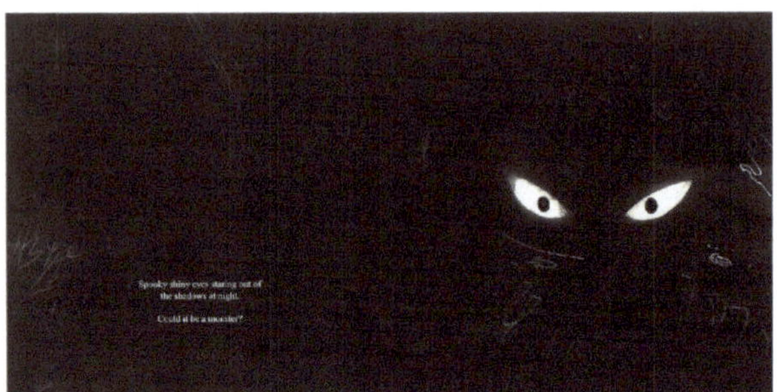

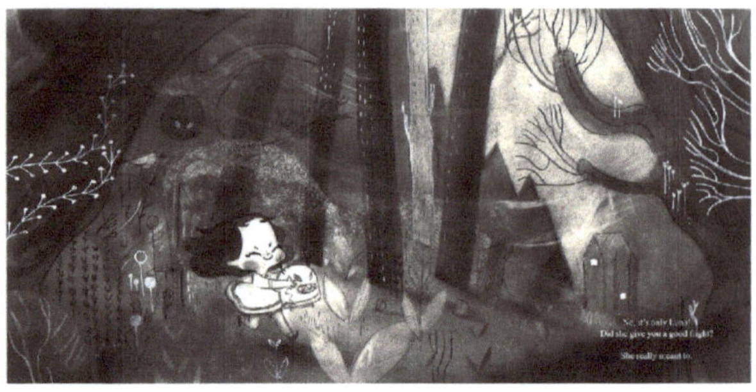

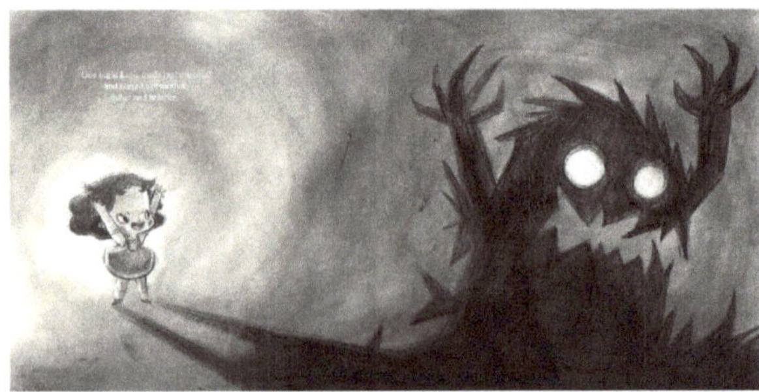

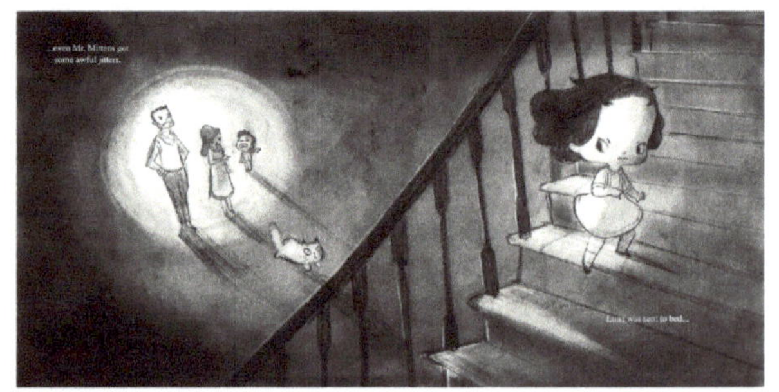

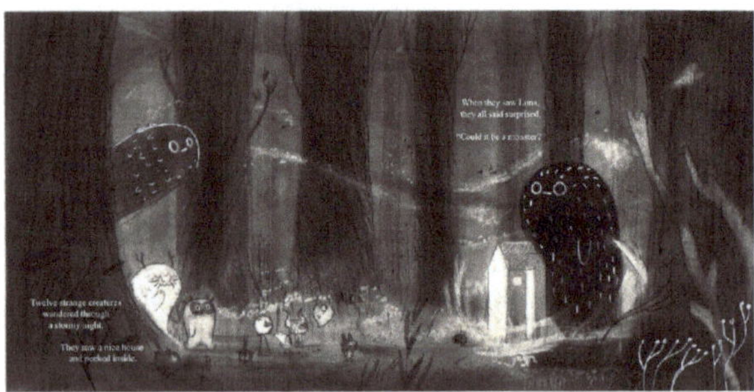

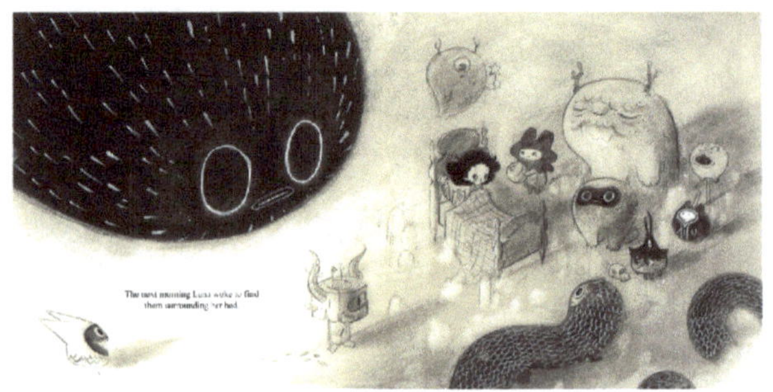

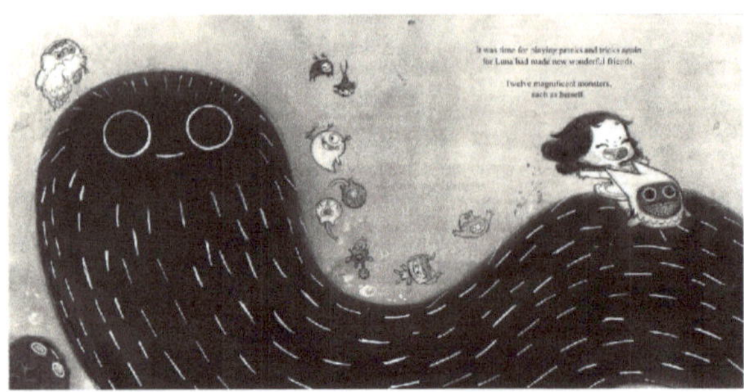

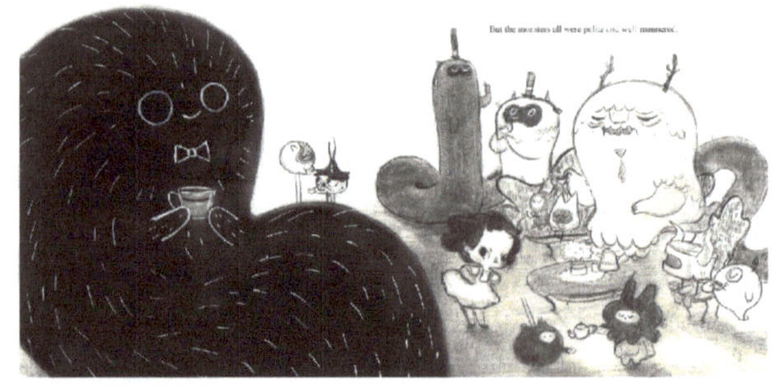

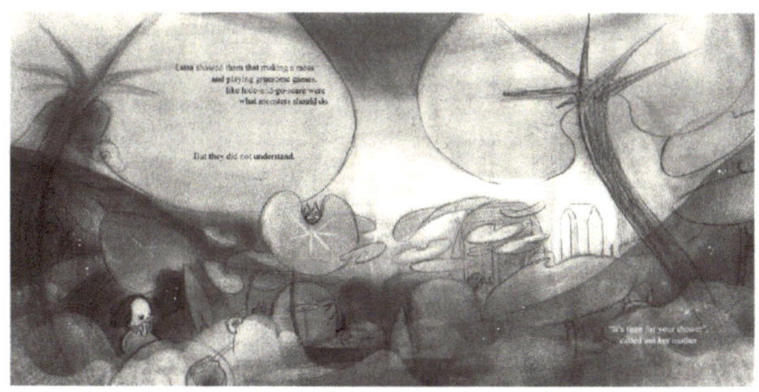

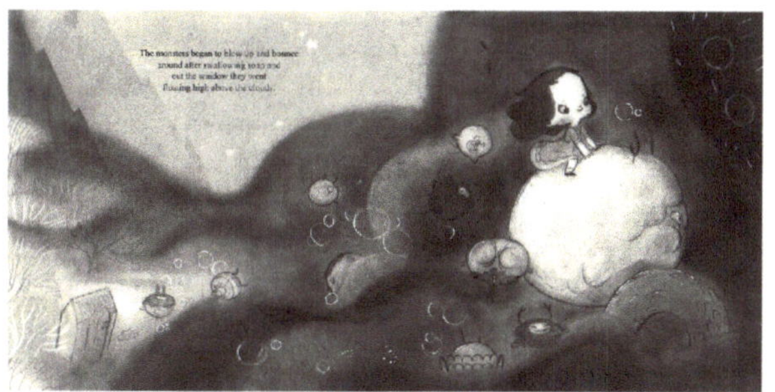

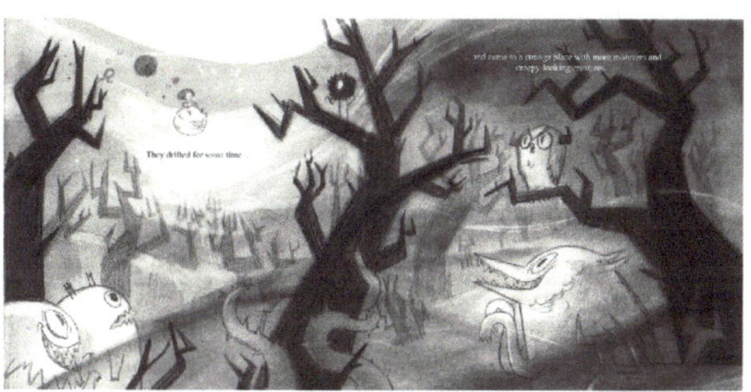

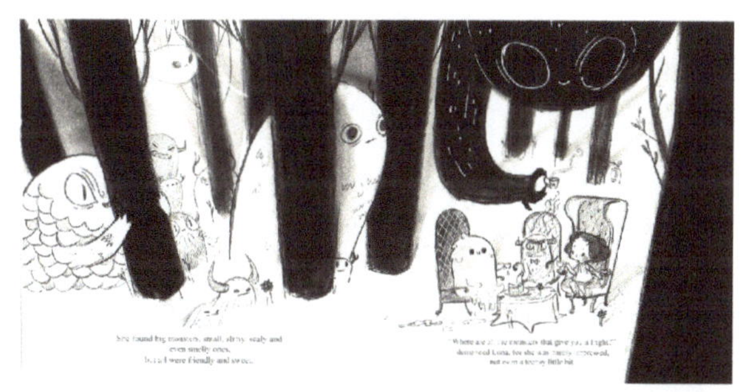

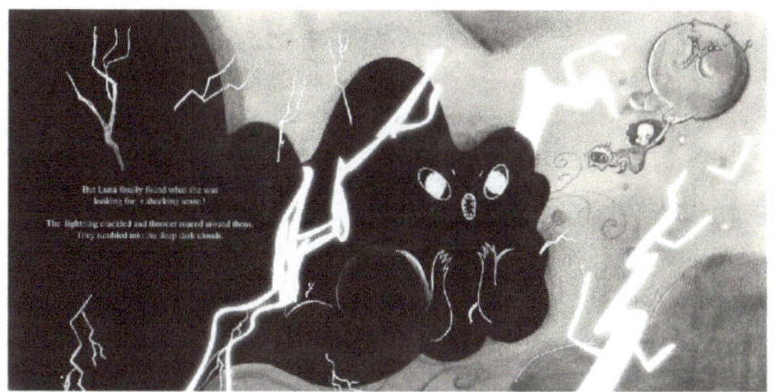

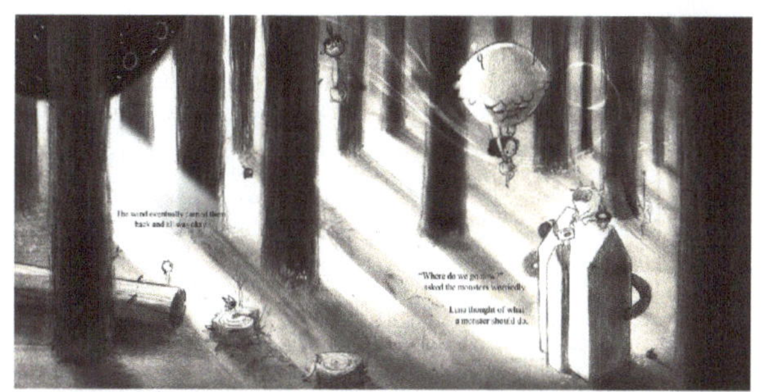

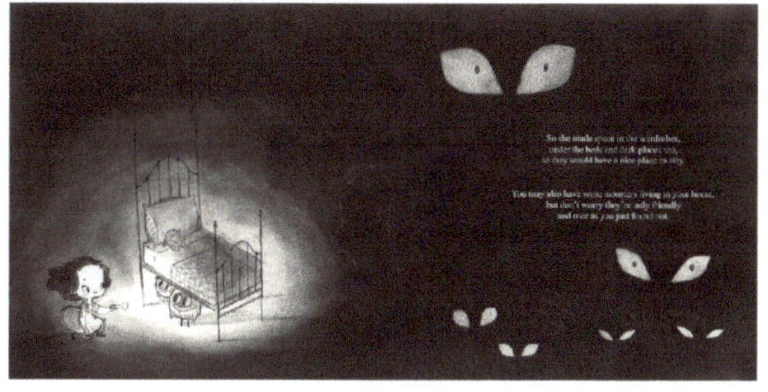

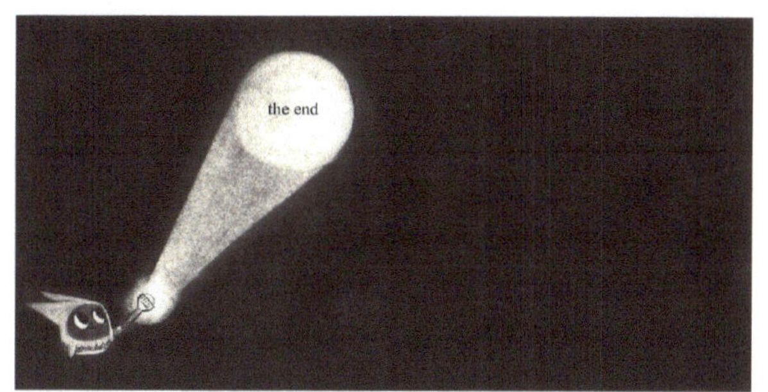
the end

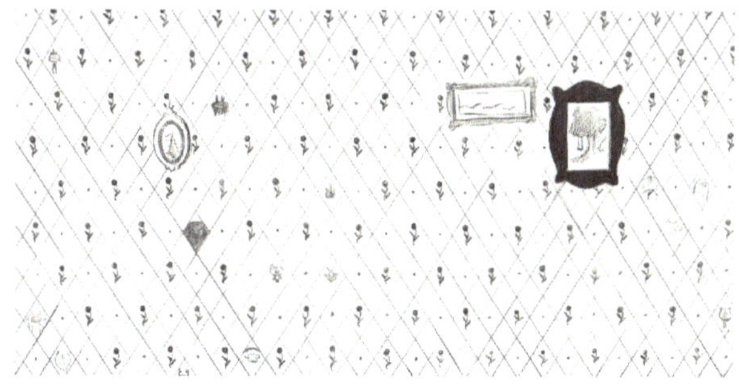

Colour Keys

Here are the colour keys I made for the book; they served as a rough guide for colour, rhythm, flow and most of all consistency even when I strayed from them a little or changed entire spreads.

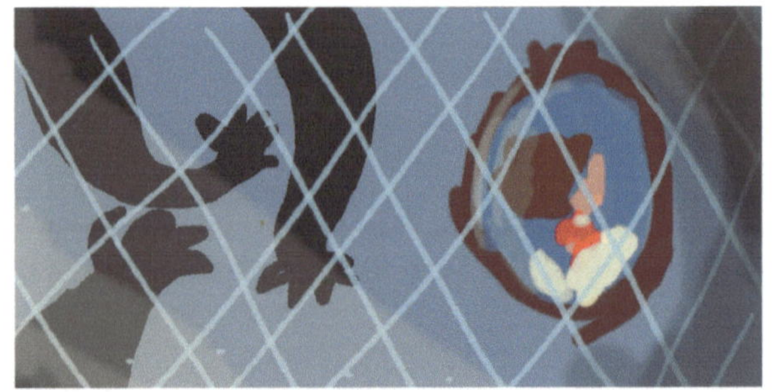

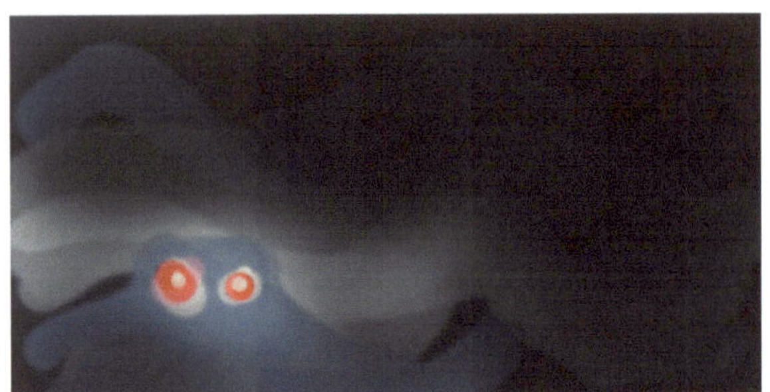

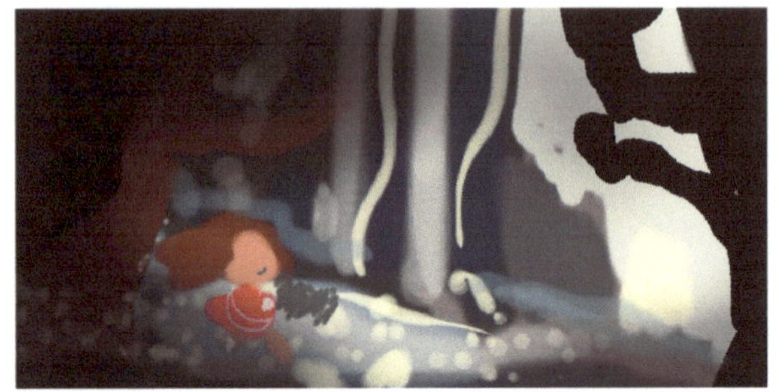

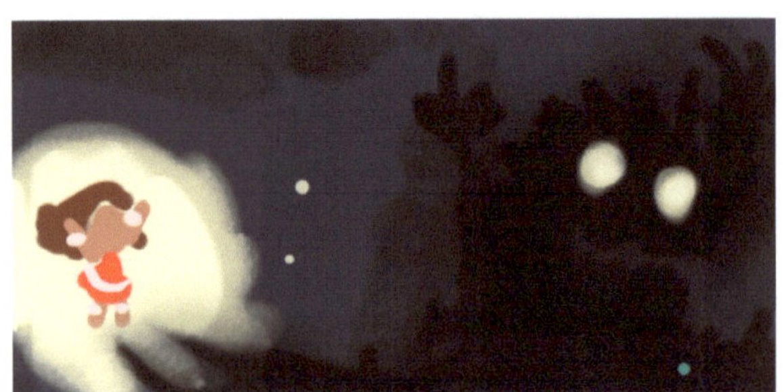

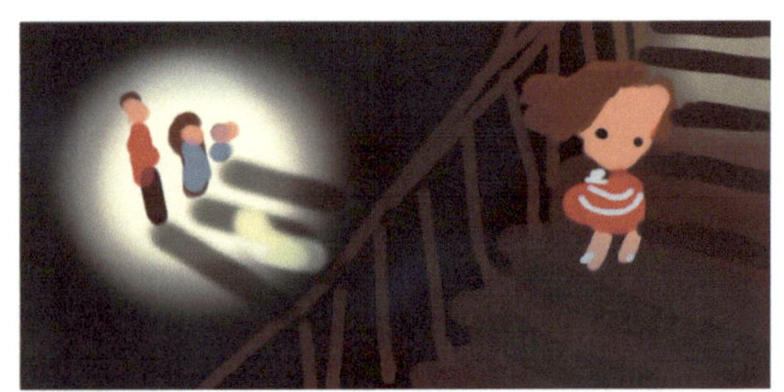

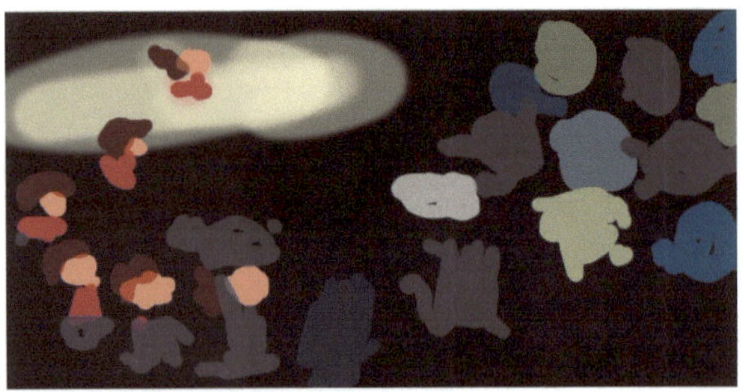

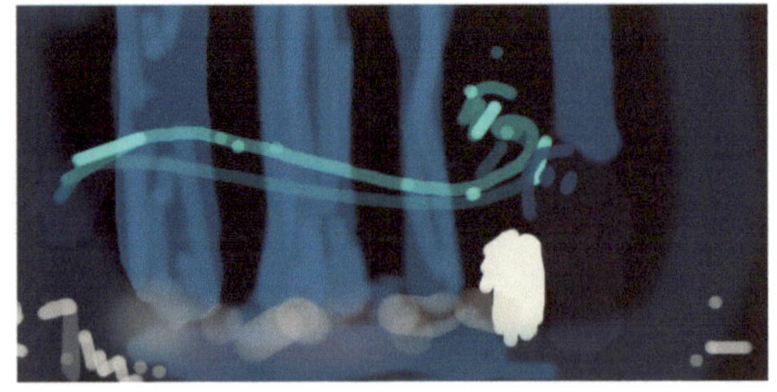

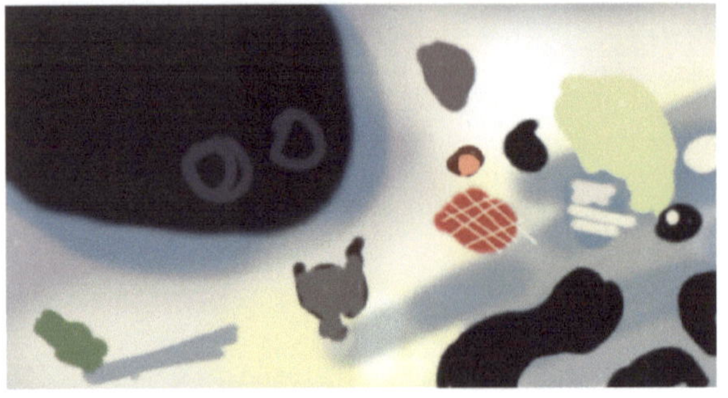

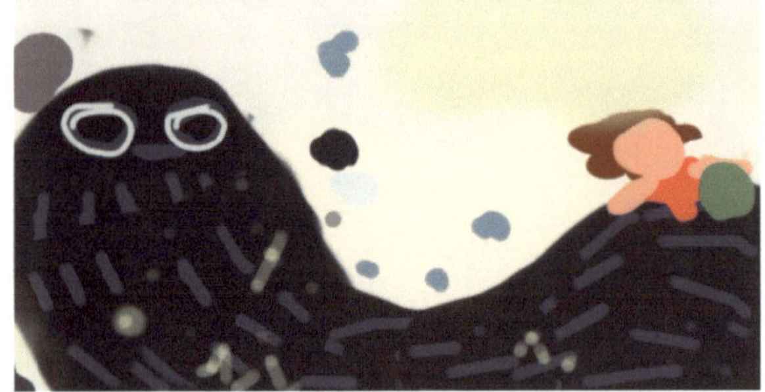

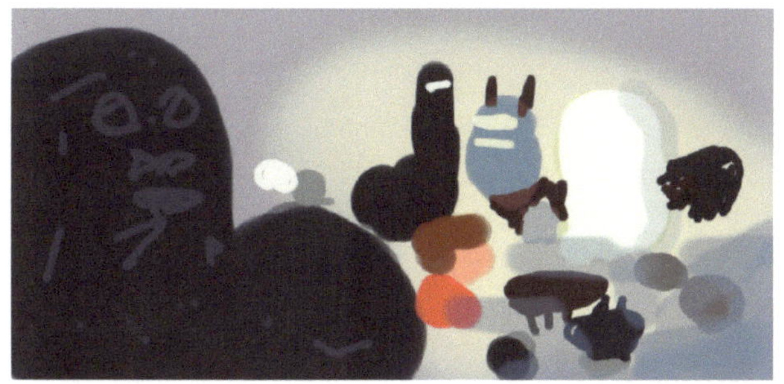

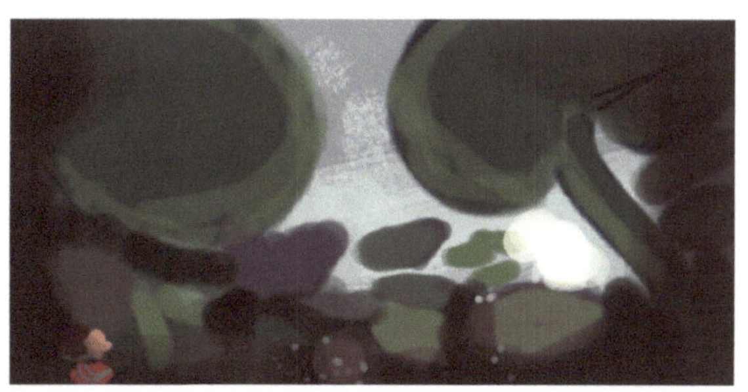

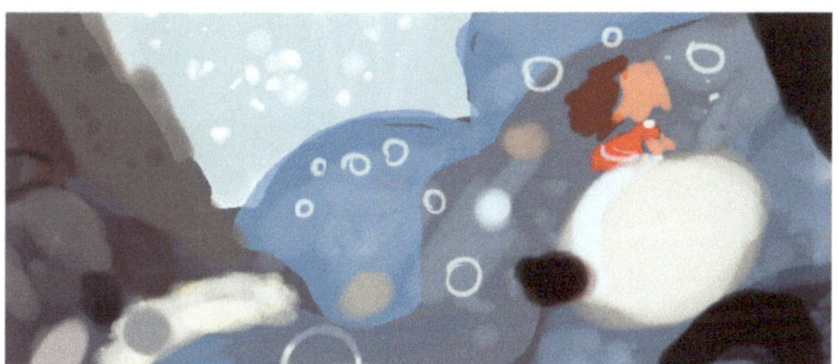

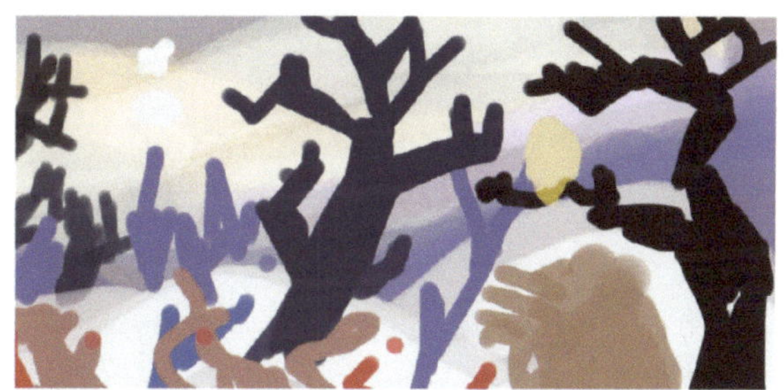

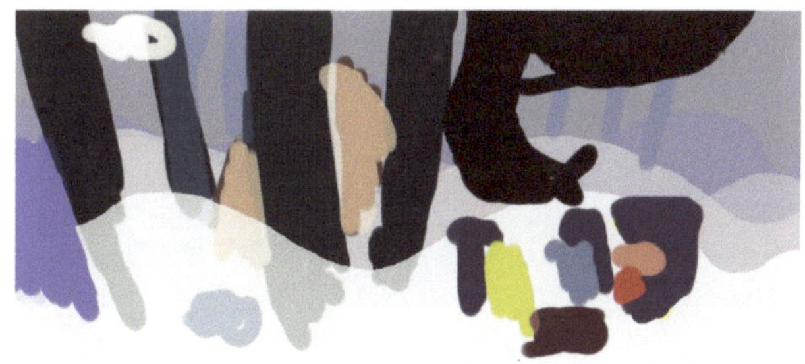

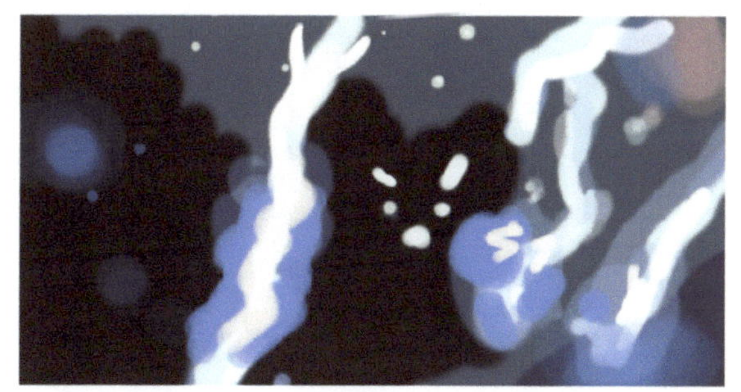

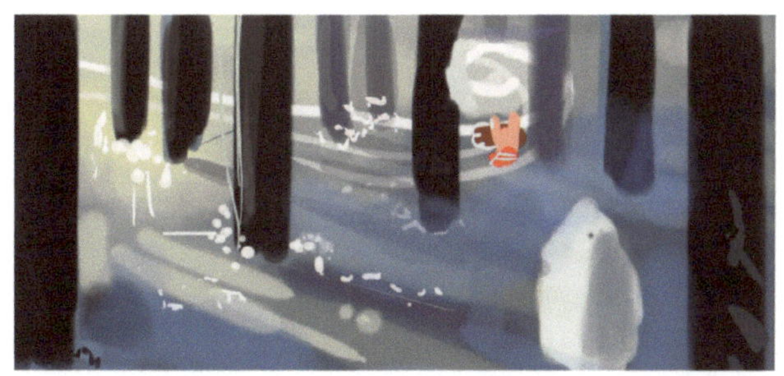

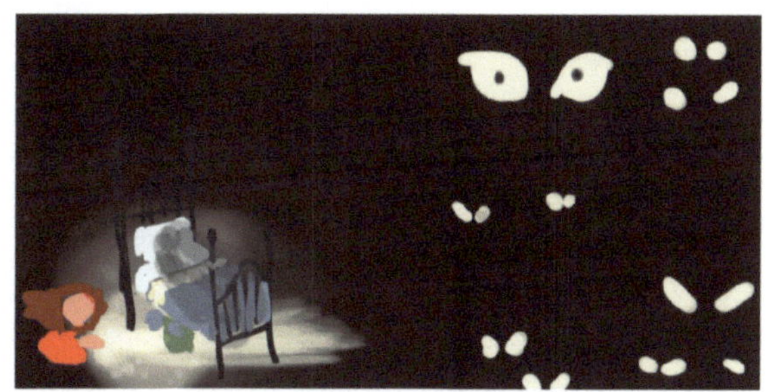

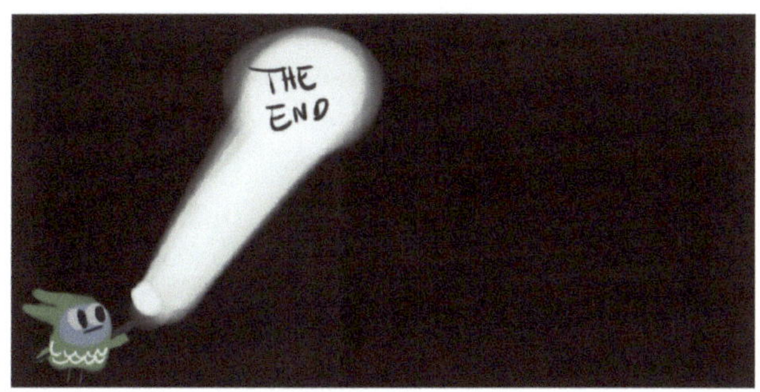
THE
END

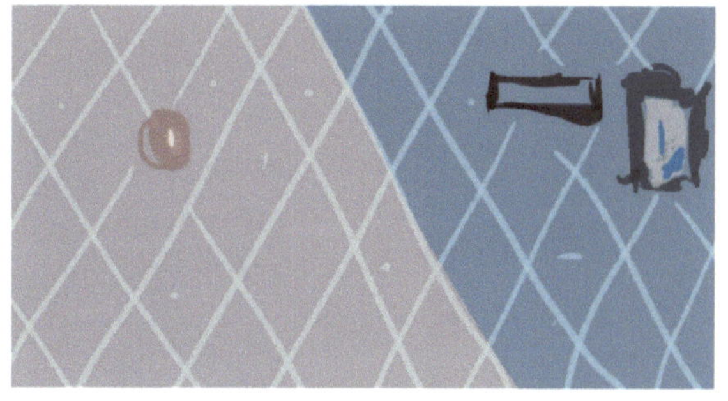

Finished Book

These are the final panels from the book.
If compared to the pencil drawings and
colour keys you will notice that they are
similar but not the same. Compared to
the first drafts, they have changed greatly
but even some elements remain.

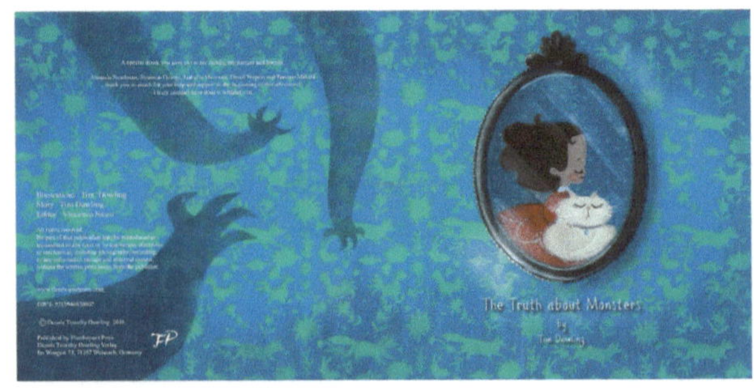

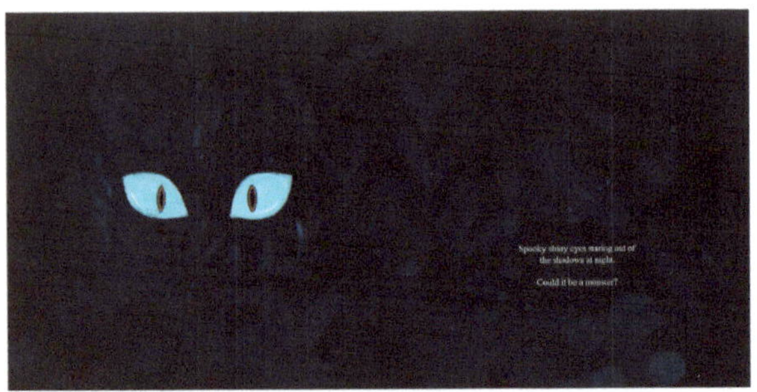

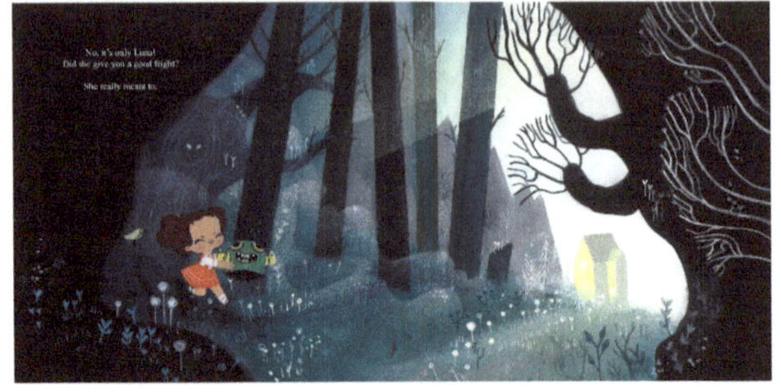

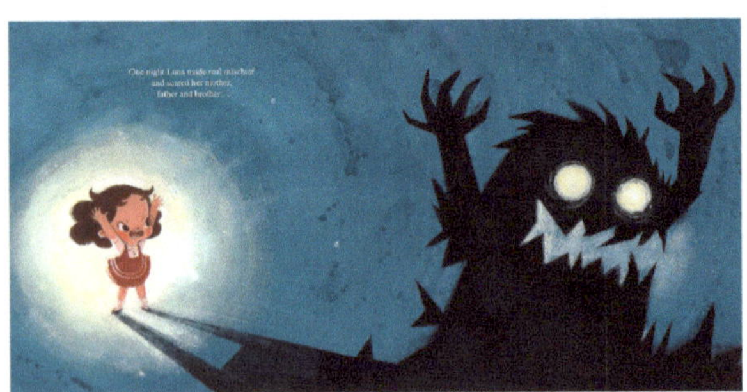

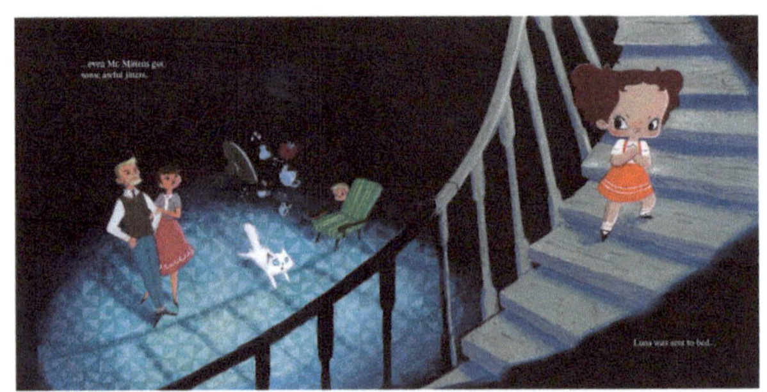

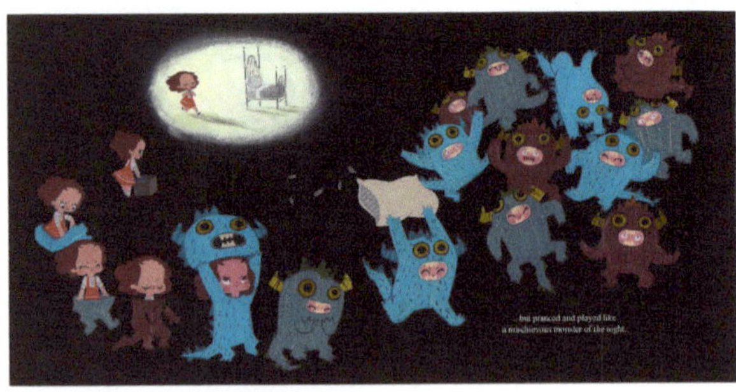

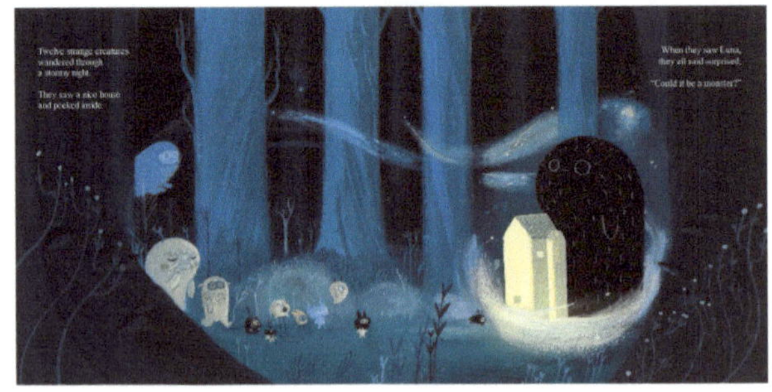

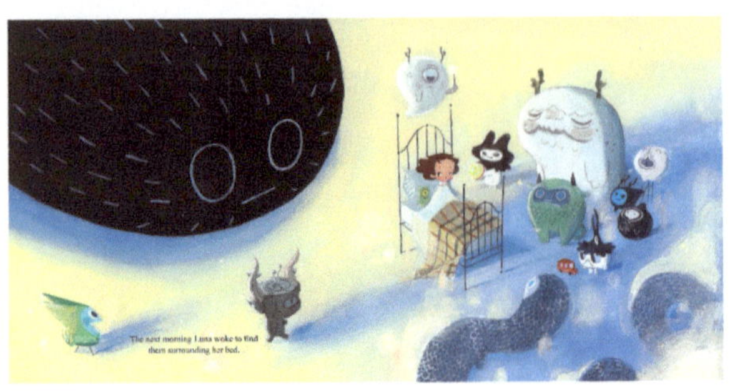

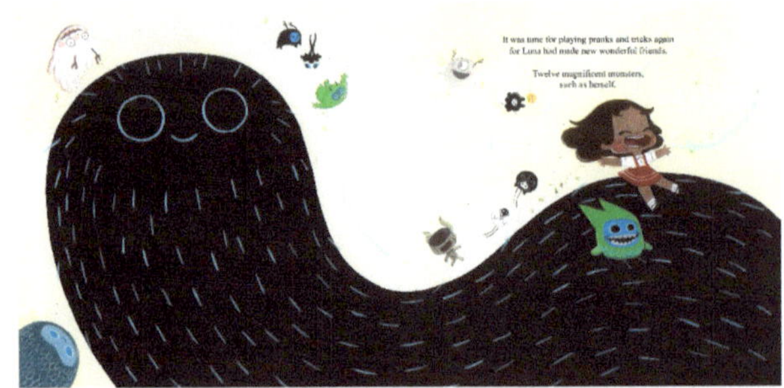

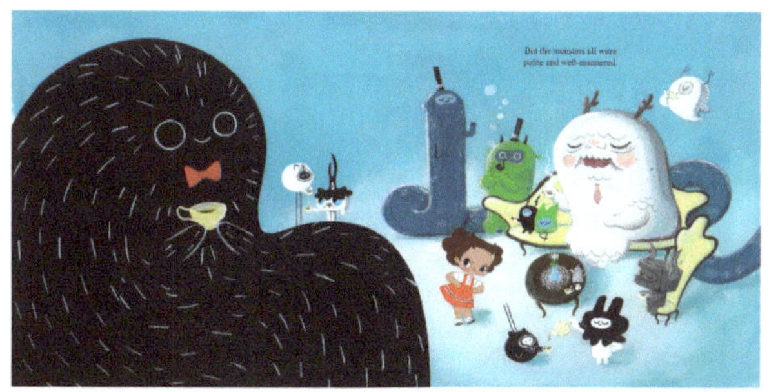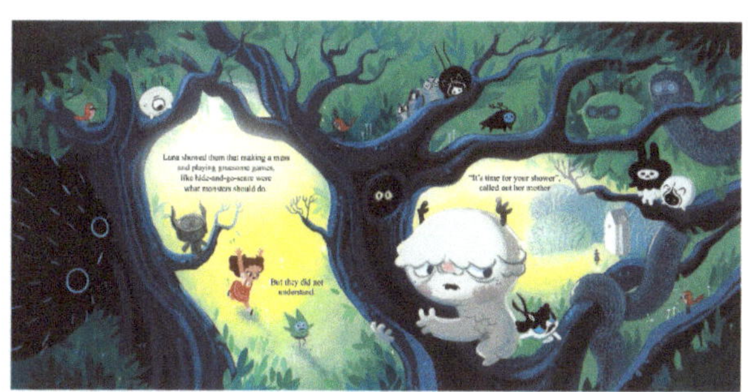
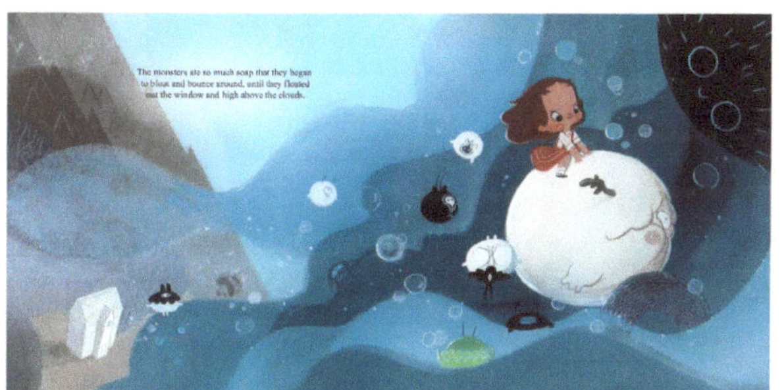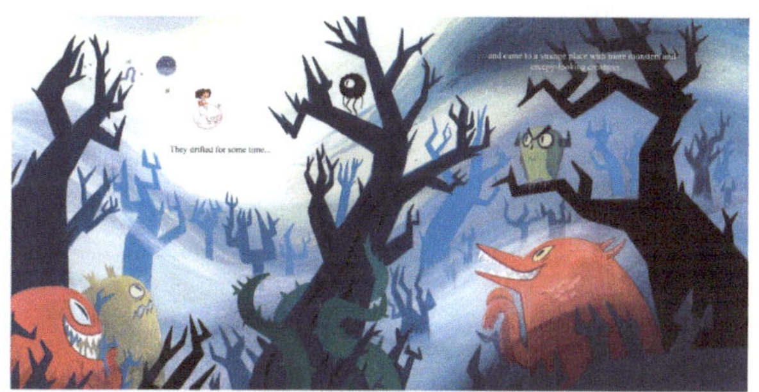
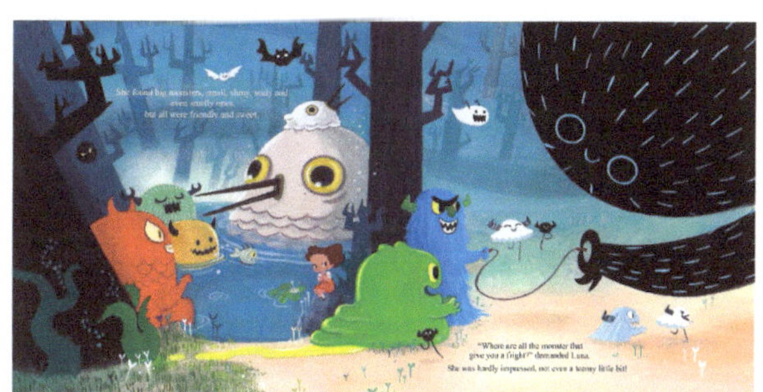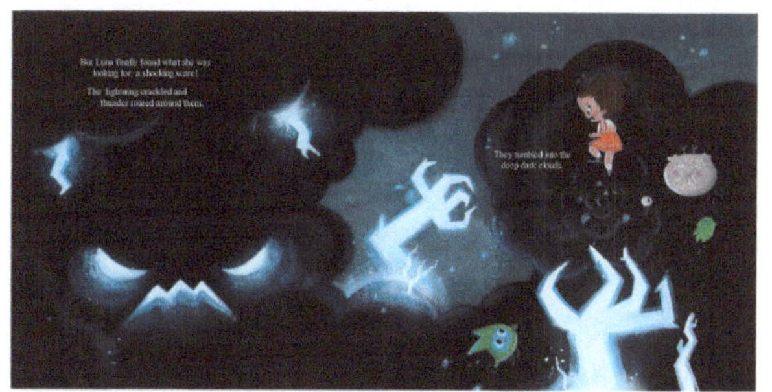
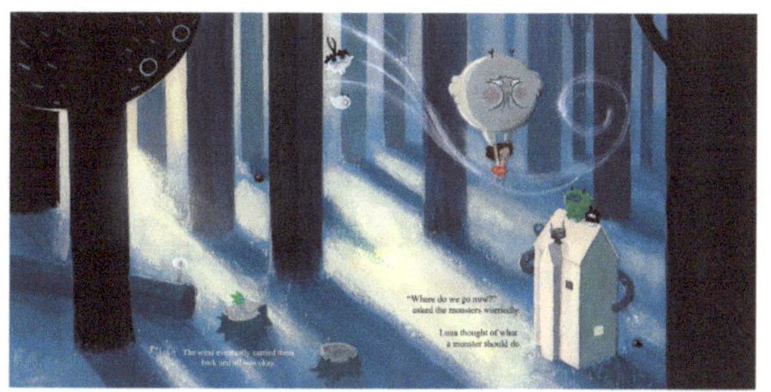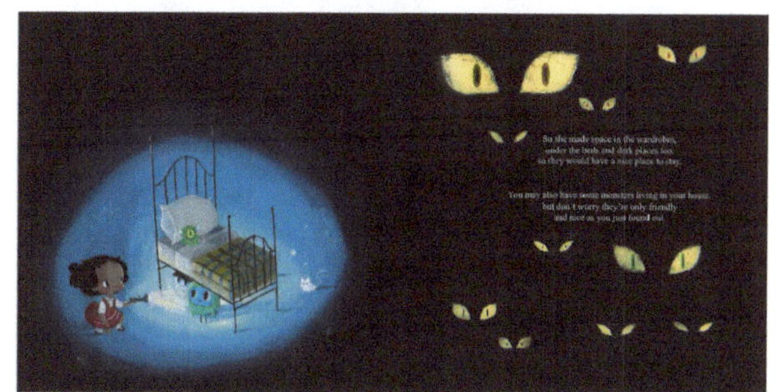
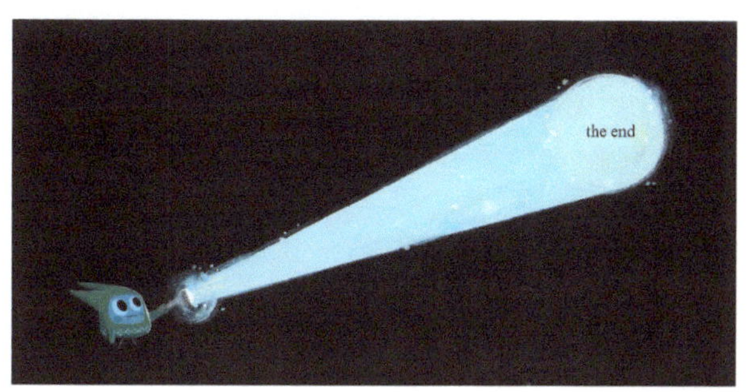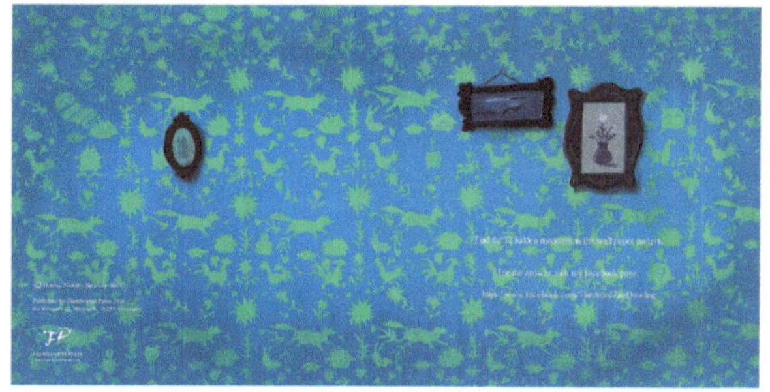

the end

Painting Process

The following pictures are work in progress steps from one of the spreads in the picture book. The first step is to make a thumbnail of your idea. This thumbnail is rather big (10x20 cm) because there are characters all over the page.

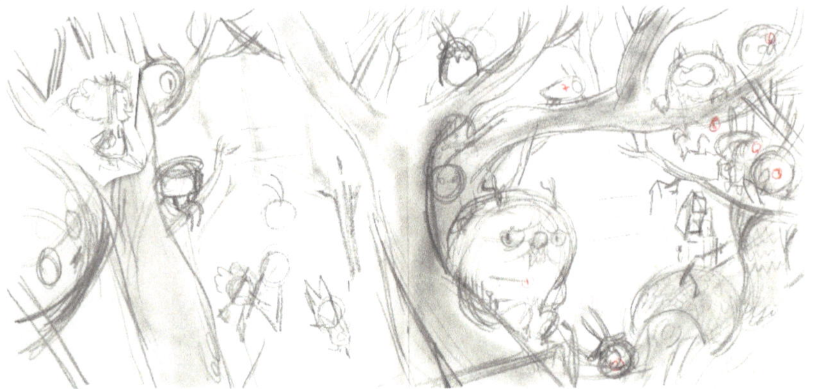

I wanted the trees and monsters to frame the background. In the following step I defined the characters and trees, working on a larger scale (20x40 cm) made this easier. At this point I added the darker areas to understand if the contrast would work with the foreground and background.

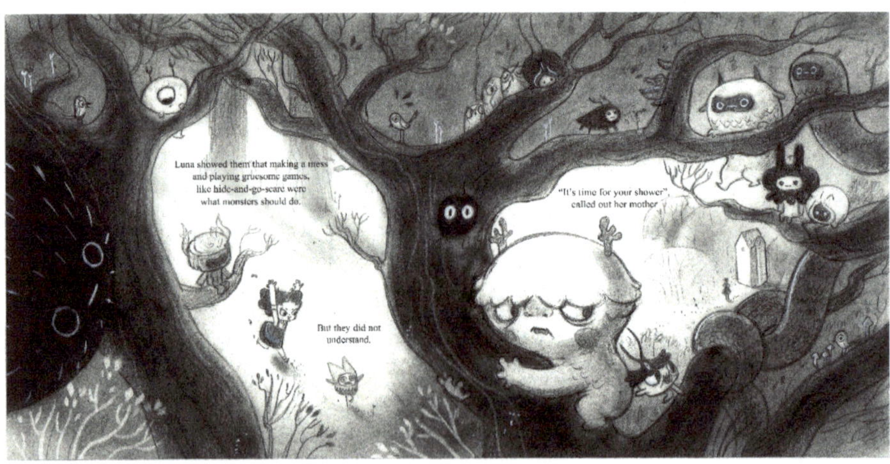

After making the defined sketch, I make the colour key (5x10 cm).
I wanted the mood to be bright and summery, so I used a lot of warm colours.
This is the last step before I move onto making the final illustration.

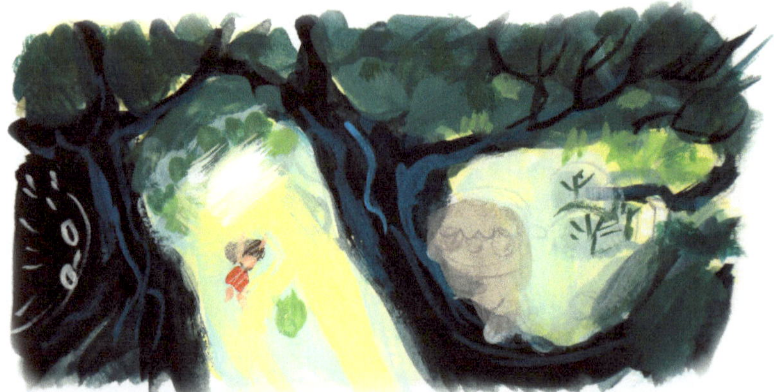

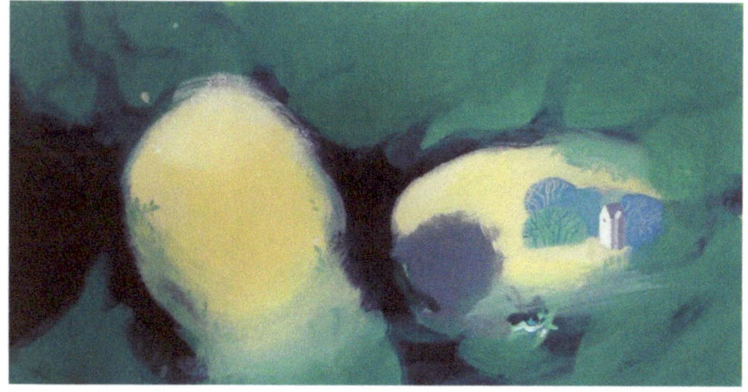

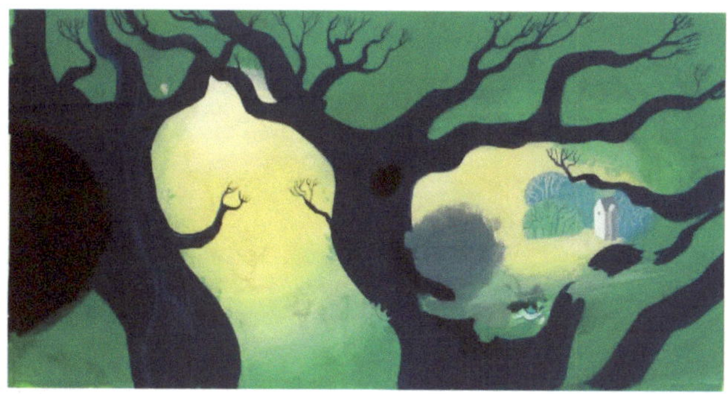

After transferring the sketch to stretched water
colour paper to wood board I begin applying
large blocks of colour of yellow and green.
I basically work from whatis furthest away in
he distance and then to what is closest by.

I lightened up the green leaves and defined the
trees a bit more. I took this approach because
the characters are all interacting with the trees
and branches so it was important to have this
nailed down first.

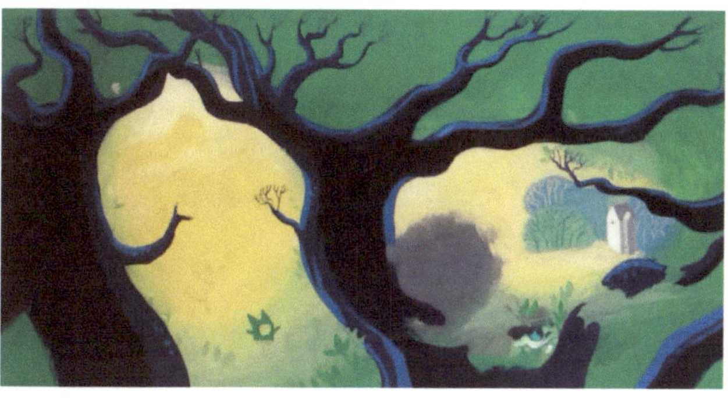

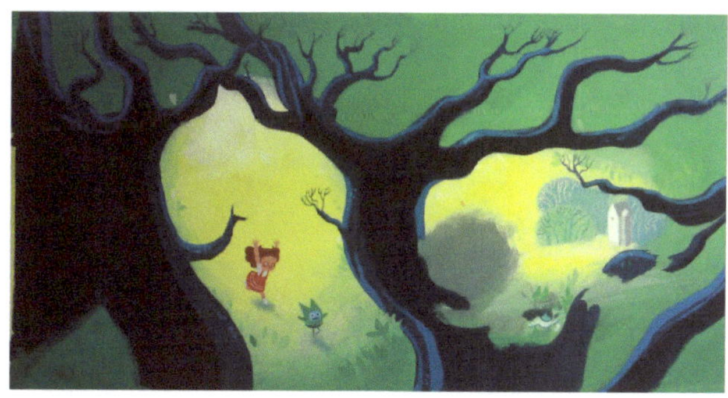

Highlights were added to the trees and also
some leaves and foliage to the background.
I painted the house and trees in the previous
steps first but thought I might have to paint
over it, luckily I didn't have to.

I added the main character to the background
and also a small monster. (lower right)
I was concerned he might disappear in the green
colours, as he is green himself but there is enough
contrast to have him stand out.

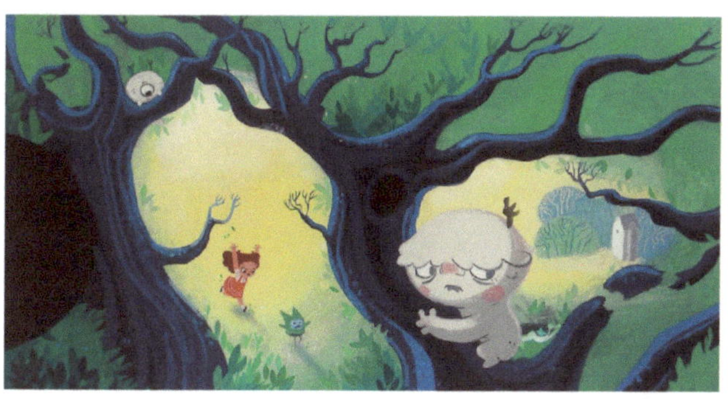

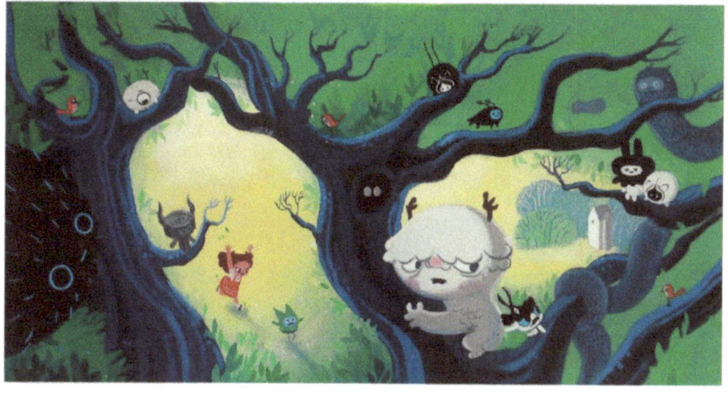

Adding more leaves helped to define the overall
look and feel I was after, I then felt comfortable
to paint the other monster characters.

Almost finished at this stage, but I still need to fill
in some more characters and small details.

When the painting is finished I have it scanned in two pieces and merge them together in photoshop. The final painting is approximately 30x60 cm and too large for an A3 scanner bed. The colours (right) look faded, more faded than the original and has to be cropped and rotated.

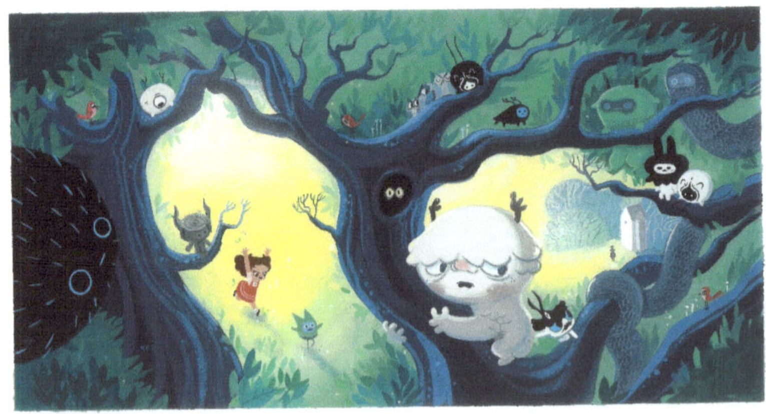

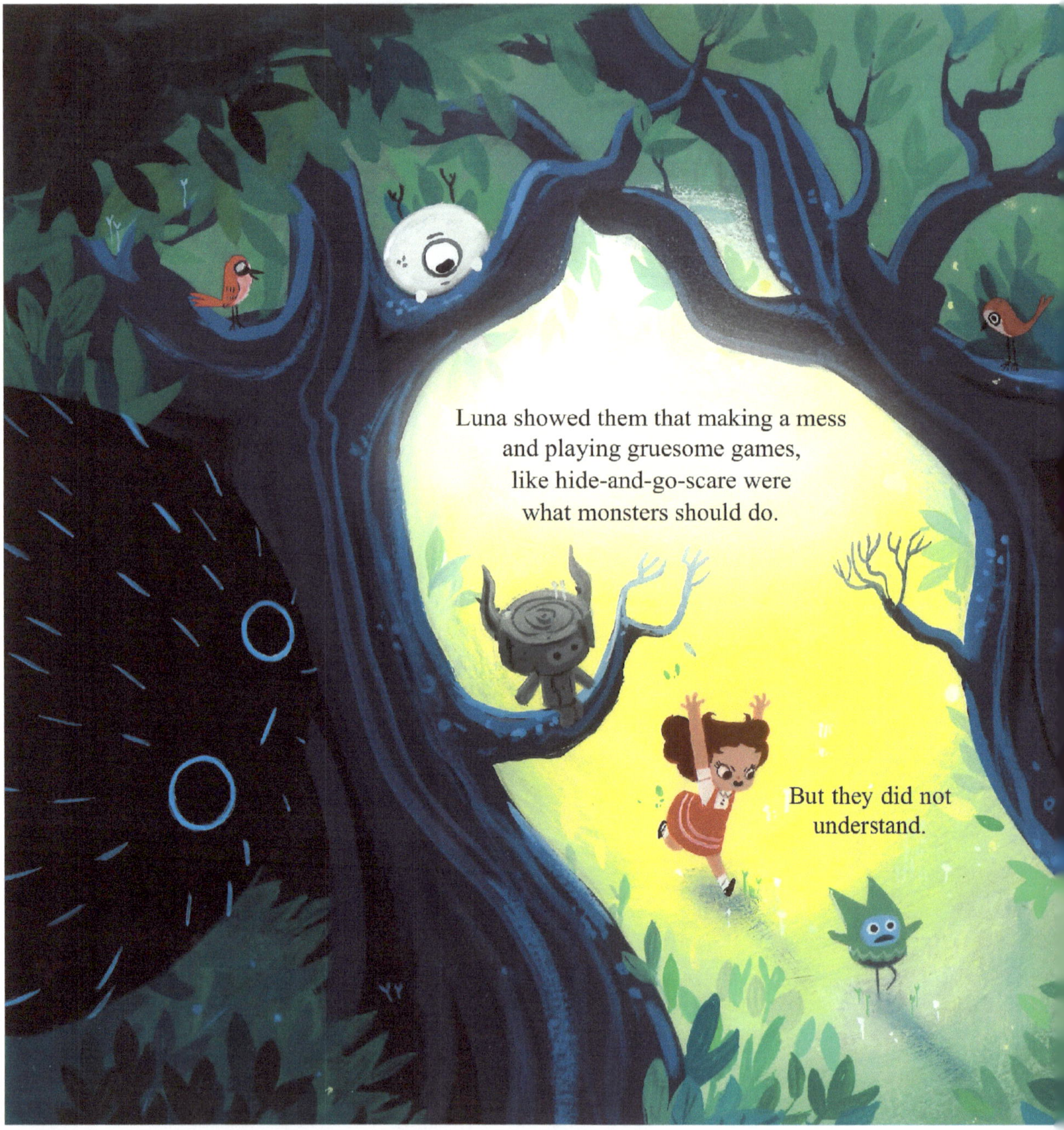

Some highlights were added to the background in photoshop so the text would be visually easy to read by contrast. I used photoshop sparingly as I wanted to have a traditional feel. I mainly used it to bring back the vibrant colours that reflect the original illustration and to add the text.

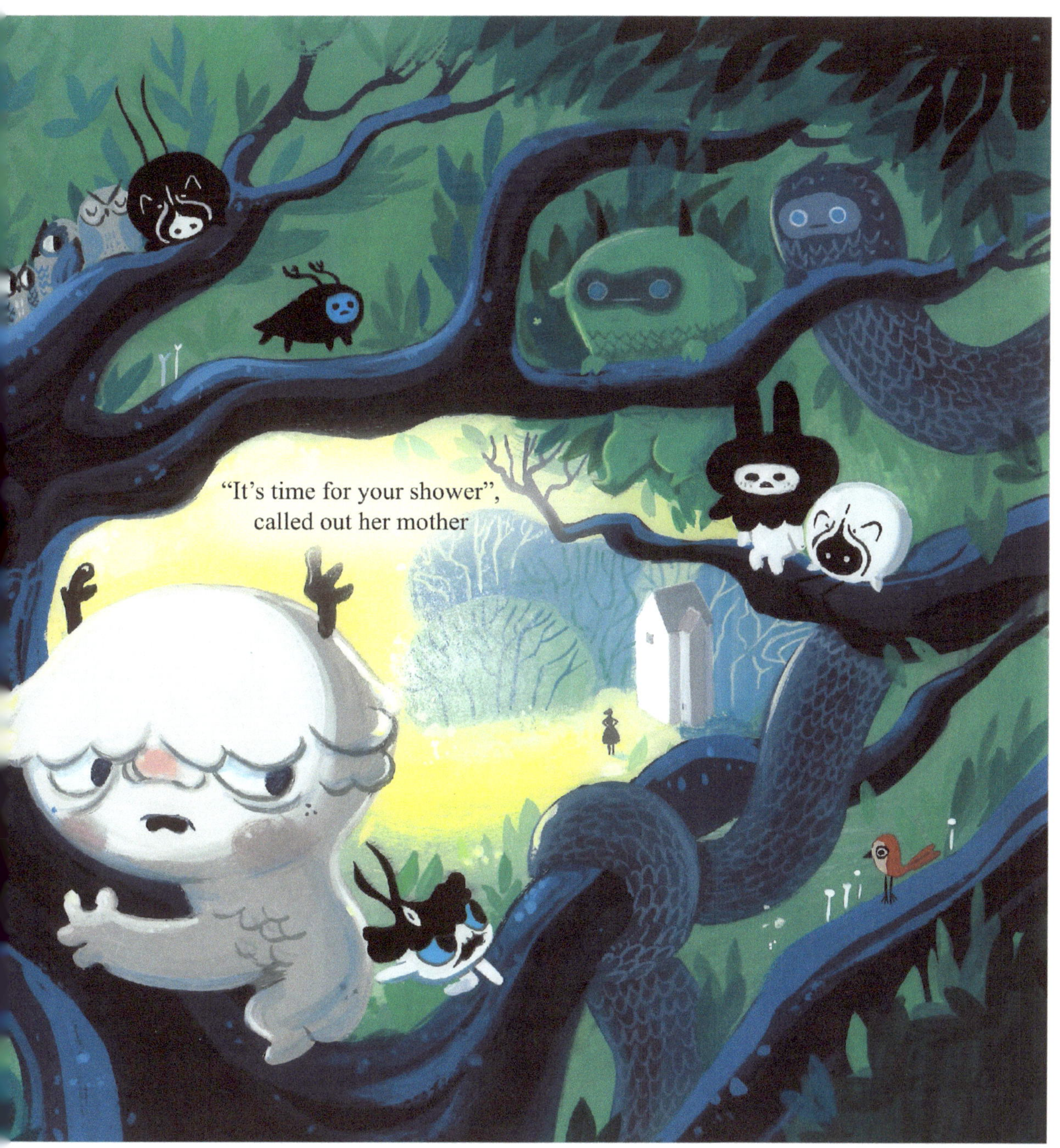

I intentionally left the cover for last because I wanted to have the content nailed down completely. Had I changed even one page, it could have affected the story and in fact I changed 3 spreads which changed the story a bit. I made 4 different pencil cover suggestions and by process of elimination and asking people on facebook, I concluded which worked best.

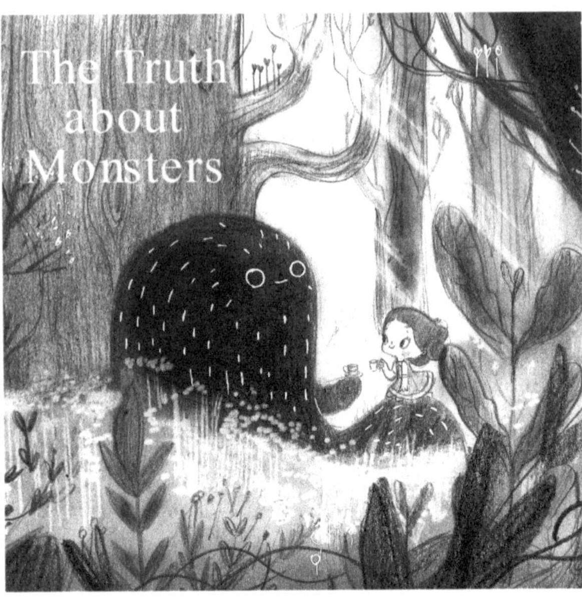

This cover did not say enough about the story and also looked a bit busy with all the foliage.

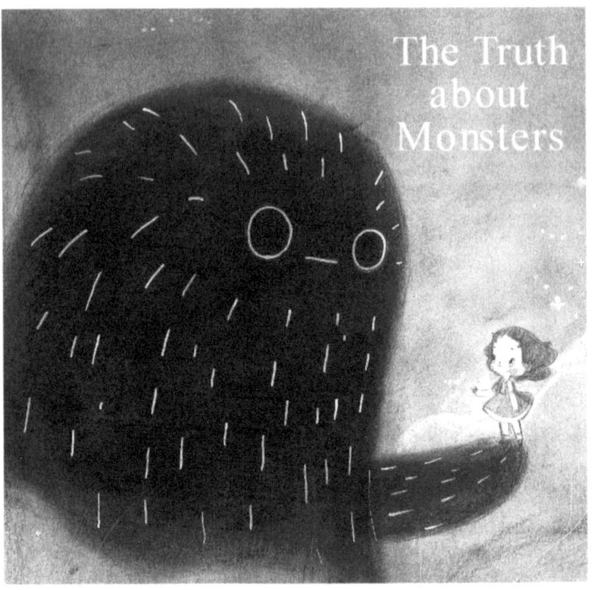

I had my heart set on this one for a long time but had to abandon it for similar reasons as the first version. (Left)

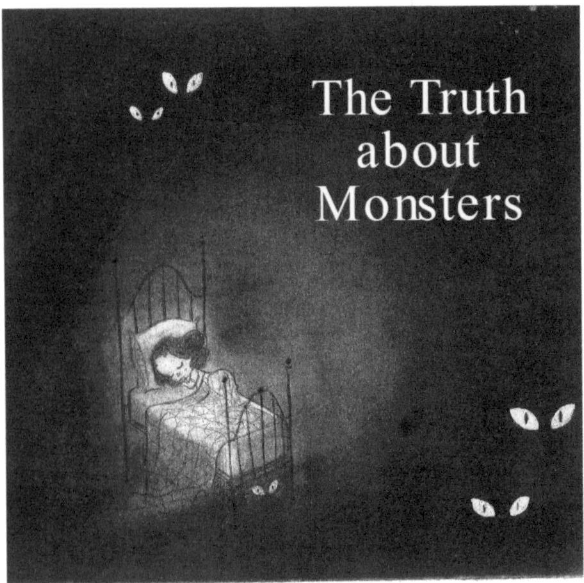

I made this one the first, but abandoned it fairly quickly because it looked too similar to the last page in the book.

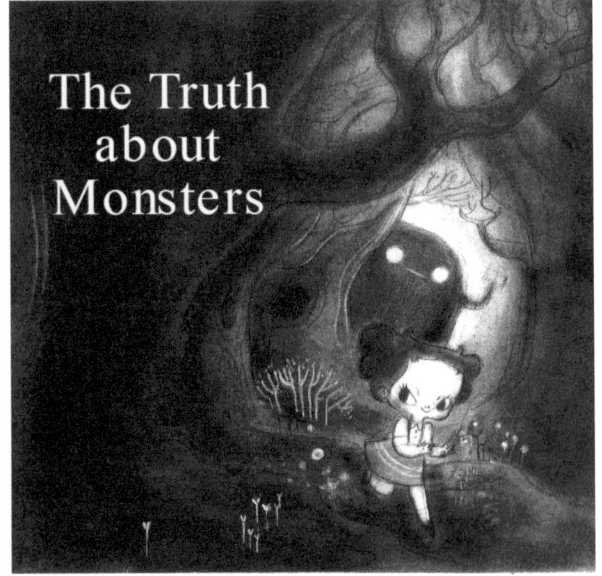

This was the last version I made for the cover which works best.

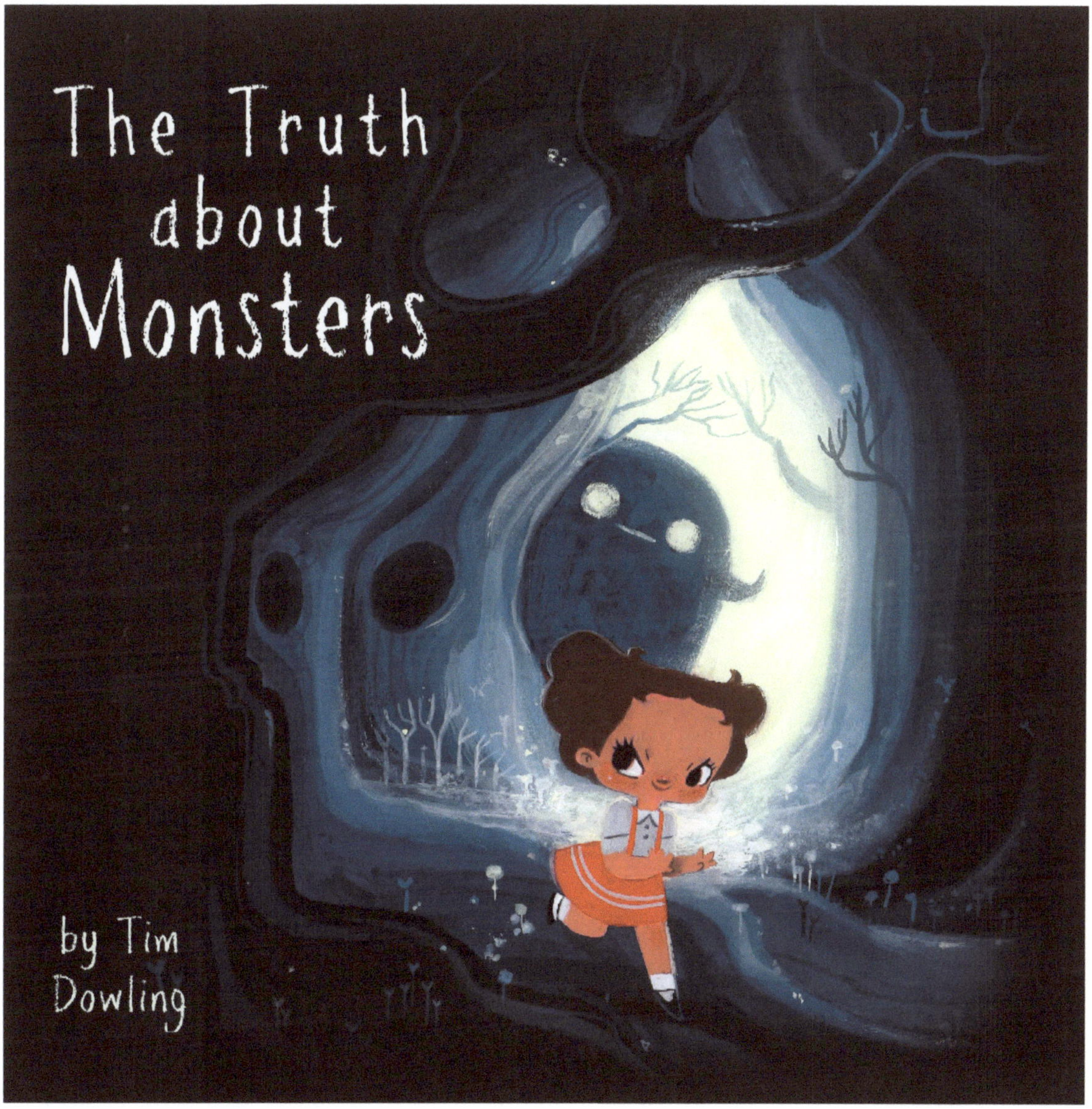

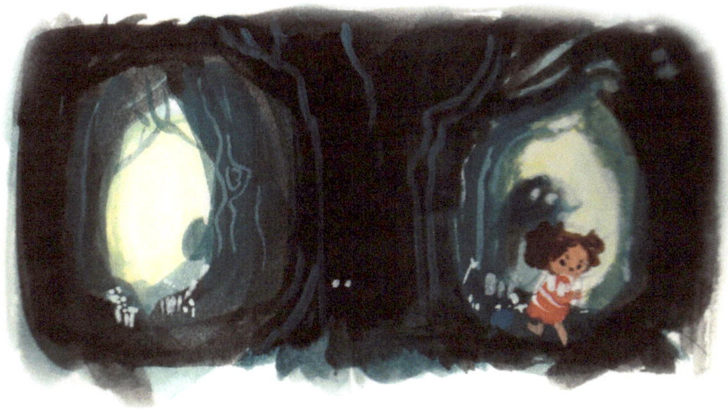

After the cover was painted it became obvious that this version worked best. The red dress stands out from the black background but does not pull away from the environment. Her expression also looks a little mischievous contrasted with the bewildered expression from the monster behind her.

The image on the left is the colour key used to help with the colour choices.

Thank you!

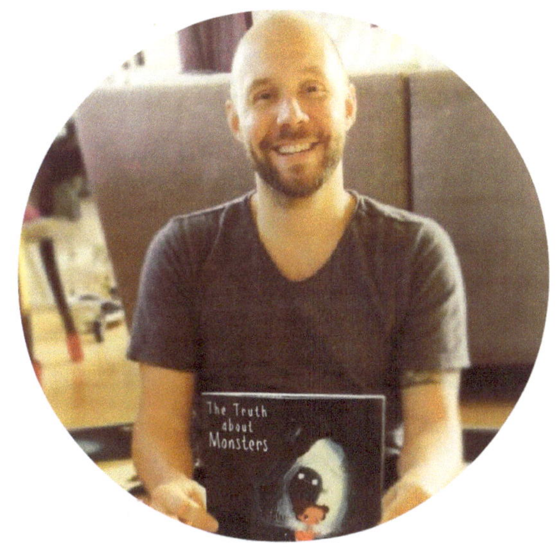

It's always a challenge to put a book together, lots
of late nights, sweat and hard work but also fun!

I created this book to de-mystify the creative process,
in particular with making children's picture books.

To start anything creative can be gruelling and taxing, even
for the most experienced artist which often leads to pro-
crastination but I do hope this book will inspire you to push
through tough periods so you can keep on being creative.

I would like to thank my family, friends and my partner,
but also you, the reader.
I hope you enjoyed the voyage through this book and learnt
something new, but mostly that you found yourself inspired
and motivated to create wonderful art!

Also available from Flamboyant Press in 2016

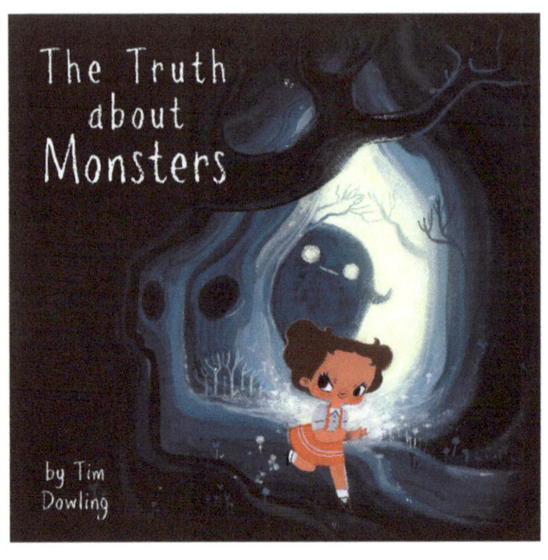

The Truth about Monsters

Tim Dowling

The Truth about Monsters
(the graphite edition)

Tim Dowling

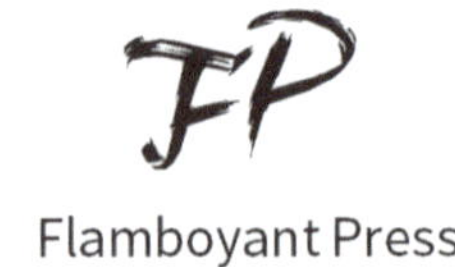

Flamboyant Press